Access your Online Resources

Supporting Children and Young People Through Loss and Trauma is accompanied by a downloadable summary chapter and printable online materials, designed to ensure this resource best supports your professional needs

Go to *resourcecentre.routledge.com/books/9781032230238* and answer the question prompt using your copy of the book to gain access to the online content.

T0388446

Supporting Children and Young People Through Loss and Trauma

Loss and trauma impacts families, communities and children and young people. This includes "collective trauma" experienced within situations such as a global pandemic, economic poverty, displacement, war, natural hazards or political turmoil. As a result, various common characteristics may be exhibited by children in school settings.

This practical book provides strategies and interventions to support the effects of loss and trauma in children and young people. It offers easy-to-understand research and theory to develop knowledge and skills, alongside hands-on strategies to support emotional responses, with practical examples of "what to do if…." Chapters consider why and how these emotions occur, recognising each child's life experiences and focus on identifying suitable approaches. The intention is to validate feelings and help each child find a way to navigate the variety of emotions experienced, using the simple "5S-Scaffold" model: *SUBSIDE–SOOTHE–SUPPORT–STRENGTHEN–SELF-CARE*.

With a wealth of information and additional downloadable resources, *Supporting Young People Through Loss and Trauma* is essential reading for teachers, senior leaders, mental health or behaviour leads and SENDCos.

Juliet Ann Taylor is an affiliate tutor and coordinator on the Postgraduate Diploma course in Social, Emotional and Mental Health (SEMH) difficulties, provided by Oxford Brookes University in partnership with SEBDA. Her writing, presenting, training and support for school staff centres around pupil's positive wellbeing, mental health and trauma-informed, attachment-aware practice.

She was a longstanding KS 3-5 teacher and key worker at a specialist school where SEND pupils, with a medical condition and SEMH diagnosis, are supported and educated utilising a graduated approach to offer a personalised curriculum and bespoke pathway.

nasen spotlight

nasen is a professional membership association that supports all those who work with or care for children and young people with special and additional educational needs. Members include SENCOs, school leaders, governors/trustees, teachers, teaching assistants, support workers, other educationalists, students and families.

nasen supports its members through policy documents, peer-reviewed academic journals, its membership magazine *nasen Connect*, publications, professional development courses, regional networks and newsletters. Its website contains more current information such as responses to government consultations.

nasen's published documents are held in very high regard both in the UK and internationally.

For a full list of titles see: https://www.routledge.com/nasen-spotlight/book-series/FULNASEN

Other titles published in association with the National Association for Special Educational Needs (nasen):

Supporting Children and Young People Through Loss and Trauma: Hands-On Strategies to Improve Mental Health and Wellbeing
Juliet Ann Taylor
2024/pb: 978-1-032-23023-8

Language for Learning in the Primary School: A Practical Guide for Supporting Pupils with Language and Communication Difficulties across the Curriculum, 3ed
Sue Hayden and Emma Jordan
2023/pb: 978-1-032-34259-7

Beating Bureaucracy in Special Educational Needs: Helping SENCOs Maintain a Work/ Life Balance, 4ed
Jean Gross
2023/pb: 978-1-032-32239-1

Inclusive and Accessible Science for Students with Additional or Special Needs: How to Teach Science Effectively to Diverse Learners in Secondary Schools
Jane Essex
2023/pb: 978-0-367-76627-6

True Partnerships in SEND: Working Together to Give Children, Families and Professionals a Voice
Heather Green and Becky Edwards
2023/pb: 978-0-367-54494-2

Teaching Reading to All Learners Including those with Complex Needs
Sarah Moseley
2023/pb: 978-1-032-11475-0

The SENCO Survival Guide: The Nuts and Bolts of Everything You Need to Know, 3ed
Sylvia Edwards
2023/pb: 978-1-032-21947-9

Supporting Children and Young People Through Loss and Trauma

Hands-On Strategies to Improve Mental Health and Wellbeing

Juliet Ann Taylor

Routledge
Taylor & Francis Group

LONDON AND NEW YORK

Designed cover image: © Getty Images

First published 2024
by Routledge
4 Park Square, Milton Park, Abingdon, Oxon OX14 4RN

and by Routledge
605 Third Avenue, New York, NY 10158

Routledge is an imprint of the Taylor & Francis Group, an informa business

British Library Cataloguing-in-Publication Data
A catalogue record for this book is available from the British Library

ISBN: 9781032230221 (hbk)
ISBN: 9781032230238 (pbk)
ISBN: 9781003275268 (ebk)

DOI: 10.4324/9781003275268

Typeset in Helvetica
by codeMantra

Access the Support Material: resourcecentre.routledge.com/books/9781032230238

Dedication

I would like to dedicate these pages to anyone who picks up this book, reads a snippet and puts some type of strategy in place, to support a child or young person who once experienced something that rocked their world in a bad-type-of-way.

While this book is not exhaustive, and I don't have anywhere near all the answers, if one adult gains an extra helping of compassion, along with a pinch of new knowledge and a heap of practical ideas, then this recipe might give a child better life prospects; together we make a difference when we don't give up on the young people in our care but believe in what they can grow to be – and resolve to simply just "be there" for them.

One adult – one good thing – for one child.

Contents

Acknowledgements

I would like to personally thank the people that made this writing possible; this book is a team effort.

Thank you to my husband Bren, for your belief, support and breakfasts-while-I-typed, all are truly appreciated. As is the care, love and offers of breaks away (while we simultaneously built a house) from my son Callum, daughter Aemelia, and their partner's Tom and Tara, respectively. Tara, thanks too for your content advice and speed reading. To my Dad, I appreciate all your support, in so many way, with love.

My indefatigable proofreader, Rob F., deserves a medal – thank you for your time, patience, care and chronic sense of humour. Thank you, Sarah, for your encouraging support, patience and being my sounding board. You both know what your friendship means to me … along with the rest of my "dance family." Happy days!

Ultimately, the book's theme was inspired through decades of teaching wonderful children at James Brindley, a city-wide, multi-site specialist Social, Emotional and Mental health (SEMH) school. The opportunities, projects and training I received all played their part – thank you to all my amazing colleagues, principal Hardip and deputy Toisin. Our young people prompted my master's studies, to research first-hand exactly what support the pupils valued the most, and why – an opportunity for everyone to hear their voice (thank you deputies, Diane and Sheilagh, for your faith in me, unending support and the opportunity to fulfil a pivotal project). Subsequently, these studies led to my role as tutor on a postgraduate specialist SEMH course – a joint venture with SEBDA (Social, Emotional and Behavioural Difficulties Association) and Oxford Brookes University – a qualification for those working with vulnerable children and young people. My SEBDA article became a presentation at "The TES SEN Show" conference (thanks to the connections of Rob L.), whereupon I was approached by the publishers to write on the theme I spoke about.

Hence, to all James Brindley and SEBDA colleagues, thank you; this weaving of events led the journey to this book.

To the publishers, thank you Clare and Molly for your calm help, friendly guidance and unending patience. Gayathree and team, thanks too for your role in bringing this book to print.

Thanks too to my family and dear friends (old and newer) who played an important part in this journey. You have drawn caricature illustrations (thank you Sue), inspired messages (thank you Carol), shared personal memories or simply asked how it was progressing (you know who you are). You've all been there during the joys and throws of life.

To my insightful friends and neighbours, Sharon, Mike and Andy; you inspired with your childhood snippets, advisory specialist teacher thoughts or political (with a small p) ex-teacher conversation and accompanying life advice.

There are parallels to be drawn between the re-building of my forever home and the contents between these pages – hopefully both offer shelter and a place of safety; dodgy foundations and cracked brickwork have been rebuilt along the way, not everything goes to plan, but patience and creativity (and skilled builders – thank you) are essential. Also, everyone needs a patient wingman, someone who sees all the layers that have gone before and, remaining calm, can step in when needed to support with something bespoke and practical (thank you kitchen and floor man). As both book and house project now near their end, I am hopeful, humbled and excited by the people-centred opportunities they both offer.

My aim is to emulate one of my favourite quotes, from *Wonder*, by R. J. Palacio which urges us to be – just a little bit kinder than needed.

Overview and Aim

The book offers practical strategies and interventions which aim to support the effects of loss and trauma in children and young people. The easy-to-understand theory provides a foundation for the practical interventions. The aim of this theory is to give a level of understanding that helps clarify why the child or young person may be behaving, or responding, as they are; it helps establish the appropriate practical strategies required to support the child or young person. With understanding comes compassion and empathy; *knowledge* gives us an opportunity to remove ourselves from our perspective and see life from another angle.

This is a rare skill, but having empathy and considering another's point of view, gives the ability to make a positive difference on small or large scales. One small act of kindness can change a life.

- It is the power that empathy gives which enables us to have compassion when trying to understand others.
- We can begin to understand emotions and experiences that differ from our own.
- Through this we can help our children and young people feel seen and known.
- We can increase our self-awareness of how our words and actions can impact others (both positively and negatively).
- Compassion brings connection, and "the sense of connection is a key element of feeling safe" (Riley, 2022, p. xiv).
- This encourages the very practical support strategies to be effective.

It is hoped that the language is accessible to all, for those with experience in education or in related professions, to those who are parents or carers or have read on this topic for the very first time.

The book is relevant for anyone wishing to understand child development, and what helps make our children and young people who they are. It is particularly helpful for those wishing to understand why the COVID-19 pandemic, the economic turmoil, the Ukraine war, grief and loss can have a tremendous impact on the youngsters in our care; practical and simply strategies are there to help us journey alongside these children and young people, whether they have an SEMH difficulty, a diagnosis or are having a blip in their wellbeing. The suggestions are not to replace specialist mental health support or care, rather the interventions should help us understand our young people and know what we can practicably do to support them.

About the Author

I'm the tutor coordinator and an affiliate tutor on the Postgraduate Certificate course in Social, Emotional and Mental Health (SEMH) difficulties, provided by Oxford Brookes University in partnership with the national charity SEBDA (the Social, Emotional and Behavioural Difficulties Association). I am a member of SEBDA's National Council, have organised and delivered at national and international SEMH conferences and have written articles for the SEBDA newsletter and website. As a result of presenting at "The TES SEN Show International Conference", I was approached by the publishers to write this book, bringing theory and practice together to support children and young people (CYP) who have experienced a "collective trauma." I have a master's degree in *"Education, Learning and Teaching: Understanding, Managing and Teaching pupils with SEMH difficulties."* My research focused on investigating short and long-term supportive interventions and their impact on pupils' mental health and wellbeing.

I worked as a specialist SEMH teacher and key worker for over 20 years, with pupils aged 10–17 years at James Brindley, Birmingham, UK. At the multi-site, city-wide school, SEND (Special Educational Needs and Disabilities) pupils with a medical condition and SEMH diagnosis are supported and educated utilising a graduated approach (assess-plan-do-review) to offer a personalised curriculum, bespoke pathway and supportive interventions. Multi-agency collaboration, individual pupil reviews, and Education and Health Care Plan (EHCP) writing all formed part of the support process. Acting as a line-manager, peer mentor and whole-school lead (for both the Equality, Diversity and Inclusion Award and Unicef's "Right Respecting School" gold award), I worked with a relational ethos aimed at building resilience and confidence, within a safe and inspiring place to learn, enabling CYP to become active citizens.

I love spending time with my family and friends, and I relax by doing art, Lindy Hop swing dance, sewing and reading. A recent house-move to the (almost) countryside has reignited a love for walking.

Introduction

Book overview

- The introduction offers a broad outline of the book, its intentions, aims and goals and its audience.
- The book is suitable to help support any child or young person who is impacted by trauma, grief or loss.
- The strategies of the "**5-S Scaffold**" (PART TWO), underpinned by theory (PART ONE) are designed to be practical and hands-on, to dip into when needed.
- A summary chapter and photocopiable resources can be found online by following the access instructions at the front of this book.

Gentle trigger warning

While in the research community there are ethical processes and safeguards to protect humans from harm (emotional or psychological), the same cannot be said for reading the content of books. The aim of the contents of this book is to support children and young people who have undergone a collective trauma, an event beyond their control. While there are purposefully no graphic details, some content deals with sensitive issues or may act as a trigger; an important ethical dilemma is that reading and writing about trauma can elicit a response in the writer or reader (Jané et al., 2022).

***

The further I researched, to write this book, the more I realised that every single subject could command an entire book of its own. Trauma and loss are huge topics, as are grief, wellbeing and support strategies. Factors such as our mental health, parental aloneness and an ever-changing world (caught up in turmoil such as pandemics, war and economic spirals), all impact our ability to support the children and young people in our care. We cannot achieve the impossible and right every wrong. However, we can take bite-size snippets of knowledge and practical *hands-on strategies* to support these children and young people. A throwback to that well-worn expression: *How do you eat an elephant? One bite at a time!*

This book is not designed to be a perfect model, nor is it exhaustive; it is there to dip into to seek out tips as much, or as little, as you want to read. The theory is written to demonstrate why these interventions may make a difference and have a positive impact. The brief *chapter overview* at the start of each chapter aims to guide your reading, similarly the *end-of-chapter summary* sections may act as "prompts" or be a quick reference guide.

The book is formed of two main parts:

PART ONE: The first half of the book lays the foundations that is the theory behind the strategies.
PART TWO: The second half of the book is more practical; the *"SUBSIDE – SOOTHE – SUPPORT – STRENGTHEN – SELF-CARE"* scaffold presents five chapters dedicated to each of the *"5-S"* supportive techniques. While they are designed to read successively, the strategies can be personalised and the sections from the **5-S** scaffold utilised in a way, and in an order, that is most appropriate for the child or young person.

The downloadable summary sections and photocopiable resources add to the book's practicality – whether the sheets are to be pinned up on a fridge, behind a teacher's desk, or displayed in a staff room, they can be utilised for individual interventions, classroom use or whole-school staff development.

If you are keen to explore additional resources available from the author, to enable your school or other professional setting to undertake their own staff development, you are welcome to contact: SEMHhelp@gmail.com

Part One
Theory
For practical application

1 TRAUMA AND COLLECTIVE TRAUMA

Chapter overview

- A brief description of "individual trauma" and "collective trauma," and the difference between the two.
- What the associated risk factors of collective trauma are, and the resulting impact of it.
- *The "six phases of disaster" chart* is used to consider emotions following a collective trauma, to understand the impact on individuals and on school staff as they seek to support children and young people in their care.

Collective trauma. The term "collective trauma" has been used to describe global events: the recent COVID-19 pandemic, natural disaster, displacement through natural disaster or as a refugee, war, economic poverty or political turmoil all impact a large number of people; *collective trauma* differs from *individual trauma*.

Individual trauma. Individual trauma is the impact an incident has on an individual or a few people, whereas *collective trauma* refers to the impact of a traumatic experience on communities, or society, as a whole (Hirschberger, 2018). Erikson (1976a, p. 302) described it, to reflect the impact that it delivers, as "a blow to the psyche that breaks through one's defences so suddenly and with such brutal force that one cannot react to it effectively." He studied the impact of the 1972 West Virginia dam collapse and subsequent flood and described two types of trauma that occur continuously and jointly in disasters, individual and collective.

Collective trauma comprises not only the event itself but also an ongoing collective memory of it; people recount their experiences long after the event itself, as an attempt to make sense of it. As a result, conversations may often include recalling and recounting personal situations and include statements such as, *"Do you remember when...,"* *"During the x event we had to..."* and *"Did you hear...."* Due to the event occurring, *collective values* may alter, and it may bring a shift in culture and mass actions. Changes to our lives or lifestyle require us to adapt, a thirst for information occurs as we try to comprehend and make sense of the situation; gaining this knowledge is a means of seeking control at a time when circumstances overtake us.

We may find ourselves living in a changing society where daily processes or government policies regularly alter; indeed, collective trauma was described as, "a blow to the basic tissues of social life that damages the bonds attaching people together and impairs the prevailing sense of commonality" (Erikson, 1976b, p. 153). Simultaneously, we experience distress and personal ramifications. Our relationships are impacted, and new social norms become commonplace. For example, with the case of a *pandemic* these may include: lockdowns, wearing masks, online shopping, "bubbles"; during *war* topics such as: curfews, near misses, injury, safe-places and bereavement are spoken of frequently. Disaster disrupts many of the usual daily activities and the human connections they entail. These many traumatic experiences can have physical, mental, relational, financial and spiritual consequences, to name but a few (Chang, 2017; Erikson, 1976b).

While individual trauma manifests as stress and grief, for example, collective trauma can separate individuals from their family, friends or community, namely *connections* that would usually provide a source of *support* during times of stress. For children and young people, there may be a loss of contact with family, friends or school. Children may find it difficult to heal from their trauma whilst still living in an unstable situation where the usual supportive community is understandably absent. Mental health interventions that also seek to establish human connections, through group contact and one-to-one positive interactions, are therefore essential to mitigate against the enormous range and depth of prevalent emotions.

Clearly, extreme *emotions* will be experienced during the time of a "collective trauma," whether they are fear or terror, anger or rage, sadness or sorrow, joy, exultation, severe boredom, surprise, denial, guilt or shame. The emotion itself can embed itself in our psyche. When we think back and ask ourselves about our *earliest, or most significant memories*, it is likely that

DOI: 10.4324/9781003275268-2

we more readily recall those times when we felt *extreme* emotions. We do not naturally recall those *mediocre* or *insignificant* times, the times when we felt nothing (partly to do with the stage of early brain development too, the brain develops its emotional regions before its cognitive regions; see chapter 4). I asked several individuals what their earliest memories were, and these were among the responses I received:

> *"It was the occasional sweet shop treat on a Friday lunchtime after nursery school, I can remember the sweet shop's smells and the excitement of choosing sweets. My other memory was being ill on holiday… I was in a pushchair as I was too ill to walk, and I had to have medicine and chewy, purple, gummy vitamins."*
>
> *"I remember my sheer fear at the holiday-site 'pirate', who dressed up and chased children around the pool, occasionally throwing them in. I stayed away from that pool in case he emerged. Although I was 3 years old, over 50 years ago, I can remember the splashing, squealing sounds from afar and the bench where I stayed."*
>
> *"I remember that rising excitement on Christmas eve with the stocking at the bottom of the bed."*
>
> *"I was playing at a friend's house when their Mum asked him to do his reading, scolding, 'Why can't you be more like Rosie [name changed] she always does her reading, and she can write her address'. I felt ashamed, rather than proud. I was embarrassed and felt sorry for the boy, but shame was my biggest feeling as I didn't want to stand out or want the others to not like me."*
>
> *"I remember being asked to go to the shop for a loaf, and on the way home I dropped it in the road. I was upset and worried."*
>
> *"My earliest memory is gardening with my Dad. He told me he'd made me my own tiny plot in the garden, he gave me some seeds and I grew some things. I felt valued and very special."*

Consequently, much of our memory is based on what we felt and experienced, on our emotional state rather than on our cognitive reasoning. Emotions are responses which help our survival; "positive emotions help us thrive, negative emotions help us survive" (Long, 2023). During an individual or collective trauma, a child or a young person may spend months or years bouncing between extreme emotions (chapter 2); additionally, their memories can be warped as they will have been stored under an extremely stressful emotional state, therefore, the learned coping mechanism at the time will be linked to being in *survival mode*. If we pause to consider this, we can begin to comprehend just how damaging this can be.

Impact of changing circumstances

It is important to note that 2018–2019 was the last stable UK academic year, before 2022–2023. As the table below shows (Figure 1.1), during the 2019–2020 year, the first lockdown (due to COVID-19) happened (Ofqual, 2021) and many changes in education delivery were seen over the following two years.

The UK Census 2021 (Office for National Statistics (ONS, 2021)) revealed some important findings regarding the COVID-19 pandemic and education. For data purposes, they categorised schools based on numbers of pupils receiving free school meals (FSM). They discovered that where no or few pupils received FSM, schools covered approximately the same amount of curriculum through remote learning as that expected by face-to-face teaching in school; high parental engagement, secure social circumstances and good access to technology were cited as reasons for this. However, unsurprisingly, in the "most deprived" schools with the greatest number of pupils eligible for FSM, teachers reported covering far less material for remote learners compared with usual in-school learning and only had contact with 50% of pupils; again, social circumstances and poor access to technology were reasons. This data indicated a widening gap between the education and experiences of the *less deprived* compared with the *most deprived* areas. Additionally, the cumulative impact on pupils, with their wellbeing and education, has been considerable.

2019-2020																																														
Teaching mode			Traditional teaching mode																					Remote teaching																							
Weeks of year	S	S	S	S	O	O	O	O	O	N	N	N	N	D	D	D	D	J	J	J	J	J	J	F	F	F	F	M	M	M	A	A	A	A	M	M	M	M	J	J	J	J	JI	JI	JI	A	A	A	A
School opening																														X	X	X	X	X	X	X	X	X	X	X	X							
Holidays																																															

2020-2021																																														
Teaching mode			New normal mode										Remote teaching								New normal mode																									
Weeks of year	S	S	S	S	O	O	O	O	O	N	N	N	N	D	D	D	D	J	J	J	J	J	J	F	F	F	F	M	M	M	A	A	A	A	A	M	M	M	M	J	J	J	J	JI	JI	JI	A	A	A	A
School opening																		X	X	X	X	X	X	X	X	X	X																				
Holidays																																															

KEY	
	Schools open
	Schools open with conditions for tiers 2 and 3.
	Schools partially open to Y10 and Y12 (rota basis)
X	Schools closed (except for vulnerable children and **children of critical workers**)

Figure 1.1 A chart to show changes in school opening between September 2019 and August 2021 (Ofqual, 2021).

Importantly, subjects such as physical activity, art and design technology were delivered the least, due to constraints in equipment access and parents feeling ill-equipped to provide *support* (ONS, 2021), yet these are the activities that people often turn to for wellbeing *support*. Clearly, the impact on our children and young people has been huge.

Data published in the British Medical Journal (BMJ) (Iacobucci, 2022) evidenced this enormous impact on children's mental health and the subsequent huge demand on mental health services. April to September 2021 saw:

- A four-fold increase in the number of children needing treatment for an eating-disorder.
- An 81% increase in referrals for children's and young people's mental health services and a 59% increase (15,000 in total) in emergency crisis care referrals, compared with the same period in 2019.

These children make up the 1-in-5 who indicate that their mental health and wellbeing had been substantially impacted by the pandemic, referred to in the final "COVID-19 wellbeing and mental health surveillance report" (Office for Health Improvement and Disparities, 2022). The report of chapter 4 refers specifically to the survey of over half-a-million children and young people and agrees with the BMJ data:

- Probable "mental disorders" and "eating problems" rose considerably.
- For children and young people with Special Educational Needs and Disabilities (SEND), of which those with a mental health difficulty or diagnosis make up a component, there was evidence of increasing behavioural, emotional and mental health difficulties. Children felt increased anxiety, social isolation and unhappiness.
- Lower income households reported more symptoms of behavioural, emotional and attentional difficulties in their children than the higher income parents.
- During "lockdown" and school closures, it was the group of children and young people who had no previous mental health indicators, who displayed the greatest increase in difficulties in this area. Symptoms they had previously kept "below the surface" simmered over and could no longer be contained.

Individual experiences

"Throughout the COVID-19 pandemic I taught vulnerable 11–17-year-old SEND pupils who have a mental health diagnosis. The specialist school supported pupils for whom Social, Emotional and Mental Health (SEMH) was their primary need or diagnosis. The pandemic lockdowns and changes in schooling brought new concerns, emotions and behaviours; pupils looked to their teachers for answers and stability. My colleagues and I witnessed the

> *enormity of the impact on children and young people; I taught pupils who developed panic attacks, some who plunged into depression (one hid under her duvet for a few weeks), others who kicked back by running away and refusing schoolwork or felt they could not control their situation, so they tried to control their eating. One pupil move (J) insisted on repeated handwashing 'because of the adverts', another would no longer leave the house, while a third ('J') would not leave his room nor open the door. For many weeks I sat outside the door passing notes under it to establish a rapport and a way for the 16-year-old pupil to understand that I would remain consistently calm, friendly and empathetic."*
>
> *"Imagine my surprise at receiving a text from an ex-colleague, February 2024, who had bumped into his Mum. She wanted to convey that 'J' is now 'is a totally different person', works on the front-line emergency services and only achieved this because you believed in him and fought for his college place "when no-one else thought he could". This incredible impact on one young life all started with a pupil who would not speak and notes being pushed under a door.*
>
> This story may hopefully serve as an encouragement to teachers and parents who cannot yet envision future possibilities.

The **SUPPORT** strategy needed was time, patience, optimism and endless sheets of paper. Thankfully it built trust, it needed months to do so but eventually resulted in regular in-person lessons, and a college place two years later. The pupils were anxious and afraid, they knew "something was out there" and that "the world was different"; they were scared. Often my colleagues would *support* the parent or carer, in order to *support* the pupil, as they were the best-placed and most-trusted adult in the child's life.

These examples show just how drastically *collective traumas* can impact individual lives. It evidences the need to ensure we are engaging in practical *support* for our pupils and have knowledge and understanding of their circumstances and plight. Whilst many other global traumatic events and natural disasters occur, there is insufficient space to do each one justice. Another event that has touched many nations though is the war on Ukraine.

Children and young people fleeing Ukraine

The Organisation for Economic Co-operation and Development (OECD) (OECD, 2022) works internationally with governments, policy makers and citizens to *build better policies for better lives*. In searching out the evidence-base to discover the best ways to foster opportunity and wellbeing for Ukraine children and young people, they established some significant facts regarding *support* for their mental health:

- The invasion has resulted in the largest forced displacement crisis in recent history, with a high proportion of those fleeing being children and young people.
- Many Ukrainian children and young people will have endured stressful and/or traumatic experiences, before leaving Ukraine and throughout their migration journey. They may also encounter a range of challenges in adjusting to life in their host country. These experiences can lead to a variety of mental health issues.
- The longer term impact of what children and young people may have experienced before, during and after fleeing Ukraine is dependent on the psychosocial *support* that they receive in their host country. Schools play a vital role in addressing refugee learners' needs and in promoting their social and emotional learning and wellbeing (because of both the high number of contact hours they have and what they can offer). This is an essential component of ensuring their inclusion in education and in society (OECD, 2022).

What these children have witnessed and experienced will cause emotions such as grief, despair, anger and guilt; post-traumatic stress disorder (PTSD), depression, anxiety disorders or sleep disturbance may ensue; unsurprisingly, refugees have a greater prevalence of mental health conditions, with rates of PTSD being particularly high compared to population norms. Many schools will play host to refugee pupils and integrating them requires that they facilitate their learning and effectively respond to diverse social and emotional needs (European Commission, 2023). Since *social needs* includes *being able to bond with peers and communities to feel a sense of belonging*, chapter 3 will be pertinent when considering attachment issues.

The OECD (2022) ascertained that supporting the emotional needs of the displaced children involved schools establishing:

a. A sense of safety, security and belonging – to feel protected, connect with peers and continue their education.
b. *Support* to help them process their emotions and cope with change, loss, trauma, separation and grief (Cerna, 2019). This includes social and emotional learning which equips children with skills, attitudes and behaviours to process their emotions, understand their environment, work with others and adapt to change in an increasingly uncertain world.
c. Access to additional psychological *support* services.

These three components form sound, supportive advice for children who have experienced other forms of trauma too. The sense is that teachers can help pupils manage their thoughts, values, emotions and actions in constructive ways by guiding and modelling these skills and qualities and by encouraging creative expression and social interaction opportunities (chapters 5–8 *support* these strategies). This requires a whole-school, genuinely supportive ethos across staff and pupils alike and a personalised, flexible approach to the school day and curriculum; issues which are considered in chapter 9 "***SELF-CARE***: Caring for the carers," where "*carers*" refers to those *doing* the caring, namely the teachers, school-staff and parental-figures.

The OECD report (2022) highlights the impressive volume of good practice that is happening internationally as part of education's response to meeting the needs of displaced children and young people. Above all, it is recognised that teachers play a pivotal role in a, b and c above (Pastoor, 2019) and to achieve this must be equipped with *knowledge and practical skills* through their professional development. This includes an awareness of mental health issues, the signs of trauma and stress so that teachers can direct students to the appropriate forms of additional *support* where necessary (European Commission, 2023).

Similarly, this book covers relevant themes such as the impact of trauma, grief and loss, feeling safe, soothing and self-regulation, encouraging supportive relationships and other interventions (Pastoor, 2016) to *support* the wellbeing of these vulnerable groups. Key findings from the COVID-19 pandemic and displaced Ukrainian refugees demonstrate increased mental health difficulties; the *constraints* plus *changing circumstances* are destabilising.

Instability itself has an impact. Each adult, child and young person experiences the same collective trauma that impacts their family, community or world, but each exhibits individual responses.

To varying degrees lives are turned upside down by loss.

Loss may be in many forms and may include: loss of contact (self-isolation), loss of a weekly rhythm or loss of a daily routine, loss of freedom, loss of identity (Farley, 2023), loss of finances, loss of a community, loss of health/abilities or loss of a loved one (breakdown of a relationship or bereavement) (Weir, 2020).

The sense of *loss* brings the feeling that there is a *loss of control*. A response to this *loss of control* may be feelings of oppression, increased anger, confusion, anxiety or stress – all part of experiencing grief. The sense of loss can be physically painful and have a social impact. An example of this is where unsupported trauma can bring behaviours incongruent with peaceful living: 57% of violent young offenders have experienced loss, whilst 91% have experienced abuse and/or significant loss (Liddle et al., 2016). Gaining timely and appropriate *support* is key.

Understanding *the phases of disaster recovery* can enhance appropriate *support*. This understanding is key to enable the personalisation of plans, targets and *support* programmes following a major event. Following their extensive work on disasters, Zunin and Meyers (2000) proposed six broad stages of community or "collective" trauma (Figure 1.2). This model focuses on mental health needs following a disaster and provides a useful framework for employers, parental-figures or professionals to visualise the journey of recovery of the children and young people in their care.

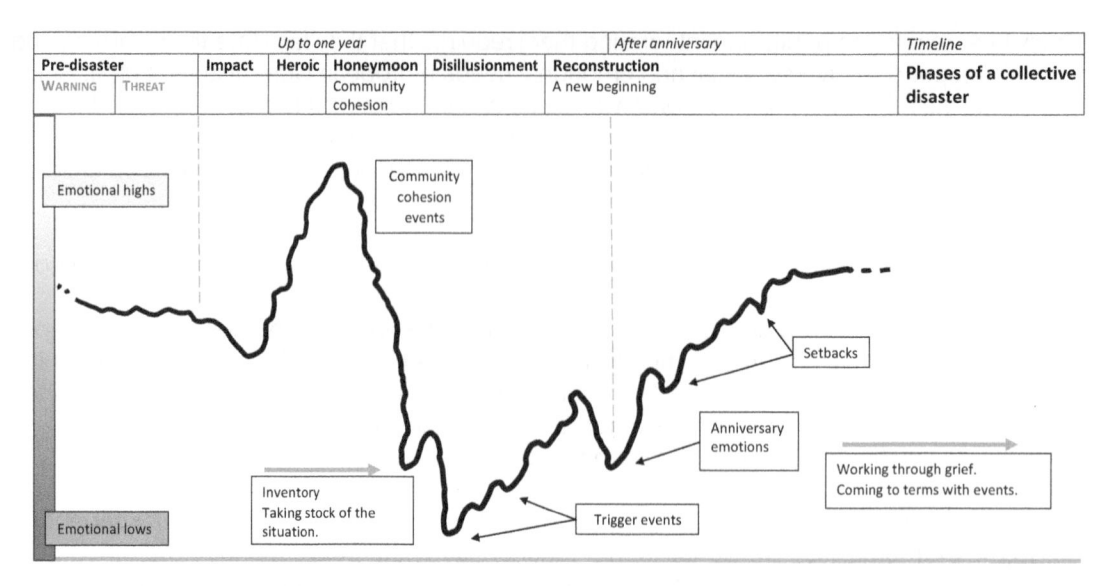

Figure 1.2 Line chart to show levels and types of emotional experience in disasters and other collective traumas. Taylor, J. (2023) adapted from Zunin and Meyers, as cited in DeWolfe, Training Manual for Mental Health and Human Service Workers in Major Disasters, U.S. Department of Health and Human Services (2000).

Describing the chart

The phases outlined, in terms of individual and collective emotional responses in the community, are:

1. *Pre-disaster Phase*: Often there is a short warning time that some trauma is looming. Generally, the mood shifts lower upon receiving the warning. In some cases, the event may feel inevitable but can still cause guilt or self-blame for failure to heed warnings or not make accurate "guesses" of the best thing to do. Feelings of vulnerability, fear of the future, lack of security and loss of control are common responses, particularly so for sudden disasters with no warning.

2. *Impact Phase*: There is a further initial dip in mood upon the impact of the disaster or announcement of the "collective trauma." Reactions and emotions can range from shock to panic. Initial confusion and disbelief are followed by a focus on self-preservation and family protection.

3. *Heroic Phase*: Rising emotions here are due to community cohesion. There is rising positivity and often an initial sense that *"we can do this"* or *"we can get through it together."* Many survivors exhibit adrenaline-induced rescue behaviour (gathering a community together to help, joining *support* efforts), high activity and low productivity. Risk assessment may be impaired as our views may be clouded, or we may not possess the full facts. There is a sense of "doing good" and self-sacrifice.

4. *Honeymoon Phase*: The emotional high peaks here and community bonding occurs; closer relationships may even bring enjoyment. Disaster assistance, or news and information, is readily available. Many are optimistic that all will return to normal. At this stage, people make "the best of the situation." In the COVID-19 pandemic, in the UK, representative features of stages 3 and 4 were events which brought connection, such as "Clap the NHS" and placing rainbows or message of *support* in home front windows; worldwide, many local-community projects or campaigns (such as with the Performing Arts) garnered *support* for those struggling because of lost employment – aiming to survive, yet bringing a sense of *support* and "being-in-it-together."

5. *Disillusionment Phase*: Rapidly descending emotions plunge us into an emotional low. In this long-lasting phase, stress and fatigue take a toll. Optimism turns into discouragement; after hoping it would "soon be over," reality sets in. Within this phase, there are "trigger events" which cause sudden setbacks, these include experiencing *losses* or a

bereavement, or significant dates such as the "one year anniversary" of the trauma. The wider community may return to some sort of normality.

6. *Reconstruction*: During this last time-period, we work through trauma, loss and grief BUT not all to the same time scale, not in the same order and presenting a whole range of intensity in emotions. Sometimes it is sensed as a new beginning or "a new normal." Individuals and communities begin to assume responsibility for rebuilding their lives. People begin adjusting to new circumstances. There is a recognition that it may be a time for growth and opportunity. This phase may continue for years or even decades.

During and following a traumatic event, there can be many people-related challenges, both at home and in the workplace. A longitudinal, action-research, case study demonstrates how employee wellbeing and performance were affected for over two years after the Canterbury earthquakes (2010–2011) in New Zealand (Malinen et al., 2018). Many organisational actions were necessary to improve staff performance, resilience and wellbeing; these actions included: acknowledgement, increased autonomy, process flexibility and a focus on wellbeing. These strategies can *strengthen* an education establishment's adaptive capacity and performance. The lengthy timeframe illustrates the impact on education staff morale in schools long after things "return to normal" and that is particularly pertinent for the time we are living in now. In June 2023, the teacher wellbeing charity, "Education Support," published a list of proposals to boost teacher retention as, "it worsened again after a short-lived Covid lull" (Walker, 2023, p. 1). Recommendations to the Department for Education, and to Ofsted, emphasised a need to consider the impact of *policy changes* that brought increased workload, on staff wellbeing (Education Support, 2023). The need to "Care for our Carers" is addressed in chapter 9 as those supporting out most vulnerable youngsters need to be able to thrive, not just survive; the recent pandemic, economic poverty and international turmoil have all taken its toll.

Children and Young People form one of the most vulnerable groups at these times, since they have the least autonomy and rely on a stable and supportive environment for their growth and secure development.

The next chapter will consider the range of emotional responses and why whilst further addressing the topic of "loss."

Summary

	Trauma and collective trauma summary table
1.	**Collective trauma** comprises not only the event itself but also an ongoing collective memory of it.
2.	While individual trauma manifests as stress and grief, collective trauma can separate individuals from their family, friends, school or community, namely *connections* that would usually provide a source of *support* during times of stress.
3.	Instability itself has an impact. Each adult, child and young person experiences the same collective trauma that impacts their family, community or world, but each exhibits individual responses.
4.	We need to ensure that we are engaging in practical *support* for our pupils and have knowledge and understanding of their circumstances and plight. Teachers must be equipped with *knowledge and practical skills* through their professional development. Understanding *the six phases of disaster recovery* can enhance appropriate *support*.
5.	Teachers can help pupils manage their thoughts, values, emotions and actions in constructive ways by guiding and modelling these skills and qualities, and by encouraging creative expression and social interaction opportunities (chapters 5–8). This requires a whole-school, genuinely supportive ethos across staff and pupils alike (chapter 9) and a personalised, flexible approach to the school day and curriculum.
6.	During a traumatic event, and in the years following, employee wellbeing and performance are affected. Staff morale is low long after things "return to normal."
7.	Organisational actions necessary to improve staff performance, resilience and wellbeing are: acknowledgement, increased autonomy, process flexibility and a focus on wellbeing. These strategies can *strengthen* an education establishment's adaptive capacity and overall performance. Ofsted (Education Support, 2023) also noted a need to consider the impact of policy change that brings increased workload.
8.	Children and Young People form one of the most vulnerable groups at these times, since they have the least autonomy and rely on a stable and supportive environment for their growth and secure development. They need to be able to thrive, not just survive.

2 EMOTIONAL RESPONSES TO GRIEF, LOSS AND FORCED CHANGE

> ## Chapter overview
>
> - The grief response is not a state but a *non-linear process*. Several *"grief models" are described and compared.*
> - *It describes how the stages, order and intensity of emotions* vary from person to person.
> - A model can help make sense of our emotional responses to grief, loss or forced change.
> - The model in chapter 1 aimed to identify a community, region or nation's response to a *collective trauma,* whilst the models in chapter 2 refer to an individual's range of emotional responses.

In the past, *mourning* was seen as a time when you "get over" or "give up" your relationship with the deceased, however, more recently there has been a shift and the thinking is to "preserve" that relationship, albeit in a different manner (Hagman, 2016).

> *One truth, which is sensed the world over, is that when we have a strong attachment to someone, (or 'something') we sense the loss when they (or 'it') are not there.*

Robertson and Bowlby (1952) first studied the impact of loss on groups of children and young people comprising WWII evacuees, juvenile offenders and lone children in hospital who were separated from their families.

These children lost all things familiar to them; family, friends, home, community and personal objects/affects.

Bowlby noted the impact that this *loss* brought on and separated it into three stages:

1. Initial separation: causing anger and resentment.
2. Indifference: a lack of emotion, apathy or void.

And if these emotions were left to continue and escalate,

3. Hatred: a desire to exact "revenge."

Bowlby posited that one of the main underlying factors was the absence of a calm, reasoning parental-figure, thus allowing the child's negative thinking to spiral and become all-consuming; ultimately this resulted in the child wishing to "self-protect" and achieve this by either disdain and indifference or (as Bowlby phrased it) "delinquency."

It was witnessed that when these children were again reunited with their parents, they showed a strong reaction, but this reaction would depend upon the type of relationship they had had with their family. However, pent-up emotions such as fury, anger, upset or destruction would also emerge; these are all forms of "active protest."

Whilst it may seem counterintuitive, "active protest" should actually be seen as a positive, expected reaction. In a later study on lone children in hospital who had been separated from their mothers, Robertson and Bowlby (1952) witnessed the silent withdrawal from life and their apathetic resignation as a sign of unhealthy development. The children went through stages in order of: protest (outbursts, crying, calling out), withdrawal (listless apathy, separation from peers) and detachment (hard to console or relate to at a deeper level, self-centred in relationships).

Bowlby was joined by Parkes (1972) who conducted a systematic study of bereavement, this time in adults, which confirmed Robertson's and Bowlby's earlier findings (1952). They postulated that anxiety is a realistic response to separation; this separation anxiety can consist of

DOI: 10.4324/9781003275268-3

anger, intense pain and overwhelming worry, angry outbursts (both to register displeasure and to "punish" to prevent the event repeating itself) and a yearning or searching for the missing person. These manifestations of separation anxiety can be extrapolated to the children this book is aimed at, since all emotions and reactions witnessed in these studies were in response to a trauma or "loss."

This early research demonstrates three components:

- **The sheer impact of loss in causing strong emotions and aggression.**
- **The importance of a parental-figure in calming, reasoning and dissipating the "destructive effects of rage in response to loss" (Holmes, 1993, p. 87).**
- **The child actively isolating themselves or disengaging and secluding as a defence mechanism "against the pain of unmet longing or anger faced alone" (Holmes, 1993, p. 88).**

The reaction to grief is seen as a *more extreme form of separation anxiety*; a permanent loss of *attachment* which causes a biological and physiological natural reaction as a response to this severe pain. Chapter 3 discusses attachment in further detail, while chapter 4 delves into the neuroscientific aspects behind those physiological and biological reactions.

Recognising, identifying and naming the emotion exhibited are aided by using a "Grief Model"; this gives a common approach to talking about the subject and helps to convey a complex state. It is more complicated than a staged linear approach in which we may expect someone to go through certain emotions, in a certain order, and then "get over" the grief. It is not a defined, predictable process.

A grief model therefore helps make sense of emotional responses to forced change, grief, loss and trauma. However, a point to note is that: the stages, the order, the emotional response and its intensity vary from person to person. These reactions may follow a rhythm over time, or they may be present within one day or even simultaneously; they do not have to follow a set order, and many may not even recognise that they are experiencing the impact of collective trauma or loss.

Next, we will consider the various models of grief, bereavement and loss to identify the common features across them and help our understanding. In these models, grief or loss is seen as a physical parting – this parting may be due to a variety of factors, including a bereavement, an absent relation or friend or lost friendships within school or other community (temporarily or permanently). In a collective trauma, there may be many aspects of life which are "lost."

Grief models

This section will discuss:

- **Freud's Four Phases of Grief Model (1917) as he was the catalyst for further theories and models that we use today. Since his initial theories are over-simplistic, three more models will also be described:**
- **The Kübler-Ross Change Curve (1969).**
- **The Dual-Process Model of Grief (Stroebe and Schut, 1999).**
- **Bowlby's Theory of Grief (1961), linked with his later (1969) "Attachment Theory" (Bowlby, 1971).**

Freud's Four Phases of Grief model (1917)

Central to Freud's (1917) view on mourning is that when we grieve, we are searching for "the attachment that has been lost." He believes that after our initial "loss," we pass through a period of mourning in which we gradually, through emotional highs and lows, *detach* from the loved person/home/lifestyle. Freud regards *detachment* as being the opposite to *attachment*.

Freud's stance on this rose from his beliefs as a psychodynamic theorist. Psychodynamic theory considers that our unconscious processes (such as our emotions, morals, our mind or personality) are what make us who we are; this brings the idea that a child or young person is affected by events and experiences in their early life which shape their thoughts, feelings and personality.

Freud's explanation for the root cause of these psychological processes was in the form of unconscious "drives," which are the energy motivating thought, action and emotion. According to Freud, a "drive" is the body making a "demand" and telling the "mind" to do something about it. The two "demands" (the drives) consisted of a need to preserve life ("libido") versus a destructive instinct ("aggression"). Freud had illuminated *the close, reciprocal connection between life-preservation and anger.* Life-instincts can mean wanting to survive and thrive, hence wanting to have "needs" satisfied, such as hunger, shelter, warmth, affection, love, belonging, healthy relationships, community and social *support*, pain avoidance; with unmet needs, strong emotions can follow. The conflict between the *life-drives* and the *destructive-anger-drives* implies that our emotions could bounce between these extremes; in bereavement that urge to be the "caregiver" can no longer happen. The resulting response may be strong, almost destructive emotions, such as anger or loss of control (dysregulation), surmised in his grief model.

Freud's "Four Phases of Grief" model, developed in the early 20th century (Freud et al., 1991), proposes that mourning a loss involves four stages:

1. Numbness or disbelief.
2. Yearning or searching.
3. Disorganisation or despair.
4. Reorganisation and resolution: identified by a gradual reorganisation of one's life and a sense of resolution.

Freud's model has been influential in the understanding of grief and mourning and has been used by psychoanalysts in two main ways (Hagman, 2016) clinically, as a quantifiable, medical model of response to loss, and secondly, "as a general psychological process which is engaged whenever a person must relinquish an attachment, whether to an object, idea, internal representation, affect…" (Hagman, 2016, p. xvii). This book will refer to this as *loss.* As established earlier, loss encompasses events or situations which require *personal adjustment* to retain stability.

This model has also been criticised for being too linear and prescriptive, and for failing to consider individual differences and cultural variations in the grieving process. Nevertheless, Freud's original paper and grief model acted as a catalyst upon which further models were based. There are three main pervasive tenements:

- "There is an identifiable, normal, psychological process of mourning", which has "identifiable, standard characteristics."
- The function of mourning is to be restorative rather than transformative; the "normal process leads to a point of resolution, rather than being open-ended and evolving" (Hagman, 2016).
- Mourning is a private, internal process rather than a social and relational one, and emotions of pain and sadness spontaneously arise from within the individual.

Whilst aspects of the model's key features are true, I emphasise that I do not hold with this standardised model as characteristics are bespoke, personal and non-linear. The traits of mourning, grief and loss are unique and highly personal for each group, community or individual; I also believe that working through grief and loss is transformative, that is, it changes us. We are not the same, we cannot be restored to what and how we were, therefore we evolve.

Fundamentally, if I held to this standard model then this book would have no place, and I would sit back and ascertain that each child and young person will automatically go through these various internal stages, and we can do nothing about it. However, I believe that we can *support* our children and young people through the range of extreme emotions that they demonstrate, in response to the desolation they feel, because of the extensive shock to their lives. In this sense, grief is not private but is a social/interpersonal/relational process. This can be seen in models that followed.

It is important to acknowledge that further theories do not suggest a final detaching, as Freud did, but rather advocate that children and young people can find a resolution to living with that loss – and this view brings hope.

Following Freud's theories came another model put forward by Kübler-Ross (1969).

The Grief cycle/change curve (Kübler-Ross, 1969)

Compiling her research, Kübler-Ross **presented a simple graph** to describe the emotional stages that a terminally ill patient may go through; it was never originally intended to be a model

The Kubler-Ross Change Curve

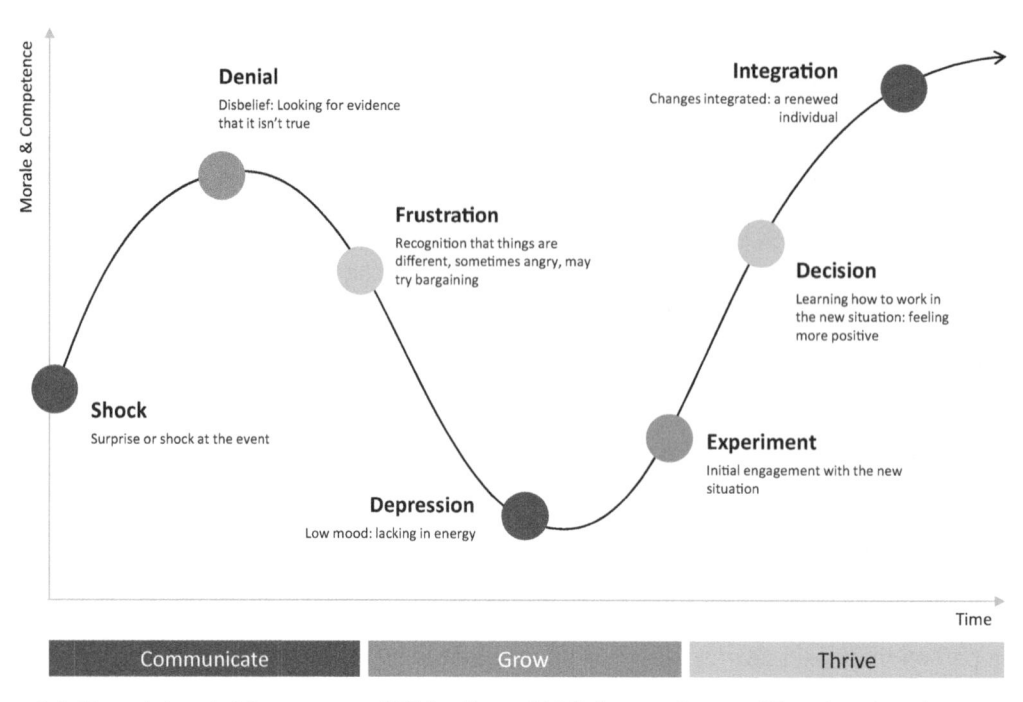

Figure 2.1 The grief cycle/change curve (Kübler-Ross, 1969). Image: PoweredTemplate (2023).

for a grief cycle neither was Kübler-Ross' intention to pigeon-hole emotions and suggest they follow a set pattern. It was a way of understanding another human at a time when they had discovered they had a terminal illness. However, it has since been used to demonstrate emotions that arise in response to other enforced change.

The Kübler-Ross Change Curve diagram (also known as the five stages of grief), above, describes the internal, emotional journey that individuals typically experience when dealing with change and transition, such as enforced workplace change. Strong links were made between enforced change (which alludes to a "loss" of *how things were*) and grief. This journey consists of seven phases that people usually go through: shock, denial, frustration, depression, experiment, decision and integration (Figure 2.1). Emotions experienced along the journey are said to include: shock and denial, anger, bargaining, depression and acceptance.

It is easy to recognise and identify the named emotion with the Kübler-Ross Change Curve; it helps make sense of emotional responses to forced change. However, it is more complicated than this linear approach and Kübler-Ross herself also asserted that the stages, order and intensity vary from person to person (to acknowledge individuality).

This change curve has therefore been translated into the following diagram (Figure 2.2) to illustrate a grieving individual's *energy* and *satisfaction* levels at each phase. The emotions linked with *low versus high energy* and *life-satisfaction versus limited satisfaction* have an implication when supporting children and young people exhibiting these responses.

These emotional responses within each "stage of grief" vary from individual to individual. They may follow a pattern over time, they may be present within one day or even present simultaneously; they do not have to follow a set order and many may not even recognise that they are experiencing the impact of a trauma or collective trauma.

The emotions represented within the stages are:

1. **SHOCK and DENIAL:** surprise or shock at the initial incomprehensible event, and a disbelief that it has happened.
2. **ANGER:** recognition that things are different: frustration and sabotage; it may also include separation anxiety or regression.
3. **BARGAINING:** bargaining is an attempt to prevent the inevitable; it is also linked with frustration.

phases of grieving

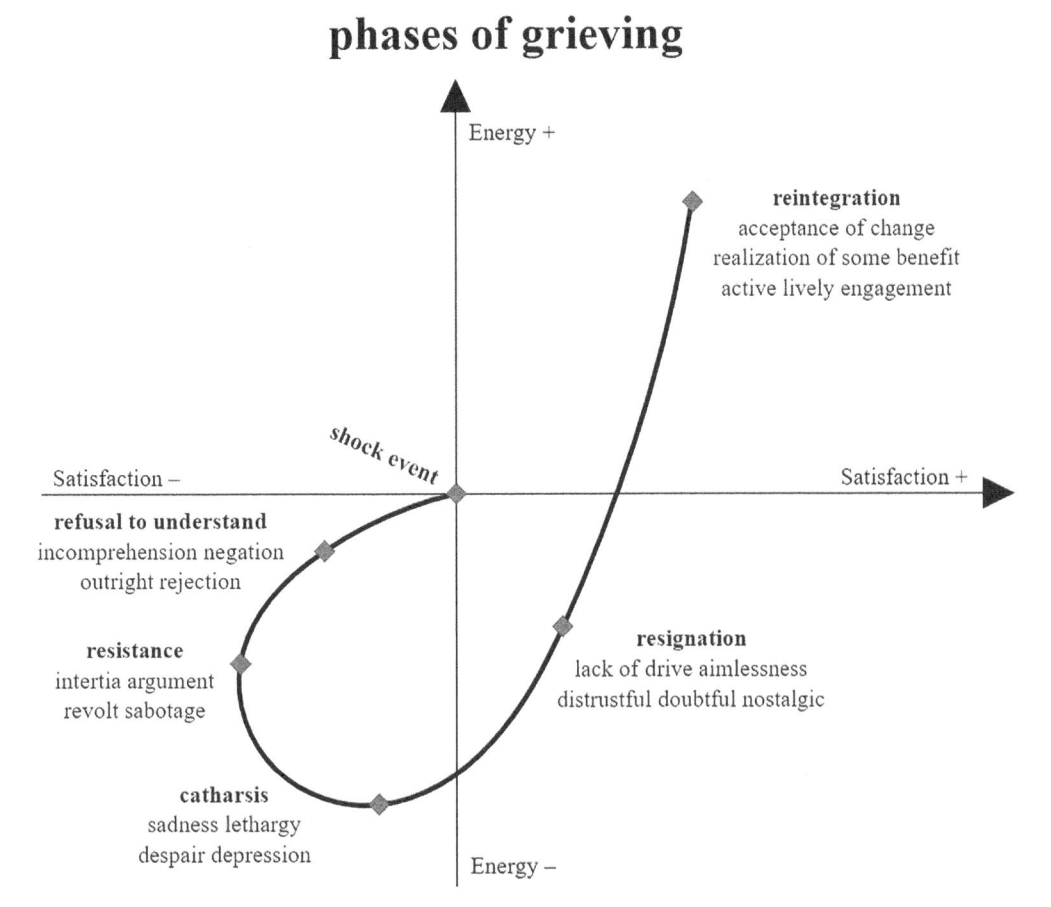

Figure 2.2 Phases of grieving. Image: Jikybebna (2021) CC BY-SA 4.0 DEED adaptation of Rebestalic (2020).

4. **DEPRESSION:** a stage of low mood and low energy: despair, lethargy and sadness are features of this stage.
5. **ACCEPTANCE:** this is depicted by calmness due to the realisation that fighting change is not going to make it go away. We stop resisting change, accept and move on. Some may explore new opportunities.

However, any stage can be "re-visited" at any point, and for any length of time. The theme of rapidly moving between emotional states is a central theme to *the dual process model of grief.*

The dual process model of grief (Stroebe and Schut, 1999)

The dual process model of grief (Stroebe and Schut, 1999) depicts the grieving person as being in a state where they bounce between two domains, one being "loss-orientated" tasks/emotions, and the other being "restoration-orientated." Loss orientation includes "grief work," that is, facing up to the loss, processing it, reminiscing, feeling emotions related to that loss (the opposite to avoiding, denying or repressing the loss), while being "restored" is the phase of adapting to life, trying new things, denying or avoiding grief and developing new relationships (Figure 2.3).

Since this diagram illustrates how a child or young person may oscillate between the two phases, it suggests that *it is ok, to not be ok.* The model *confirms and accepts* that experiences rebound continually between those linked to *grief and loss* and those which are *forward-looking* again. It sees the positive phase as being expected and therefore suggests that "trying new things out" or starting a new relationship is not something to feel guilty about. However, how frequently a child or young person bounces between, or resides in, each of these two sides is very individual. This model depicts a dynamic process characterised by a roller-coaster of emotions.

A further theory which posits that grief evolves through a sequence of emotions is Bowlby's theory of Grief (1961).

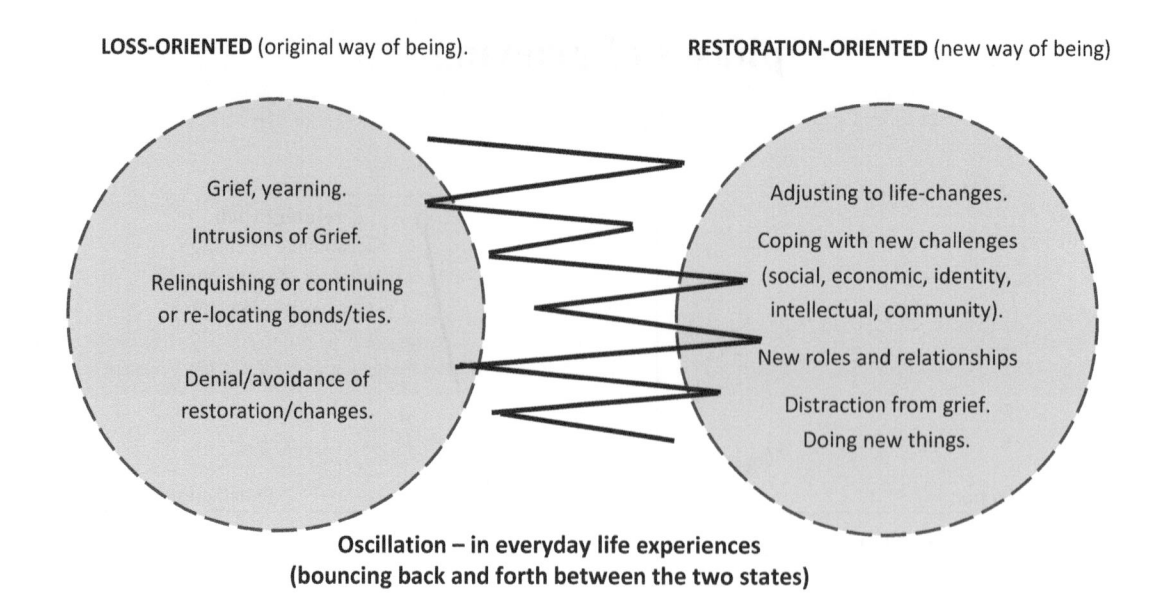

LOSS-ORIENTED (original way of being).   RESTORATION-ORIENTED (new way of being)

Grief, yearning.

Intrusions of Grief.

Relinquishing or continuing
or re-locating bonds/ties.

Denial/avoidance of
restoration/changes.

Adjusting to life-changes.

Coping with new challenges
(social, economic, identity,
intellectual, community).

New roles and relationships

Distraction from grief.
Doing new things.

**Oscillation – in everyday life experiences
(bouncing back and forth between the two states)**

Figure 2.3 The dual process model of coping with grief and loss. Taylor (2023) as described in Stroebe and Schut (2010).

Bowlby's theory of Grief (1961)

Bowlby (1961) built his theories after Freud's ideas resonated with him; the idea that the child or young person is searching for their *lost attachment* is a key theme. The emphasis on personal attachment conveys the importance of human relationships (attachments) and bonds developing in early life. Bowlby held the view that these attachments form a system where the individuals continually impact each other, aiming to "attune" to maintain their relationship in various ways. Consequently, when a "loss" occurs or that bond is broken, when we "miss" that human, we experience grief; he regarded grief as a *normal*, *adaptive response*. Bowlby (1961) believes that grief evolves through a sequence of flexible phases; he broke it down into these stages:

1. Shock; numbness, physical distress, somatic symptoms.
2. Yearning and protest; aware of the void, we try to fill it.
3. Despair: hopelessness and helplessness, anger at the change, questioning, perhaps even depression. Realisation that the "loss" (bereavement or trauma) has removed the person(s) to who we would usually turn, as well as the person/people themselves. The young person feeling the "loss" is thrown into turmoil, that secure base has vanished.

Later, Bowlby's colleague Parkes (1972) added a fourth stage:

4. Recovery: reorganisation, realisation that life can still offer some positives, grief does not fully disappear but recedes in our thinking, but it may still influence us. The past inner world has been broken down, and it is now being rebuilt without the person or community in it.

Robertson (Robertson and Bowlby, 1952) and Parkes (1972) supported Bowlby's theories and earlier work, which developed into Bowlby's 1969 *theory of attachment* (1971, 1981); this will be discussed further in the next chapter.

This theory offers us reasons why we experience emotional distress when those attachment bonds are irreversibly broken (and we suffer within that loss). It has been "done" to us, it was not our choice to sever that mutual relationship that had actively built over years or decades of that life together. Bowlby viewed the emotional reaction as normal development; he regarded expression of anger as a *healthy positive response*, and as a sign of *active protest*, whereas repressing anger was seen as unnatural, since, "a violent reaction is normal and an apathetic resignation a sign of unhealthy development" (Holmes, 1993, p. 88). The reactions to bereavement are, essentially, an extension of reactions to loss or separation. Bowlby views anxiety as being one reaction to separation or threatened separation; here a link can be made between the anxiety of threatened separation and the "perceived threat" that is present during times of pandemic, war or economic downturn. We can assume that since the relationship is reciprocal (parent-child, spouse-spouse, caregiver-care seeker, friend-supporter, adult-companion, partner-partner), the "attachment dynamic will continue throughout adult life" (Holmes, 1993, p. 89) and consequently separation anxiety will exist whenever that relationship is threatened. Symptoms of this threat include emotions such as worry, a yearning or searching (for the person), pain and tension and angry protest (as a punishment, to prevent this occurring again). Bereavement is a special case of separation anxiety; it is a permanent and unalterable separation.

Bowlby (1980) used childhood experiences (involving separation) to explain these emotional reactions; grief and loss are seen as responses to a more permanent mode of experiencing "separation." The **next chapter** will consider his attachment theory – as our reactions to trauma or loss also stem from the *base* that we are each operating from.

Summary

	Emotional responses to grief, loss and forced change summary table
1.	Anxiety is a realistic response to separation; *it* can consist of overwhelming worry, intense pain, angry outbursts (both to register displeasure and to "punish," to prevent the event repeating itself) and a yearning/searching for the missing person. These manifestations of separation anxiety, the emotions, are in response to a trauma or loss (Parkes, 1972; Robertson and Bowlby, 1952).
2.	Early research demonstrates three components: • The sheer impact of loss in causing strong emotions and aggression. • The importance of a parental-figure in calming, reasoning and dissipating the "destructive effects of rage in response to loss" (Holmes, 1993, p. 87). • The child actively isolating themselves or disengaging and secluding as a defence mechanism "against the pain of unmet longing or anger faced alone" (Holmes, 1993, p. 88). The reaction to grief is a *more extreme form of separation anxiety*; a permanent loss of *attachment* causes a biological and physiological natural reaction as a response to this severe pain.
3.	Using a *grief model* gives a common approach to talking about the subject and it helps to convey a complex state; it is not a defined, predictable process. A grief model therefore helps make sense of emotional responses to forced change, grief, loss and trauma.
4.	**Freud's Four Phases of Grief Model (1917):** a child or young person is affected by events and experiences in their early life which shape their thoughts, feelings, morals and personality. The four stages: (i) Numbness or disbelief, (ii) Yearning or searching, (iii) Disorganisation or despair and (iv) Reorganisation and resolution; gradually reorganising one's life and gaining resolution. The three main pervasive tenements: • "There is an identifiable, normal, psychological process of mourning", which has "identifiable, standard characteristics." • The function of mourning is to be restorative rather than transformative; the "normal process leads to a point of resolution, rather than being open-ended and evolving" (Hagman, 2016). • Mourning is a private, internal process rather than a social and relational one, and emotions of pain and sadness spontaneously arise from within the individual.
5.	**The Kübler-Ross Change Curve (1969)** (also known as *the five stages of grief*) describes the internal, emotional journey that individuals experience when dealing with transitions and enforced change. Strong links were made between enforced change (a loss of *how things were*) and grief. Emotions experienced along the journey are said to include: *shock and denial, anger, bargaining, depression and acceptance*. However, any stage can be 're-visited' at any point, and for any length of time.
6.	**The Dual-Process Model of Grief (Stroebe and Schut, 1999)** illustrates the theme of rapidly moving between emotional states. It suggests that *it is ok, to not be ok*. The model accepts that experiences rebound continually between those linked to *grief and loss* and those which are *forward-looking* again. It sees the positive phase as being expected, and therefore not something to feel guilty about. This model depicts a dynamic, individual process characterised by a roller-coaster of emotions.
7.	Bowlby's **Theory of Grief (1961)** proposes that the child or young person is searching for their *lost attachment*. This emphasises the importance of human relationships (attachments) and bonds developing in early life. Consequently, when a *loss* occurs or that bond is broken, we experience grief as a *normal*, *adaptive response that* evolves through a sequence of flexible phases: • Shock: numbness, physical distress, somatic symptoms. • Yearning and protest: aware of the void, we try to fill it. • Despair: hopelessness and helplessness, anger at the change ("active protest" is a healthy, positive response), questioning, perhaps even depression. Realisation that the "loss" (bereavement or trauma) has removed the person(s) to who we would usually turn, as well as the person/people themselves. The young person feeling the "loss" is thrown into turmoil that secure base has vanished. • Recovery: reorganisation, realisation that life can still offer some positives, grief does not fully disappear but recedes in our thinking, but it may still influence us. The past inner world has been broken down, and it is now being rebuilt without the person or community in it (Parkes, 1972).

(Continued)

	Emotional responses to grief, loss and forced change summary table
	This theory offers us reasons why we suffer emotional distress when those long-standing attachment bonds are irreversibly broken. A link can be made between the anxiety of threatened separation and the "perceived threat" that is present during times of pandemic, war or economic downturn. Symptoms of this threat include emotions listed above. Bereavement is a special case of separation anxiety; it is a permanent and unalterable separation. This theory links with his later (1969) "Attachment Theory" (Bowlby, 1971) (chapter 3).
8.	Put simply, what these theories and systems of grief concur is that: • We exhibit strong emotions (as part of our instinctual survival) when we experience grief, loss or trauma. • Grief and loss models largely agree that responses such as anger, denial, hopelessness, despair, depression and questioning are likely to form part of the responses post-trauma. • These responses can occur and recur in short or lengthy bouts, by themselves, or all at the same time! There is no set pattern or series of stages that we all go through in a predetermined order, it is highly personalised and depends on the individual. • In a *collective trauma*, many people are experiencing strong emotions simultaneously.

3 UNDERSTANDING ATTACHMENT THEORY

Chapter overview

- Early experiences make the template for relationships.
- The base the child is operating from can, in turn, impact their response to grief, or loss or forced change.
- Describing attachment theory helps in understanding its practical out-workings such as the range of responses to the same trauma.
- The responses may range from resilience, due to strong wellbeing and secure attachment, through to a traumatic response, including anger, anxiety or depression; the latter requires a supportive intervention.
- A child's attachment relationship with their teacher develops independently to their attachment relationship with their parent; if this relationship is positive then a secure, trusting bond makes *support* more effective.

Attachment Theory offers us reasons why we need to form strong relational bonds with others. To offer a common understanding to the concepts discussed in this chapter, it will begin with an illustration.

Picture the scene, you are walking in a dark forest in the Spring, birds are singing, flowers are out and it's sunny. You're enjoying the tranquil atmosphere and the cool in the shady branches. Now imagine that you are there during a dark, silent night; senses are heightened as you are aware of every sound, each snap of a twig, or call of an owl. If you had, for example, a phobia of small creatures, then every rustle at ground-level would have you on high-alert with extra vigilance needed; you would not be able to think of anything else as your eyes darted everywhere and your heart-raced... you would likely be unable to concentrate to answer any logical question. However, if that night adventure is accompanied by a fellow human (or dog) in whom you have a close trusting bond, then, generally, the heightened awareness, anxiety or racing-heart reduces, you feel safer – and therefore in a better place emotionally to explore or embark on a different adventure.

Children need to feel safe and secure to explore and have the confidence to venture out. Bowlby (1988) would call this having a *secure attachment* to our main caregiver(s) (Bomber, 2011; Geddes, 2006). Children and young people who have this secure foundation in place will feel the security that comes from consistent, reliable *support*; this gives a strong sense of belonging. When we are with someone who we trust, we can move out of our comfort zone, we can engage with *challenge and learning* as we are open to new experiences (Ainsworth and Bell, 1970). When children trust the adult, they can learn – and this includes learning a language and a culture. We call these positive aspects **protective factors.**

Conversely children and young people who do not experience *support* they can trust in may feel unsafe or powerless. They may not have the security or self-esteem to venture out if they have an "insecure attachment" to their primary carers (Rose et al., 2015). These negative experiences we refer to as **risk factors** and they may include experiencing early trauma or "adverse childhood experiences" (ACEs) (WHO, 2020); these will clearly have an impact on their personality and their reactions to experiences or events. Early trauma or "ACEs" can result from a whole host of factors (NHS, 2023) such as:

- families experiencing care-giving challenges,
- neglect,

DOI: 10.4324/9781003275268-4

- very inconsistent or absent parental-figure(s),
- abuse (emotional or physical),
- witnessing violence in the home and
- isolation or enforced separation.

Since any young child is impacted by their lived situation, those closest to them have an impact. Their "child development" begins with the first three years of their life.

What children are impacted by (early child development)

Over the decades, there have been several models of child development, all of which focus on how children grow and change throughout childhood and into adulthood. These models help us understand how children may acquire cognitive, social-emotional, physical (gross and fine motor skills) and educational (speech and language) growth.

Cognitive skills include intellect, memory and reasoning, which lead onto skills such as problem-solving and decision-making. It is the stimulus of the world around them that causes a child to learn; as their brain develops, it rewires itself in response to its environment. If we consider that every day children acquire new information, learn skills, process information and form new or different opinions, then it follows that this will include knowledge regarding opinions of their own self-worth. This suggests an interlinking of cognitive and social-emotional development. When *self-esteem* is considered alongside their *social and emotional (psychological)* development, then it stands to reason that a fundamental necessity is an adult caregiver who meets these needs and provides a nurturing environment; the National Childbirth Trust (2023) website offers explanations and examples in abundance to *support* these early years (Tronick, 2017). The *Centre for Early Childhood* (2022) commissioned research, titled "Big Change Starts Small." It considered the first 1,000 days of a baby's life with respect to physical, social and emotional development (NCT, 2023) and demonstrates that the largest influence in early childhood is adults.

The resulting impact

Early developmental theories suggested that the right side and the left side of the brain were responsible for different functions. Whilst this theory has been largely refuted, it will be briefly described.

The left side was regarded as being responsible for speech and language, reading, maths and writing. It was said to be ordered, literal, logical and sequential and therefore it focused on the detail. Its analytical capabilities were described as enabling us to put our experiences into words and make predictions based on past events – its use was to evaluate, make a choice and plan (McGilchrist, 2009).

The right side was said to be our feeling side of the brain, to comprehend *meaning* in a situation, the emotions, not the words; it helped us understand those non-verbal cues in communication: paralinguistics (voice tone and volume), gesture, posture, eye gaze, personal space, touch, facial expression and body language. It was described as holistic and concerned with "the big picture," using sensory information to intuitively perceive our experiences. Being non-verbal, it communicates in symbols or images, caring about the meaning and the feel of an experience; it is highly attuned to the emotional world, past experience and personal memory.

Recent research suggests that these functional specialisations of the brain are complex and distributed across various regions of the whole brain, rather than be strictly confined to one side or the other. The brain operates through intricate networks and connections with both hemispheres working together in most tasks (Gazzaniga et al., 2019). These *functions*, previously attributed to the "right" and "left" hemispheres, do exist; however, they are the result of *dynamic interactions* across different regions in the whole brain (Barrett, 2021). One example is a child becoming aware of how they *feel* after a negative experience; the emotional "feeling" response could be anxiety or fear. The brain, linking the experience and the unpleasant emotion, deduces that we should strive to prevent enduring that situation again. Another relevant factor is that being with someone who makes you feel safe is less energy-depleting, which allows a wider range of brain regions to be available for problem-solving (Rose and Gilbert chapter, in Colley and Cooper, 2017); it is another example of the emotional and the cognitive brain functionality working in harmony. Neuroscientific approaches are discussed further in chapter 4.

Research is ongoing, nevertheless earlier resources often state that a young child has a "left side" of the brain that is not fully developed but that we know when it springs into action as that is when they begin asking questions, sometimes continually, such as, "why? what's that? why?" If we refer to this as *cognitive development*, rather than "left brain development," it reflects the fact that the young child is aiming to gain knowledge at a pace that is correct for them and about a topic in which they are interested, to help their brain grow and build. This logical development wants to understand the connections in the world, whereas prior to this surge in brain growth, children under three years old generally do not have the ability to use words to communicate their feelings, they do not have their *reasoning* knowledge-base, they just "feel" (Siegal and Bryson, 2011). Reactions at a young age are not wilful, just a response to what they are feeling – they communicate through crying or throwing themselves on a floor as they do not yet have sufficient cognitive and language skills. A baby, toddler or child at that developmental stage will mainly detect the emotion in a situation.

> *A toddler may spend ages in awe of moving trees or crawling ants, it is fascinating to watch them point and laugh in glee as ants carry leaves, or branches wave in the wind. We marvel at their sense of awe and wonder.*
>
> *They may become absorbed when playing with sticks and stones, all based on what they are experiencing in that moment – how it makes them feel is the thing most important to them.*
>
> *Senses are used as objects are held to their mouth to bite on or shaken to determine if they can elicit a sound.*
>
> *Infants react emotionally to the situation they are in, there is no cognitive filtration system, and it can be joyful to watch them dance unhindered by social norms.*

The adults who matter to the young child have the greatest impact on what they *feel*, what emotions are evoked and what sense they have of the situation they are in – whether they feel fear, confusion, safety, calmness or joy. Ultimately children need to sense comfort and warmth from the adults caring for them.

Staying safe and staying close are recognisable evolutionary traits, they are natural, biological, survival instincts as those infants who were protected and kept safe were those who were most likely to survive. We also see this happening in the animal kingdom too, and we call this "attachment." A strong attachment helps a baby thrive; to do so, they need to bond with an adult.

Babies have a limited ability to regulate their own emotions or calm themselves when distressed. A natural survival reaction is that the baby will try to make the caregiver interact with them – succeeding in *forming a secure bond* means an adult will carry you close and offer protection and safety. The aim of smiling, frowning or crying out is to gain the adult's attention; babies can signal an emotion in various ways, for example, when they turn away or focus their attention on another object, it is an attempt to *hold-in* their distress, this turning away (or throwing themselves face down on the floor) is a means of showing disapproval. However, when they stroke themselves or clasp their own hands together, they are trying to calm (self-regulate) themselves as a response to a stressful situation (Music, 2016); these actions also suggest that they have given up trying to gain the caregivers' attention. *The "still face experiment"* (Tronick, 1989, 2017) shows that babies are upset by bad communication experiences, hence try to avoid them and do all they can in their power (laughing, pointing, making eye contact, small distress cries and so on) to regain a positive interaction. However, when a baby's caregiver responds to the baby, smiles when the baby smiles, sings and observes joy or reactions in the baby and comforts when the infant is crying, then the bond is "attuned." There is a two-way relationship as they respond to each other and communicate together; time spent together is a positive experience and gives that "feel-good" sensation. This happy, secure and safe relationship between the parental-figure and child brings contentment and joy. Natural bonding and enjoyment occur in *positive shared experiences*; laughter and fun during play, smiling at dancing butterflies, and calm tiredness during a bedtime story, all *strengthen* the two-way connection, the reciprocal bond between infant and caregiver (Colley and Cooper, 2017).

This reciprocal bond is known as "attachment," and a secure attachment is forged during these consistent, emotional interactions and communications (both verbal and non-verbal). Attachment is the part of this relationship that involves protection; therefore, the infant understands how safe they feel. As well as giving this sense of safety, it helps with regulating their security and regulating emotions; it provides that confidence in their safe base, from which they can go out to explore (Bowlby, 1988).

When those happy, joyous, playful, calm times give way to times when the infant is distressed, crying or in pain, it is the adult figure who will act to *support* the infant, alter the situation, act to relieve distress and bring comfort. That awareness of the infant's emotional state where the parent-figure picks up on cues and responds appropriately is known as *"attunement."*

Even good mothers don't *attune* 100% of the time; in reality, good mothers attune 30% of the time (Ham and Tronick, 2009). Times of mis-attunement occur when a mother fails to immediately notice her newborn's reaction (smile or cry) and act accordingly, but this break in attunement can be repaired. Thus, a gap or "wait time" is experienced between the infant alerting the parent to their needs and getting their needs met; it is not a wholly negative occurrence since the "wait-time" helps to build resilience *if* the parent soon notices and acts appropriately.

It is also an encouragement that this is classed as *"good enough" parenting*, and that *"perfect parenting"* does not exist (Winnicott, 1973). Resilience starts to be built in these early months of an infant's life. Resilience is a quality that enables children to regulate their emotions and be able to think and reason, even when under stress (Clark, 2019). Children and young people who have been *well-supported* emotionally will develop a tolerance to frustration and an ability to persevere when faced with difficulty.

> *"Oh, you want your cuddly toy, I think you dropped it *picks it up* here it is [hands toy]"*

Being "well-supported" involves the carer being *"attuned"* and, for example, "chatting" to the baby about a concurrent event.

This chatting helps a baby make sense of the world as it gives meaning to their reactions; their emotions have been ***regulated*** as their inner or mental state has been explained back to them in words and actions. Both positive and negative emotions can be regulated, when structured through the feedback of an adult attuned to them (Meins et al., 2003). This leads to a trust that their thoughts and feelings have been accepted and understood. If they have been upset, understood and calmed down, then the infant gains insight into what they were feeling and how they are viewed from another person's point of view, thus giving the baby an internal representation of themselves. This view of themselves is sometimes referred to as their "Inner Working Model" (IWM) (Bowlby, 1988).

When the parent-figure responds to the infant in a suitable manner, offering a balanced reaction rather than an overreaction, they empathise with the infant's negative experience, acknowledge their pain, *soothe* them and subsequently provide opportunities for distraction. This approach enables the infant to effectively navigate and surpass the obstacles posed by the "bad experience." Bion (2019) describes this as **"containment"** of emotions, in which the caregiver has "edited" or "modulated" those strong emotions and fed them back to their baby in a digestible form. This reassures the child that the moment was not as scary as they first thought, hence it builds trust, mutual understanding (Music, 2016) and a secure attachment. This containment can be as simple as allowing a toddler, or young child, to repeatedly tell you the same story over-and-over in order that you can talk it through with them and feedback to them how to respond – it helps the child make sense of the world. Dan Siegel (Siegel and Bryson, 2011) refers to this as **"integration"** where the negative experience, or mild shock, eventually becomes just another one of life's experiences. Talking with a toddler or older child about their "bad" experiences will help them develop resilience to call on in later life – it is a time for growth and brain rewiring (Siegel and Bryson, 2011). This brain rewiring (neuroplasticity) is discussed further in chapter 4, but put simply, the parent-figure directly shapes their child's growing brain; talking about feelings helps them develop emotional intelligence. Consequently, by the time they reach adolescence, a young person is more equipped to understand their own and other people's emotions and respond appropriately (Siegel and Bryson, 2011).

When children lack integration, they experience "dysregulation," which manifests as an inability to effectively control (regulate) their emotions. They exhibit signs of being overwhelmed, and potentially appear out of control, confused and unable to maintain a state of calm. This dysregulation may result in tantrums, meltdowns or even aggression. It typically takes approximately

20–25 minutes for adrenalin levels to decrease before a highly aroused child can commence the process of self-regulation (and certainly before engaging in a discussion about the incident); implementing a calming "time out" strategy proves effective where the child understands that they are not being reprimanded or *"in trouble."* Key points to remember about *how* we respond (described in chapters 5–6) are preferably: remaining calm and patient, imposing no fear or threat and choosing age-appropriate words to convey that you understand. A child who is frequently fearful of a parent/carer, or regularly scared of another person/situation and are not kept emotionally safe by their parent-figure experiences a level of trauma and **neglect.**

Originally, Sigmund Freud (1917) and John Bowlby (1988) believed that neglectful parents (their early research only considered mothers) were the only cause of ***Attachment Disorder***. However, recent research has determined that Attachment Disorder can also occur more frequently within other groups of infants: premature babies (Carpenter et al., 2015), in disabled children, in blind babies with sighted mothers (Music, 2016) or in a family where parents may have addictions or substance-abuse. Here, "Attachment Disorder" is largely due to the higher number of occasions where it is difficult to "attune" to the babies needs to build the essential sense of safety.

Since relationships and attachment are highly important in forming who we are (Freud's 'idea of 'self', 1917; Bowlby's 'Inner Working Model', 1971), it naturally follows that healthy relationships and strong, successful *attachments* are important in sustaining our wellbeing and developing our emotional regulation (Carpenter, 2017, in Colley and Cooper, 2017).

Secure attachment and life outcomes – the need to feel safe

Consequently, *attachment* style is inextricably linked to the child's emotional experiences within their family setting, with their primary caregiver(s).

A crucial point to emphasise is that even if we did not get the best start in life, then we can still **break this cycle**. It is possible to learn and develop the skills needed to raise our children in a way that was different to how we were raised. For further reading on this subject, read "Growing up Again: Parenting Ourselves, Parenting Our Children" (Clarke and Dawson, 2009); Clarke refers to *not being parented well ourselves* as **uneven parenting.** The book, among many other good reads on this topic, considers effective ways to break this cycle and raises awareness that while it may feel a negative experience, something must have gone *well enough* to raise a child to an adult.

A report, written by a highly specialist team (Harvard University specialists from its "Center on the Developing Child," together with UK-based neuroscientists and academics) identified a direct link between *early childhood experiences* (ECE) and *life outcomes*. It also considered wider impacts such as financial wellbeing, addiction and crime (Centre for Early Childhood, 2022) and clearly shows that the early years lay the foundation for "our future selves." Our experiences and our interactions shape and mould us – and this can have a permanent impact on our mental and physical wellbeing. It is when and where, "we first learn to manage our emotions and impulses, to care and to empathise, and thus ultimately to establish healthy relationships with ourselves and others" (HRH The Duchess of Cambridge, in Centre for Early Childhood, 2022, p. 4).

Not-so-healthy relationships

However, when those relationships are not healthy and the attachment bond is weak or non-existent, a child may be considered to have an Attachment Disorder. It is believed that Attachment Disorder originated directly because of a poor attachment formed with the main caregiver – an "insecure attachment" style can lead to social, emotional and mental health (SEMH) difficulties in children and young people, an indicator of this was often given the descriptor "poor behaviour," whereas this **behaviour is their communication** tool to signal something is wrong.

*It is important to note that even if the child has attachment trauma in the relationship with their parent, they can still have a positive relationship with their teacher. This is because a **child's attachment relationship with their teacher develops independently to their attachment relationship with their parent**; if the teacher-pupil relationship is positive and the teacher is emotionally available, then a secure, trusting bond makes support (chapters 5–8) more effective.*

Table 3.1 A table describing features of the attachment styles

Attachment style	How it presents	The impact	Implications for later in life
Secure (healthy) The child's primary experience is a secure and loving relationship which provides a template for future relationships with a positive view of the world.	A healthy emotional bond that arises when the child learns to associate the presence of the parent with safety, love and comfort resulting from • repeated experiences of their feelings and needs being attuned to, validated and met, • of consistently being received by their parents with love and joy, • of being protected and kept safe, and of being calmed and *soothed* by their parents when in distress.	*Benefits:* The child develops a strong identity and awareness of their own and others' feelings. The child feels loveable and worthwhile. They feel safe and have a "secure base" from where they feel able to explore their environment, move out into the world. This stimulates curiosity, develops their sense of competence and autonomy; this *supports* their ability to learn. It leads to good future social and emotional development and healthy relationships. **Secure attachment** can be comforted. May get upset when their caregiver leaves, however knowing they will return will be easily *soothed* [observed in the "Strange Situation" experiment (Ainsworth and Bell, 1970)].	Children with a secure attachment style tend to display the following (Levy, 2016a, 2016b): • positive self-esteem; • the capacity for independence and autonomy; • resilience in the face of adversity; • the ability to manage impulses and feelings; • the ability to maintain long-term friendships; • positive relationships with parents, caregivers and other authority figures; • prosocial coping skills; • trust, intimacy and affection; • positive, hopeful belief systems about self, family and society; • empathy, compassion and conscience; • good behaviour in school; • academic success; • ability to promote secure attachment in their own children when they become adults.
Insecure (unhealthy) The child has learnt from their early attachment relationships that other people cannot be trusted to meet their needs and feelings, that other people cannot help to *soothe* their distress and that such people may even be a source of threat. Furthermore, the child or young person is likely to have developed a core belief that they themselves are fundamentally bad, unlovable and worthless and that the world is a dangerous place.	A child learns to associate the presence of the parent with a lack of comfort, pain and distress and develops defensive behaviours such as avoidance or clinginess to cope with that. This could be because, for whatever reason, the parent is unable or unwilling to meet the child's needs, they are repeatedly unable to *soothe* the child when they are dysregulated or may even increase their dysregulation; additionally, they may respond to the child with indifference, hostility or cruelty.	*Depending on the particular features of the relationship they had with their primary caregiver, the child or young person will have developed a range of behavioural strategies designed to help them survive:* **Anxious-resistant attachment** children do not trust adults as they cannot predict how they will respond, having experienced inconsistencies in parenting. They may be seen as clingy, attention seeking, and have negative self-worth.	By contrast, children with an insecure attachment style may exhibit some of the following: • low self-esteem; • needy, clingy or pseudo-independent; • lack of resilience when faced with stress or adversity; • lack of self-control; • difficulty with developing and/or maintaining friendships; • sense of alienation from and/or oppositional with parents, caregivers and other authority figures;

(Continued)

Table 3.1 (Continued)

Attachment style	How it presents	The impact	Implications for later in life
Insecure attachment *includes the following three types:* • *Anxious-resistant attachment* • *Avoidant attachment* • *Disorganised-disorientated attachment.*		**Avoidant attachment** children are often self-reliant or self-sufficient, having learnt from an early age that adults are not there for them. These children have a strong need to control situations and may appear withdrawn. Accordingly, a child may have learnt to suppress their feelings and needs; they avoid or withdraw from intimate relationships since their parent consistently ignored their needs and feelings. **Disorganised-disorientated attachment** children found their caregiver's behaviours were so unpredictable they never learned how to feel safe. The caregivers may be a source of fear to the child; consequently, they display high levels of anxiety and a need to control their environment and the people within it. This frightening inconsistency (sometimes responding, sometimes ignoring, sometimes shouting at them or even hurting them), causes the child to remain in a permanent state of terror and hypervigilance; this could express itself as agitation, as violent behaviour or as a frozen dissociative response.	• antisocial attitudes and behaviours; • aggression and violence; • difficulties with genuine trust, intimacy and affection; • negative, hopeless and pessimistic view of self, family and society; • lack of empathy, compassion and remorse; • behavioural and academic problems at school.

In school, teachers are a key person to the child or young person; they will be the ones to act as a buffer between the traumatic event and their future life. In school, they will be the ones to help them regulate and set them off on a better life-trajectory.

Attachment styles

Bowlby (1979) identified the following first three attachment styles and his student added the fourth. The psychologist, Mary Ainsworth, is known for devising "*The Strange Situation*" experiment to assess the security of a child's attachment to their caregiver (Ainsworth et al., 1979); the accompanying video is enlightening and in it the following attachment types (see Table 3.1) can be observed in toddlers.

Secure attachments are clearly essential for healthy development, and when they are not there, the children who are insecurely attached may have later issues. If unsupported, children and young people with an insecure attachment develop significant problems as they progress through school and into adulthood; this may include difficulties with learning, mental health problems and poor relationships.

Understanding responses to aid *support*

Understanding how pupils respond to events because of their attachment style can help the adults instigate appropriate strategies, particularly when supporting those who have an "insecure attachment" and during times of acute stress or loss, such as may be felt during (or after) a collective traumatic event. If supported, these children and young people potentially can experience positive outcomes with learning, wellbeing and relationships, both as they progress through school and into adulthood. When we consider the hours that a primary/ elementary pupil may spend with their teacher, 600–700 hours per year in the classroom (Burgess, 2013), there is a reliance on teachers and school staff recognising children's needs, and being knowledgeable in providing effective *support*, particularly when considering that specific attachment interventions may be needed. Supportive interventions are discussed further in chapters 5–8.

However, even the most "securely attached" children and young people may feel unsafe and insecure at times of collective trauma, caused by a lack of stability and a whole series of unknown possibilities.

In the current climate, with economic instability, the impact of war felt worldwide and having lived through a pandemic crisis, there is an increased risk of experiencing events that have an adverse effect on wellbeing and child development. For many families that risk is even greater as 1.3 million children and young people in England live in poverty (that is over a third of children under five in the UK), many others face adversity; half a million children live in the *most* vulnerable circumstances (Centre for Early Childhood, 2022).

Sadly, it is those who are already living in disadvantaged situations who feel the greatest impact in any difficult or traumatic situation. The COVID-19 pandemic made things harder for everyone; however, those in the most precarious situations had additional stress placed on their mental health and wellbeing. Research, news reports and witnesses to those affected made it apparent that our children and young people have felt the weight of the situation. Some of the impacts have been seen by teachers of *early years children*, who, when comparing the personal development of those who are starting school, find that there is a *developmental delay* – their speech, language and social skills were not at the higher levels expected (The Children's Commissioner, in Centre for Early Childhood, 2022, report; Andrews, 2023). This *developmental delay* impacts how teachers' respond and *support*, since pupils' attention and listening skills have been significantly limited; except with regard to using mobile phones or television, where Early Years specialists observed an increased skill set (Andrews, 2023). Some practical supportive interventions will be described in Part Two.

During times of a pandemic, or other situations where rules are imposed and lifestyles undergo drastic changes, the ability of the closest adults to meet the needs of infants may be compromised for various reasons; economic poverty, displacement as refugees or times of war, all bring severe challenges. For whatever reason, adults may be unable to "attune" to their child and needs may remain unmet.

This lack of *attunement* leaves the infants with unmet requirements. When a child lacks consistency, *support* or positive experiences, it significantly impacts their developmental progress. They may struggle with a poorly developed stress-regulation system, have difficulty utilising their thinking and reasoning skills, exhibit low resilience and experience feelings of frustration, pain, hurt or confusion (Music, 2016).

These challenges often manifest in outward expressions and behaviours. It is important to recognise that such behaviour is not inherently "bad," but rather a form of communication. "Children do not have bad behaviour, but merely inappropriate coping techniques" (Long, 2023, conference). All behaviour serves as a means for children to convey their needs and emotions.

For a child who has experienced neglect, trauma and/or abuse before they are three years old, the impact will be profound. The child will not feel safe and secure, their basic needs may not be met, they will feel helpless and scared and will act or react accordingly. Then, in addition, a serious life event is added to that mix, such as a "loss," a trauma, grief, a pandemic, displacement or poverty. The feeling of "helplessness, terror and rage" that was felt as a baby may emerge at whatever age that "new" trauma or loss is experienced.

Past trauma re-emerging

When faced with a trauma, some may be strongly reminded of a previous event and catapulted back to a prior time. We can be reminded of past events, both good and bad, through something we see, hear, feel, smell or experience. A song can jog our memory, a taste can remind us of an outing and a meal we had, similarly an emotion or a fear (however irrational) can evoke a traumatic response; it is as if we were experiencing that original trauma, or situation, all over again. It can conjure up a strong, unconscious emotional reaction.

Opportunity in brain "plasticity"

However, while experiencing this feeling is painful (as indeed is experiencing any grief, trauma or loss), it is also an opportunity to have those needs met. What is needed is a supportive environment, and knowledgeable and understanding adults, who can use or adapt strategies to *support* the child's needs. This requires a relational approach with appropriate interpersonal experiences (more on this in chapters 6 and 7).

Importantly, the environment, relationships and experiences all impact early child development and their evolving brain. Their brain circuits are all formed in the earliest years. Whilst genetics and the environment play a small part, it is the *brain circuits* which govern their responses – it underpins *how* they regulate their emotions, feelings and behaviour and build their sense of agency and confidence to ultimately navigate their physical and social worlds independently (Centre for Early Childhood, 2022).

From a neurobiological perspective, a secure attachment relationship is vital for the healthy development of the child's brain and wider nervous system. This is because babies are born with their nervous system relatively unformed and much of the development of this system takes place after birth through the interactions with their primary carer. If these interactions are warm, loving and responsive to the child's needs, the attachment will be *secure*. Therefore, the child will develop a healthy nervous system, including a well-developed stress-regulation system. This is critical for social and emotional development, as it gives them the resilience to cope with life's stresses and the capacity to regulate their emotional states and impulses.

However, even for children with an *insecure attachment*, or past trauma, there is hope.

In their early years, the brain has extreme "*plasticity*" which means it is easy to reshape; a child's or young person's thinking and responses can be altered. Therefore, it is possible to change an attachment style throughout our lives, depending upon our experiences within relationships. This is because our attachment style is effectively a *survival strategy*; when that strategy is no longer needed, it becomes possible to change it. Indeed, ultimately this reshaping can be beneficial too when we consider that a common initial response to trauma (or reminder of it) is the *fight-flight-freeze-fawn-flop response* (*chapter 4*); thinking about a child on full alert, fearful, anxious and possibly angry, helps us begin to understand how exhausting and scary this response must feel to the young person. It brings a compelling need to learn how we can rewire young brains.

During adolescence, there is increased plasticity of the brain which means that this is a fertile time for giving young people *support* to help them develop more security in their relationships. What this means in practice is that it is possible to give young people who are *insecurely attached* a positive experience of relationship that moves their attachment style from insecure to secure with positive and reparative consequences. Additionally, the pupil-teacher attachment relationship develops independently to a parent-child relationship, hence applying relationship-building strategies (described in Part Two), to build epistemic trust (chapter 8), always has value. Likewise, *how* teachers and education staff collectively model behaviour and their interactions directly influences pupil behaviour; collective experience is a core component in developing a positive environment conducive to thriving. Therefore, adults are crucial in the role of nurturing wellbeing and healthy development to turn a traumatic situation into an opportunity.

To understand *why* and *how* this is, the next chapter will delve further into aspects of the brain. Knowledge about neurodevelopment and more recent advances in neuroscience will help us begin to comprehend what is happening inside of the brains of our children and young people. The description of *neuroplasticity* (the brain's ability to evolve) brings hope; it shows how, despite adversity, with appropriate *support* there is opportunity for change.

Summary

	Understanding attachment theory summary table
1.	**Feeling safe and staying close** Children need to feel safe and secure to explore and have the confidence to venture out. Bowlby (1988) would call this having a *secure attachment* to our main caregiver(s) (Bomber, 2011; Geddes, 2006). The adults who matter to the young child have the greatest impact on the child, on what emotions they *feel* and what sense of safety they have of the situation they are in. Ultimately, children need to sense comfort and warmth from the adults caring for them. A strong *attachment* helps a baby thrive.
2.	**Regulation, attunement and IWM** Within this attachment bond, a parent-figure chatting out loud helps a baby make sense of the world as it gives meaning to their reactions; their emotions have been **regulated** as their inner or mental state has been explained back to them in words and actions. Both positive and negative emotions can be regulated, when structured through the feedback of an adult **attuned** to them (Meins et al., 2003). This leads to a trust that their thoughts and feelings have been accepted and understood.
3.	**Containment** When the parent figure responds to the infant, offering a balanced reaction rather than an overreaction, they empathise with the infant's negative experience, acknowledge their pain, *soothe* them, *support* and subsequently provide opportunities for distraction. In this **"containment"** of emotions, the caregiver has "edited" or "modulated" those strong emotions and fed them back to their baby in a digestible form (Bion, 2019). This approach enables the infant to effectively navigate and surpass the obstacles posed by the "bad experience." This reassures the child hence it builds trust, mutual understanding (Music, 2016) and a *secure attachment*.
4.	**Integration and resilience** This *containment* can be as simple as allowing a toddler, or young child, to repeatedly tell you the same story over-and-over in order that you can talk it through with them and feedback to them how to respond; it helps the child make sense of the world. Dan Siegel (Siegel and Bryson, 2011) refers to this as **"integration"** where the negative experience, or mild shock, eventually becomes just another one of life's experiences. This helps develop resilience to call on in later life and is a time for growth and brain rewiring (Siegel and Bryson, 2011).
5.	**Dysregulation and insecure attachment (Attachment Disorder)** When children lack *integration*, they experience *dysregulation*, which manifests as an inability to effectively control (regulate) their emotions. They may exhibit signs of being overwhelmed, appear out of control, confused and unable to maintain a state of calm. This dysregulation may result in tantrums, meltdowns or aggression. It typically takes approximately 20–25 minutes for adrenalin levels to decrease before a highly aroused child can commence the process of self-regulation. Time-out is needed, whilst the adult or teacher remains calm, patient, imposing no fear or threat and choosing age-appropriate words to convey that they understand (chapters 5–6). A child who is frequently fearful of a parent/carer, or regularly scared of another person/situation and is not kept emotionally safe by their parent-figure experiences a level of **trauma and neglect,** which leads to *insecure attachments* forming. **Not-so-healthy relationships** An "insecure attachment" style can lead to SEMH difficulties in children and young people, an indicator of this was often given the descriptor "poor behaviour," whereas this **behaviour is their communication** tool to signal something is wrong.
6.	**Healthy relationships, emotional regulation and wellbeing.** Since relationships and attachment are highly important in forming who we are (Freud's 'idea of self', 1917; Bowlby's 'Inner Working Model', 1971), it naturally follows that healthy relationships and strong, successful *attachments* are important in sustaining our wellbeing and developing our emotional regulation (Carpenter, 2017, in Colley and Cooper, 2017). There is a direct link between **and *life outcomes*** (Centre for Early Childhood, 2022); the early years lay the foundation for "our future selves" (including wider impacts such as financial wellbeing, addiction and crime). Our experiences and our interactions shape and mould us – this can have a permanent impact on our mental and physical wellbeing. It is when and where, "we first learn to manage our emotions and impulses, to care and to empathise, and thus ultimately to establish healthy relationships with ourselves and others" (HRH The Duchess of Cambridge, in Centre for Early Childhood, 2022, p. 4). *A child's attachment relationship with their teacher develops independently to their attachment relationship with their parent; if this teacher-pupil relationship is positive and the teacher is emotionally available, then a secure, trusting bond makes support (chapters 5–8) more effective. In school, the teachers are the key person to the child or young person; they will be the ones to act as a buffer between the traumatic event and them living their life. In school, they can be the ones to help them regulate and set them off on a better life trajectory.*

(Continued)

		Understanding attachment theory summary table
7.		**Understanding responses to aid** *support.* Understanding how pupils respond to events (and what their "behaviour" is trying to communicate) because of their attachment style, especially during times of acute stress or loss, surrounding a collective traumatic event, helps the adults instigate appropriate strategies. If supported, these children and young people potentially can experience positive outcomes with learning, wellbeing and relationships, both as they progress through school and into adulthood. There is a reliance on teachers and school staff recognising children's needs and being knowledgeable in providing effective *support* (chapters 5–8). However, even the most "securely attached" children and young people may feel unsafe and insecure at **times of collective trauma,** caused by a lack of stability and a whole series of unknown possibilities. Sadly, it is those who are already living in disadvantaged situations who feel the greatest impact in any difficult or traumatic situation placing additional stress placed on their mental health and wellbeing. During times of a pandemic, or situations where rules are imposed and lifestyles undergo drastic changes, the needs of infants may go unmet for various reasons: economic poverty, displacement as refugees or times of war, all bring severe challenges. This may prevent **attunement** to their needs. When a child lacks consistency, *support* or positive experiences, it significantly impacts their developmental progress. They may struggle with a poorly developed stress-regulation system, have difficulty utilising their thinking and reasoning skills, exhibit low resilience and experience feelings of frustration, pain, hurt or confusion (Music, 2016). These challenges often manifest in outward expressions and behaviours. It is important to recognise that such behaviour is not inherently "bad," but rather a form of communication. All behaviour serves as a means for children to convey their needs and emotions. **Past trauma re-emerging** When faced with a trauma, some may be strongly reminded of a previous event and catapulted back to past events, both good and bad, through something we see, hear, feel, smell or experience. A fear (however irrational) can evoke a strong, unconscious traumatic response – the emotions react as if we were experiencing that original situation all over again.
8.		**Opportunity in brain "plasticity."** However, while experiencing this feeling is painful (as indeed is experiencing any grief, trauma or loss), it is also an opportunity to have those needs met. What is needed is a: • Supportive environment. • Knowledgeable, understanding adults, who can use/adapt strategies to *support* the child's needs. • Relational approach with appropriate interpersonal experiences (chapters 6 and 7) and secure attachment. These experiences impact early child development and their evolving brain (chapter 4); the *brain circuits* govern their responses – this underpins *how* they regulate their emotions, feelings and behaviour and build their sense of agency and confidence to ultimately navigate their physical and social worlds independently (Centre for Early Childhood, 2022). **However, even for children with an** *insecure attachment,* **or past trauma, there is hope.** In their early years the brain has extreme "*plasticity*" which means it is easy to reshape; a child's or young person's thinking and responses can be altered. Therefore, it is possible to change an attachment style throughout our lives, depending upon our experiences within relationships. This is because our attachment style is effectively a *survival strategy*; when that strategy is no longer needed, it becomes possible to change it.

4 NEUROSCIENCE
Stress response – anxiety impacts learning

Chapter Overview

- This chapter examines advances from the realms of neuroscience to further our understanding of brain structure, functioning and brain changes when under stress.
- It demonstrates why a learner in our classroom who has trauma or anxiety is unlikely to learn. A pupil experiencing big emotions, such as anger, sadness, panic, anxiety and fear, cannot make reasoned decisions; their brain will be in fight-flight-fawn mode, or even worse, a freeze-flop response!
- Breathing is impacted and emotional regulation needs to occur to return the child or young person to a peaceful state. They cannot calm themselves down, so they need supportive adults to help them think, play and experience bodily control.
- These emotions can feel intense and unmanageable, particularly when given the changing nature of a teenager's brain construction.
- The good news though is brain plasticity; its ability to change and adapt gives hope and enables **SUPPORT** strategies to have a positive impact (described in Part Two of this book).

Introduction

Children are affected by their surroundings, and anyone who encounters them will know that their development (whilst partially dependent upon genetics) is largely impacted by the environment in which they develop. Their setting, their experiences and their relationships influence children's progress and their evolving brain. As we read in the previous chapter on "attachment," adults are crucial in their role of nurturing children, of being responsible for promoting good well-being and meeting physical needs.

Child development specialists have produced decades of research showing that the environment of a child's earliest years can have effects that last a lifetime. The long-term effects of neglect, maltreatment, poverty or early stress are well-established (Felitti, 2016). Just how these alter the brain can be more fully understood through the recent advances in neuroscience and imaging technology. Neuroscientists can now demonstrate how some early negative experiences result in certain patterns of brain activity; there is a direct link between experiences of trauma or neglect and which regions of the brain become wired (Lipina and Colombo, 2009).

Since the original brain circuits are being formed during their earliest years, *how* they are wired helps children navigate their emotions and regulate their feelings and behaviour. Generally, this brain-wiring is not "fixed," the brain has "plasticity" which means it can be re-wired; this reshaping can help alter thinking and responses to any stimulus or event in the environment. This "plasticity" is what gives hope for children and young people who have experienced individual or collective trauma; this "plasticity" is also the reason that adults, teachers, social workers and health visitors can hope to bring change to a young, traumatised brain.

Neuroscience has helped us for several reasons:

- If imaging techniques can help identify exactly how "Adverse Childhood Experiences" (ACEs) affect children and young people, then we might gain insight as how best to provide *support* to reduce (or reverse) this negative impact (Lipina and Colombo, 2009).
- Understanding how the brain works and responds gives insight that brings more effective *support*. We gain an awareness of how situations can trigger certain responses and behavioural reactions. This increased awareness may bring greater empathy which, in turn, paves

DOI: 10.4324/9781003275268-5

the way to a stronger relationship between the supportive adult and the child or young person.

It is for this last reason that this chapter is included. It is hoped that understanding this theory better equips us with knowledge, inherent to effectively *support* a vulnerable child; gaining insight into the general workings of our brain will help explain some of the reactions and behaviours we may witness.

The contents of this chapter will include:

- What our brain is for – to predict, maintain stability and keep us alive.
- Brain anatomy – the three main parts: cerebrum, brain stem and cerebellum. The outer surface of the cerebrum is the cerebral cortex. The prefrontal cortex and amygdala (in the limbic system) have key roles.
- How we actively construct our emotions.
- How the brain responds to stress or trauma.
- Key brain changes during adolescence that impact a teenager's development, thinking and actions.
- Brain plasticity – that brings hope.

What is our brain for?

In evolution terms the most primitive "brains" were akin to a few cells that detected light, or other sensory information, that allowed them to eat to survive (Human Genome Project, 2023). This is the case with the amphioxus, also known as a lancelet, a long tadpole-shaped creature that would plant itself in the seabed and wait until it sensed food drifting past (Barrett, 2021; ShapeofLife, 2023).

The Cambrian explosion (500 million years ago) saw rapid change. Originally life only existed in the sea, however, evolutionary development resulted in the three-part brain, along with the move from soft to hard bodies (Ortega-Hernández, 2014, 2015a, 2015b) and predatory creatures began to hunt (Pearson, 2014).

Consequently, this pushed the evolution of more complex brains, as they now needed to both recognise potential danger and coordinate movement to flee, in order to survive (Ma et al., 2015).

However, if they used up their energy when fleeing from a potential threat that never arrived, they wasted resources that they might have needed later; energy efficiency was the key to surviving (Barrett, 2020). Creatures needed to judge if a distant being would eat them or if they had spotted one good enough to eat. The brain evolved to keep the animal that housed it healthy and alive.

Although current brains are vastly complex, they are still restricted by the need to be energy efficient. A term used to describe this has been "body budgeting," a simplification of the scientific process of "homeostasis." We may be aware that if we have over-exerted ourselves one day, the next day we may need to relax and recover; this is a way of budgeting our body's resources.

However, when it comes to the vigilance required to hunt and eat, rather than be eaten, there could be no chilled "duvet days" due to over-exertion the day before. So, *prediction* emerged as an energy-saving strategy – *prediction* beats *reaction*. If a creature was prepared in advance, then it was more likely to live. Hence, the brain developed to help us survive and stay regulated to stay alive; *thinking* is a by-product of this need to stay alive (Barrett, 2021).

The brain – as a tool of prediction, to maintain stability and keep us alive!

The brain is an organ that actively makes predictions using information gathered from our external surroundings – it infers this sensory input in order to steer a vulnerable body through an unpredictable world (Friston and Picard, 2014). The brain is not so much a singular *organ*, but a whole metabolic process. Its main role is to maintain stability (homeostasis) within the internal workings of our body by controlling our physiological processes and our behaviour. If the brain predicts needs before they arise, then it *does the right thing* to aid our survival (Tranter, 2021). We invest in food, shelter, warmth, affection and physical protection; these plus all our mental capacities and our social-emotional reactions are part of the core mission to keep us alive. The brain achieves this through regulating all aspects of our body, from basic automatic ("autonomic") bodily functions such as breathing, blood pressure and heart rate, through to interpreting and processing our surrounding sensory information; this results in generating thoughts and emotions – and informs complex cognitive processes such as decision-making. The brain also plays a crucial role in social interaction, learning and memory – all towards the ultimate aim of aiding our continuing existence (Clark, 2019).

Recent advances in neuroimaging and other techniques have allowed scientists to study the brain's neural circuits, and the interplay between its different regions, in more detail. This has led to new insights into how the brain controls behaviour, emotions and cognitive processes such as decision-making, attention and memory.

Latest research suggests that the brain is a *highly complex and dynamic system… it functions to integrate information from the external environment, the body and internal mental processes* (Clark, 2019).

Furthermore, research has shown that the brain is highly adaptable and can change over time in response to environmental stimuli and experiences, a process known as neuroplasticity. This has important implications for understanding how the brain responds to various forms of therapy and how it recovers from injury or disease (Carter et al., 2014).

The brain is an incredible creation, an object of awe and wonder. With that in mind we will first delve into the structure of the brain.

An overview of brain anatomy

Getting to know the brain's main structures helps us understand how these relate to the brain's functioning (Figure 4.1). The relationship between brain structure and function is never simple. Although we often hear claims about the "language area" or "emotion centre" of the brain, statements like these are simplifications; in reality, even the simplest mental activities involve multiple brain regions (Barrett, 2021).

The brain can be divided into three major parts (Dingman, 2017).

1. **The brain stem**, shaped like a wide stalk, connects the spinal cord to the cerebrum and cerebellum. It controls reflexes and automatic, involuntary processes like breathing, blood pressure and heart rate.
2. **The cerebellum**, behind the brain stem and below the upper brain, is involved in balance and coordination. It receives information (from the cortex) about any movement we plan to make and uses information (from the spinal cord) about our body position, to allow us to move smoothly whilst maintaining balance and equilibrium.
3. **The cerebrum**, the largest part (85%) of the brain, sits above the brain stem and cerebellum. The **cerebrum** is the area most involved in higher processes like memory and learning. Many structures form the cerebrum; these include the lobes, limbic system and cerebral cortex.

The cerebrum's outer covering is called the **cerebral cortex** (or the *cortex*). It is merely 6-mm thick (in adulthood) yet takes responsibility for the brain's most advanced activities, such as planning and decision-making, and all higher order conscious activities such as imagination and creativity, language and abstract thought. It houses our memory which includes our biographical memory and all automatic memories related to familiar activities, including talking, walking, dance routines and playing a musical instrument (colloquially referred to as *muscle memory*).

The folds of the **cerebral cortex**, which give the brain its wrinkled appearance, are used to divide the cerebral cortex into smaller units called **lobes** (Urban Child Institute, 2023).
The four lobes.
There are two halves to the brain, the right and left hemispheres. Each hemisphere has four lobes (Nikoni, 2011).

A. **The occipital lobes**, at the back of the brain, control vision.
B. **The parietal lobes** are associated with bodily sensations like heat, cold, pressure and pain.
C. **The temporal lobes** are involved with hearing, language skills and social understanding, including perception of other people's eyes and faces.
D. **The frontal lobes** are associated with memory, abstract thinking, planning and impulse control.

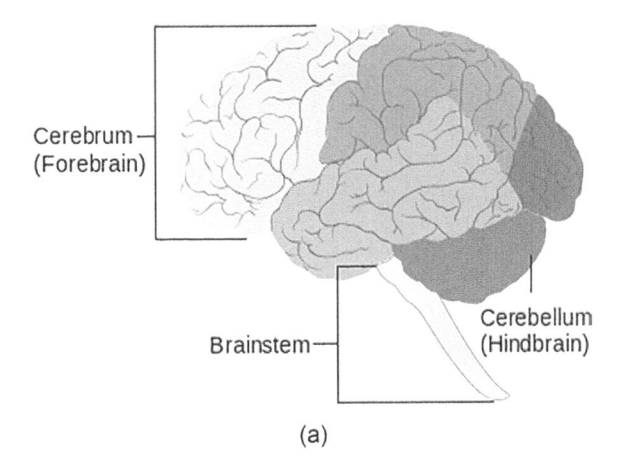

(a)

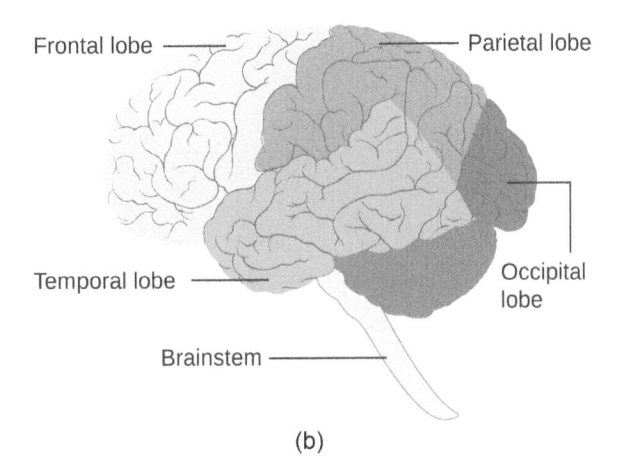

(b)

Figure 4.1 Human Brain Anatomy. (a) Human Brain Anatomy. Cancer Research UK, CC BY-SA 4.0 via Wikimedia Commons; (b) Human Brain Anatomy – the four lobes which make up the cerebrum. Cancer Research UK,CC BY-SA 4.0 via Wikimedia Commons.

The forward-most section of the frontal lobes is a distinct area referred to as:

The prefrontal cortex – is the part of the cerebral cortex which covers the front part of the frontal lobe. This is the **last brain area to mature**, undergoing important developmental changes as late as adolescence. Housed here are our most advanced cognitive functions, including decision-making, attention, motivation, expression of personality, moderating social behaviour and goal-directed behaviour. A term often used to describe these internal goals is *executive functioning*. We saw the important role the parental-figure has in their role of guiding and modelling these behaviours (chapter 3, but pertinent to chapter 6 too); playing peep-o, rules inherent in role-play games, following routines to control impulses, all act as a scaffold for this executive functioning – it builds resilience, encouraged through "wait times," and develops self-control. Executive functioning skills underlie our ability to stay focused on a task despite distractions, follow multiple-step directions, plan ahead to achieve goals and display self-control. Feeling remorse, acknowledging guilt or social control (i.e., *not* perform socially unacceptable behaviour) all require an "adult" fully functioning, *prefrontal cortex* (Center on the Developing Child at Harvard University, 2011). Since practicing mindfulness has been shown to activate the prefrontal cortex, increase wellbeing and reduce anxiety, it has sometimes been recommended as a practice for school practitioners.

This region, **the prefrontal cortex, is shifting and changing during adolescence**. Hence, knowledge about it is particularly relevant to anyone working with young people who hope to implement strategies to *support* the impact of loss or trauma. Our "thinking" prefrontal cortex can be taken over by our "emotional, reflexive" limbic system (the amygdala, discussed later). Therefore, our limbic system is quicker to respond to a perceived threat, especially pre-adulthood, before the prefrontal cortex is fully formed. Emotions occur faster than thoughts. Therefore, when under traumatic stress, the ***limbic system*** rules with the purpose of keeping us safe and alive (Hill and Dahlitz, 2022).

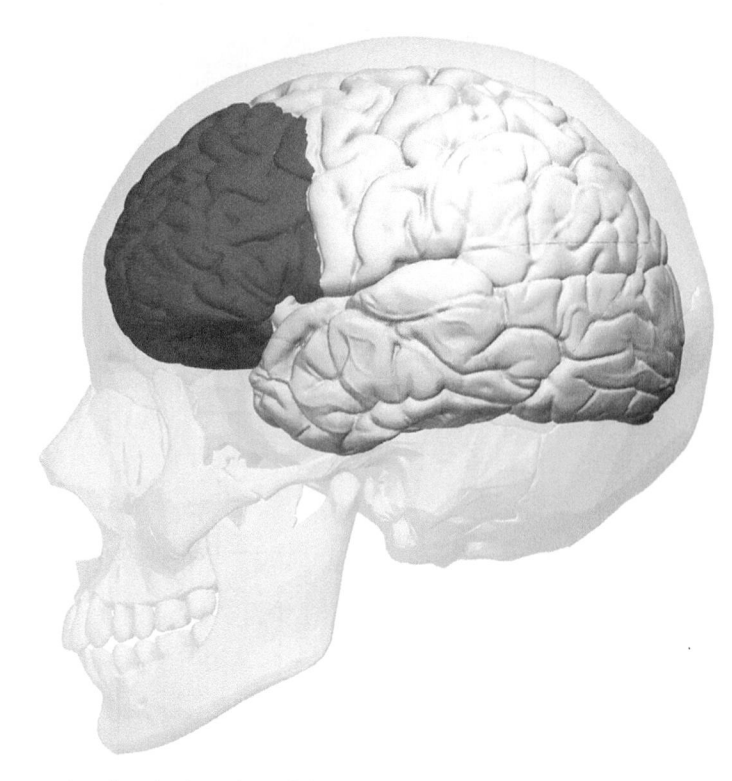

Figure 4.2 A diagram showing the location of the prefrontal cortex. Polygon data generated by Database Center for Life Science(DBCLS), CC BY-SA 2.1 JP DEED.

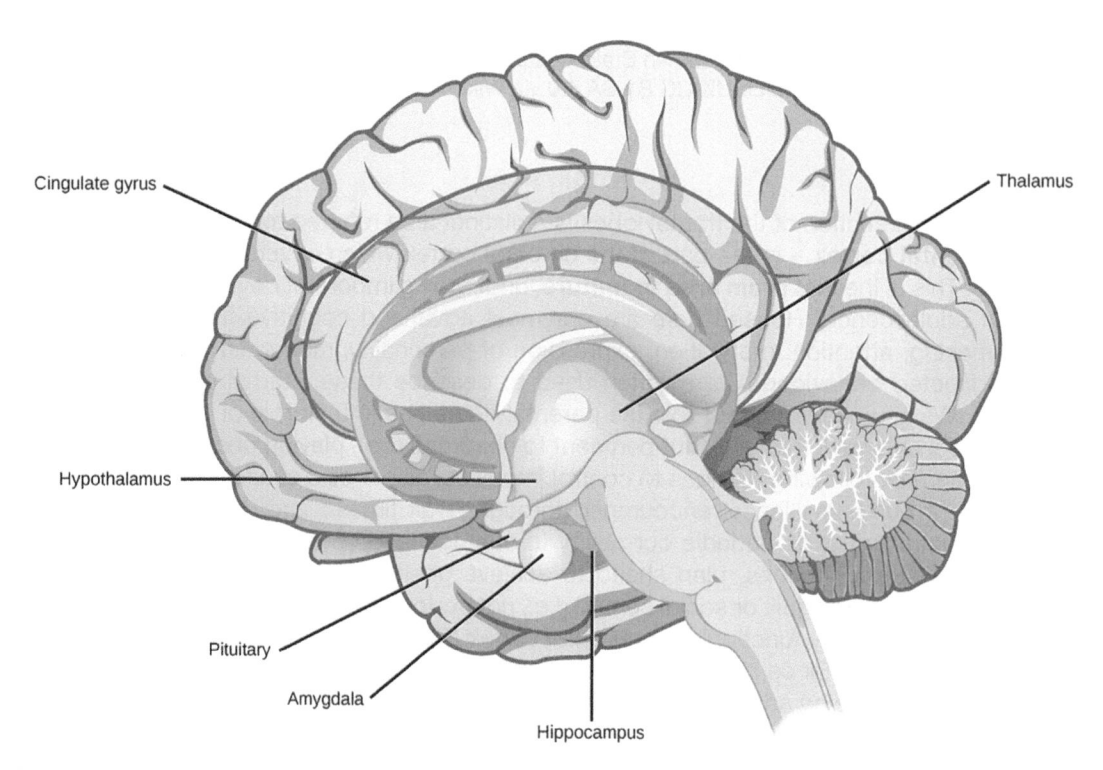

Figure 4.3 Diagram showing important components of the limbic system. CNX OpenStax, CC BY 4.0, via Wikimedia Commons.

Limbic system (Figure 4.3)

Although our advanced cognitive abilities are dependent on the **cerebral cortex** (the outer layer), it is not the only part of the brain relevant to education and child development.

The limbic system is located in an arc around the brain stem and deep inside the cerebrum (in the inner brain beneath the cortex). The term limbic system refers to a collection of small structures involved in more **instinctive behaviours** such as:

- Emotional reactions, and emotional memory.
- Stress responses.
- Pleasure and reward-seeking behaviours (in adolescents this includes "getting a kick" from risk-taking).

Key components of the limbic system are:

The **hippocampus**: involved in forming new memories and spatial learning. Therefore, it is important for navigation and orientation. Interestingly, London taxi drivers have an enlarged hippocampus (Maguire et al., 2000).

The **hypothalamus:** the control centre for the body's key stress systems, regulating the release of cortisol and other stress hormones. It is also the command centre for the autonomic nervous system which controls involuntary processes such as breathing, heart rate and blood pressure.

The **amygdala**: a small part with a big job. Often called the emotional processing centre, it connects memories with positive and negative emotions. Since it also remembers past fear-inducing events, it evaluates threat and triggers the body's stress response. The amygdala manages the processing of information between prefrontal cortex and the hypothalamus (AbuHasan et al., 2022).

The **pituitary gland:** makes, stores and releases hormones that control growth and metabolism. As it also controls other hormone glands, it affects physiological processes throughout the body. It is controlled by the hypothalamus, and together they control the involuntary nervous system, all with the aim of achieving body stability (homeostasis) (Dingman, 2019).

The orange-plum illustration.

The below visual illustration (Figure 4.4) can be described like this:

- Imagine a fork is first dug into a small plum, and this fork (with plum in situ) is then placed into an orange.
- The orange peel represents the bumpy, thin layer of the cerebral cortex.
- The plum underneath is the cerebellum.
- The wider prongs of the fork represent the brain stem.
- The fork handle below gives a representation of the spinal column.
- The orange segments represent the lobes beneath.
- In the orange centre, the pips represent the amygdala and hippocampus.

It may not be to an accurate scale, but the strong visual image can be used in the classroom as a visual, tactile resource. The last decade has seen a burst in research using brain-imaging scans to determine structure and function (LeDoux and Pine, 2016). Magnetic Resonance Imaging (MRI) is used to scan brain structure changes over time, whilst Functional MRI (fMRI) scans act

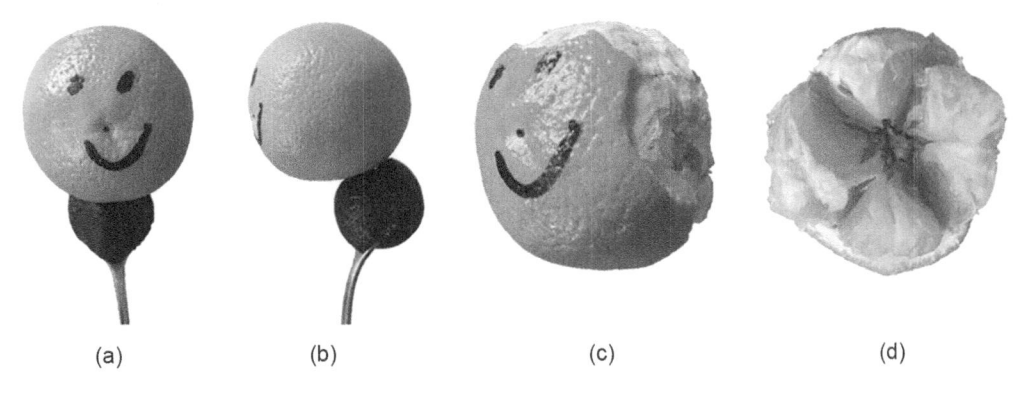

(a)　　　　　(b)　　　　　(c)　　　　　(d)

Figure 4.4 Visual resource to illustrate a simplified brain structure (not to scale). Taylor, J. (2023).

more like an incredibly high-resolution video recording to determine changes in brain functioning whilst carrying out a particular task (Blakemore, 2019). Having described the structure of the brain, its functioning will be described next.

Functioning of the brain

Modern advances in brain-imaging have determined two very important facts:

1. Brain development is not *over* during early-childhood, but it continues to change and develop throughout adolescence and into the 20s and 30s.
2. The brain regions, described above, do not act alone and independently, rather a variety of regions of the brain are always active together in any *one* experience, whether that is during autonomic (breathing and heart-beat), emotional (feelings) or rational (cognitive) functioning (Barrett, 2021).

Current neuroscience research emphasises the interactions and connections between different brain regions (Gazzaniga et al., 2019); however, an outdated but widely circulated theory has often been used to describe brain functioning. *The Triune Brain Theory* presents a simplified account of the various functions the brain carries out. Formed in the 1960s, MacLean (1970) proposed that the human brain was divided into *three distinct regions which each acted independently*. His hierarchical, evolutionary model (Holden, 1979) purported the three regions consist of:

1. *Reptilian brain (also called Lizard Brain, Primitive Brain, Primal Brain or Basal Ganglia)*: the brain stem and cerebellum, responsible for life-maintaining processes, such as breathing and heart rate, our *primal instincts*.
2. *Mammalian Brain (also called Mammal Brain, Paleomammalian, Emotional Brain or Limbic System)*: consisting of grouped structures, referred to as the emotional centre or stress response system, said to be responsible for emotions, memories, habits and attachments.
3. *Neocortex (also called Human Brain, Neomammalian or Rational Brain)* neo meaning "new": the cognitive or "thinking" component, thought to be responsible for cognition, language, reasoning, rational, abstract or objective thought.

The outdated view is that each region (Figure 4.5) was added, in evolutionary terms, as the need arose (MacLean, 1994). MacLean's model claims that activity in the three brain regions is largely distinct when we are engaged in each of the activities for which they are responsible. Whilst this has since been disproved, it is, nevertheless, a good model for explaining the main *functions* which the brain is responsible for (Gould, 2003). These functions are *life-maintaining*, *thinking* (cognition) and *feeling* (emotional and stress responses).

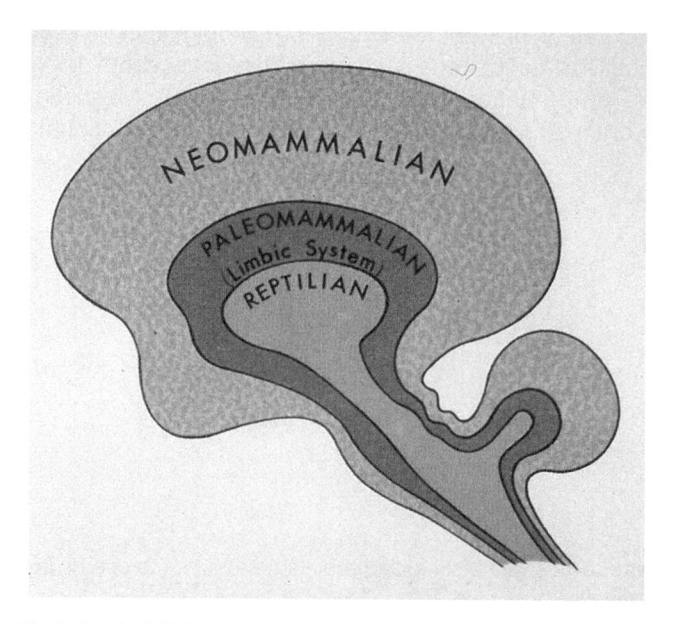

Figure 4.5 The Triune Brain Myth. Bill Benzon triune-brain-theory CC BY-SA 2.0 DEED.

Some key points differentiating Triune theory from recent neuroscience findings:

- Brain structures do not function independently of one another. During emotional responses, there is activity in many regions simultaneously. Additionally, emotion (limbic system) and cognition (cortex) are interrelated functions (Blakemore, 2019; Steffen et al., 2022).
- The limbic system is not purely for emotions, for example, the hippocampus is a key area involved in memory, which is more closely associated with cognition. The limbic system's parts together impact many interrelated processes, including processing internal (bodily) and external stimuli, arousal and memory.
- The brain does not act by simply responding to a stimulus. Instead, it predicts our internal and external needs and adapts accordingly. Incoming stimuli interact with the current state of our brain.
- Current neuroscience research shows that brain networks always have some level of activity. For example, there is no *fear-brain-circuit* that springs into action during a fear response but otherwise stays inactive (Steffen et al., 2022).

Importantly, we are active, not passive. We actively receive the sensory information, so **we actively construct our emotions** (Blakemore, 2019; LeDoux, 1996).

We construct our emotions from a whole range of information. The *ingredients* are:

- Sensory input and bodily sensations.
- Previous life experiences, and our expectations of if "X" happens I will feel "Y."
- The people we are with.
- The situation we are in.
- What occurred moments before we felt that emotion (sometimes this directly relates to the emotion, but sometimes it causes us to make an irrational link too).
- Learning, memory, language and culture; culture is important as it can give us priorities and a belief system.

One brain, creating an emotion

All these listed *ingredients* are required for our brain to interpret them and make **the emotion** that we feel at that moment in time. Even if the ingredients come together in an unconscious manner, our brain constructs meaning and recommends a course of action (LeDoux, 1996). This means we can often assess any "threat" (fear, stress or anxiety) we may feel and apply rational thinking using the ingredients above.

We experience many emotions such as love, passion, hate, grief, greed, envy, peace, elation. We feel *emotionally* and *bodily* (see "*interoception*"). How we respond to these feelings is a choice designed to help us survive. These *responses* shape our experiences, our future life and our future self (Blakemore, 2019). In doing so, we may also engage the human quality of *empathy* which consciously links our inward wellbeing with the wellbeing of others.

The hand-fist brain model

We often consider that one of the most important decisions we can teach our children is to make ethical and moral judgements, to think about the feelings of others, to pause before acting and to consider *consequences*.

This translates as the important skill of *making good decisions in a high-emotion situation*.

Dan Siegal (Siegel and Bryson, 2011) imagines the brain as a house with the downstairs and an upstairs connected by a staircase (Momentous Institute, 2019). This is a useful *metaphor* rather than a scientific theory.

The downstairs brain, in his model, includes the brain stem and the limbic region, located in the lower parts of the brain from the top of our neck to the bridge of our nose. It is the place where basic needs get met (Figure 4.6). Since the model has its roots in the disproven Triune Brain Theory, for the purpose of combining this hand-fist brain model with modern neuroscience findings, we will regard the downstairs and upstairs brains as "functions," rather than "regions." Functions include: breathing and blinking, fight-flight reactions and impulses and strong emotions (anger and fear).

The upstairs brain was regarded as completely different. Described as being made-up of the cerebral cortex and its various parts (including the ones directly behind your forehead, called the medial prefrontal cortex) and responsible for logic, reasoning, problem-solving and decision-making.

Figure 4.6 Upstairs and downstairs brain illustration. Taylor, J. (2023), using Wikimedia stairs icon CC BY-SA 2.0.

The more basic *downstairs brain* needs the *upstairs brain* to give a fuller perspective on our world. This is where more intricate mental processes take place, such as *analytical thinking, imagining and planning*. It controls many higher order thinking skills (and *executive functioning*); therefore, it is responsible for some of the qualities we would wish to see in our children:

- Sounds decision-making and planning.
- Control over emotions and body.
- Self-understanding.
- Empathy.
- Morality.

This theory (Siegel and Bryson, 2011) considers that only if a child's brain is effectively functioning, can it carry out highly *important self-regulation tasks* and will: (a) *regulate their emotions*, (b) *consider consequences*, (c) *think before acting* and (d) *consider how others feel*. This works best when the upstairs and downstairs brains are *integrated* with each other. The upstairs brain can monitor the actions of the downstairs brain and help calm strong reactions, impulses and emotions that originate there. Our downstairs brain consists of the emotional and physical feelings and reactions before it uses the upstairs brain to decide on a course of action (Figure 4.7). Neuroscience and attachment theory (chapter 3) interlink here, as through the attachment figure's co-regulation we gain the ability to self-regulate, as we learn and practise these *important (a-d) self-regulation tasks*.

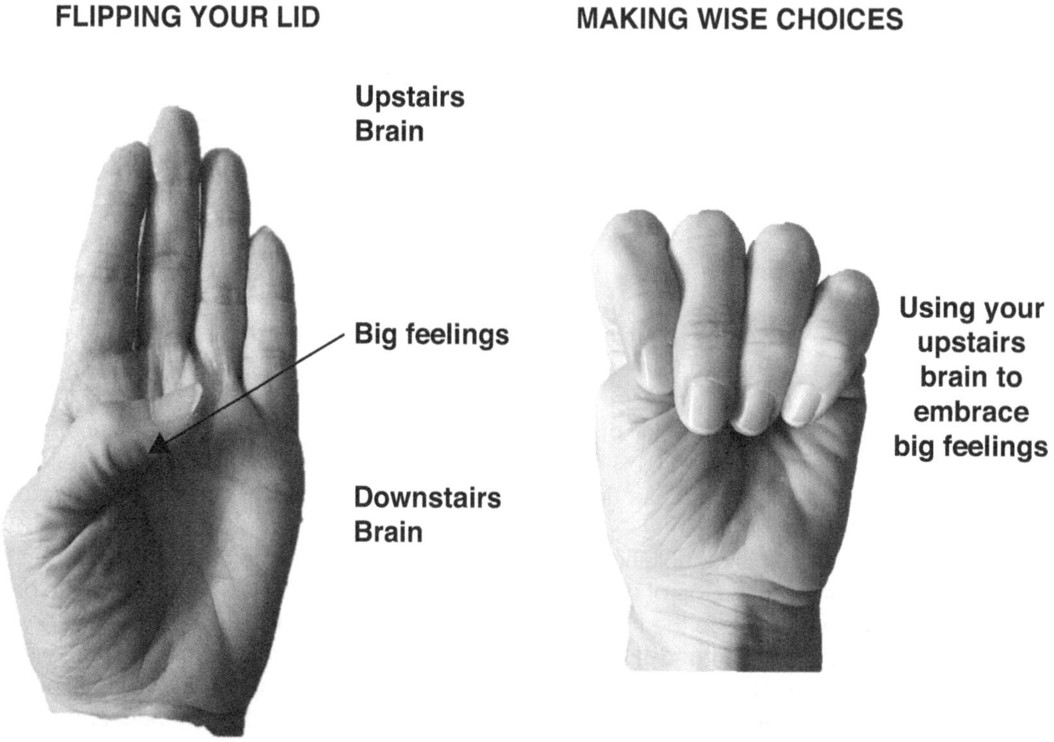

FLIPPING YOUR LID   **MAKING WISE CHOICES**

Upstairs Brain

Big feelings

Downstairs Brain

Using your upstairs brain to embrace big feelings

Figure 4.7 Flipping the lid hand-brain model. Taylor J. (2023), adapted from the NHS Sheffield Hand Model of the Brain.

He demonstrates this with **the hand-fist brain model**: holding an arm up in a fist, with the thumb inside the fist, the wrist represents the brain stem, the thumb inside represents the emotional centre (limbic system) and the fingers surrounding the thumb represent the cerebral cortex. With the fingers closed tightly around the limbic system, the brain is functioning well, able to reason, consider consequences and remain calm. However, using the expression "a flipped lid," he describes the fingers springing off, the absence of rational thought and big emotional reactions. This "flipping their lid" illustrates a child or young person who suddenly reacts to an event or to a situation, it may be a door slam and storm out, it could be a torrent of ill-chosen words or experiencing overwhelming emotions in the face of experiencing a trauma.

This model is a good visual example of how a child experiencing big emotions cannot reason and act calmly or logically. They are responding to what their body is feeling inside, through *interoception* (see next section). It can be useful to explain this to children and young people and can be utilised in *emotion coaching* (Gilbert et al., 2021).

The adaptive brain

Accurate knowledge of brain structure and *function* determines that it is *interdependent*, not independent, brain networks that have evolved to increase adaptation thereby survive as a species and, consequently, be around to reproduce. Recent neuroscientific research has found that the brain regions and interconnected networks team-up to maintain and regulate our internal state (*homeostasis*), based on how we feel and what we think (our emotion and our cognition), to *adapt* to our ever-changing needs.

Neuroscientists at Johns Hopkins University (Kanjlia et al., 2016) made a fascinating discovery regarding the brain's adaptability. They conducted an experiment involving two groups of individuals: (group A) sighted people wearing blindfolds and (group B) individuals who had been blind since birth. During the experiment, both groups were given maths and language problems to solve while their brain activity was monitored using fMRI brain scans.

What the researchers found was remarkable. The brain network responsible for numerical reasoning was found to be virtually identical in both blind and sighted individuals. However, there was a crucial difference. In blind individuals, the occipital lobe, typically associated with vision, was highly engaged during the maths tasks. In contrast, the sighted group did not utilise this region at all for mathematical processing Figure 4.8 illustrates the regions engaged.

This finding provides compelling evidence that the brain is significantly adaptable and flexible. It suggests that the brain can repurpose areas, typically dedicated to vision, to perform complex mathematical tasks – that is, *visual* areas of the brain can be taken over by *nonvisual* functions. The study highlights the brain's remarkable capacity to reorganise and adapt its neural networks to compensate for sensory deficiencies, shedding new light on our understanding of brain plasticity.

Further, emerging findings suggest that the brain uses interoceptive (internal) and exteroceptive (external) information to predict future conditions and needs, to enable optimal adaptation to continuously changing internal and external environments (Zhao et al., 2022). Based on better

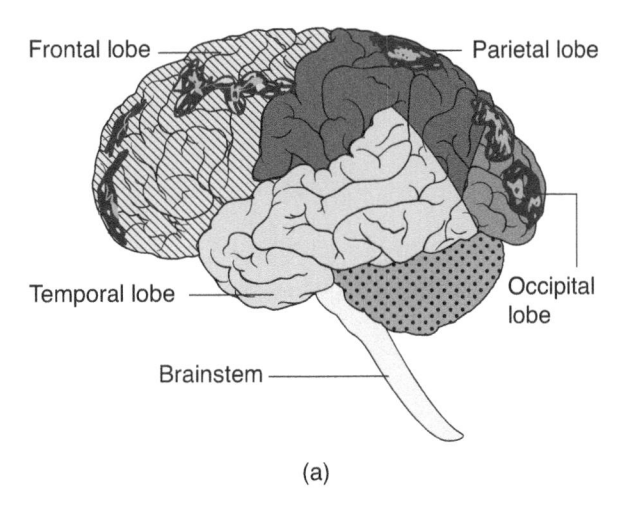

(a)

Figure 4.8 Illustration showing blind participants using part of the brain usually used for vision. Taylor, J. (2023), adapted from MRI scans of the brain as shown on: http://fotisliarokapis.blogspot. com/2016/10/adaptive-brain.html using a figure of the brain from *Cancer Research UK, CC BY-SA 4.0.*

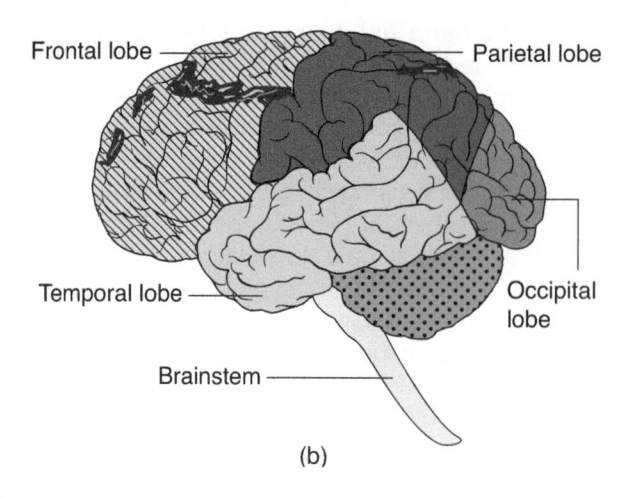

(b)

Figure 4.8 (Continued).

understanding of how the brain works, various recent researchers and academics have suggested replacing "*triune brain*" with the term that better captures current understanding of brain function: **the adaptive brain**. In this concept, the term adaptive brain emphasises the interdependence and plasticity of brain regions, and the brain's ability to predict and adapt to future needs and conditions.

For the brain to have this amazing ability to adapt to conditions, it needs to *collect information*. It does this by using a network that *includes and extends from the brain;* this network is known as *the Nervous System.*

The Nervous System

The nervous system has two main parts to it (Figure 4.9):

- The *Central Nervous System* (*CNS*) which consists of the brain and spinal cord.
- The *Peripheral Nervous System* (*PNS*) – this is everything else outside the CNS and also includes the sensory fibres at the very edges of our body. These are shown in the diagram below.

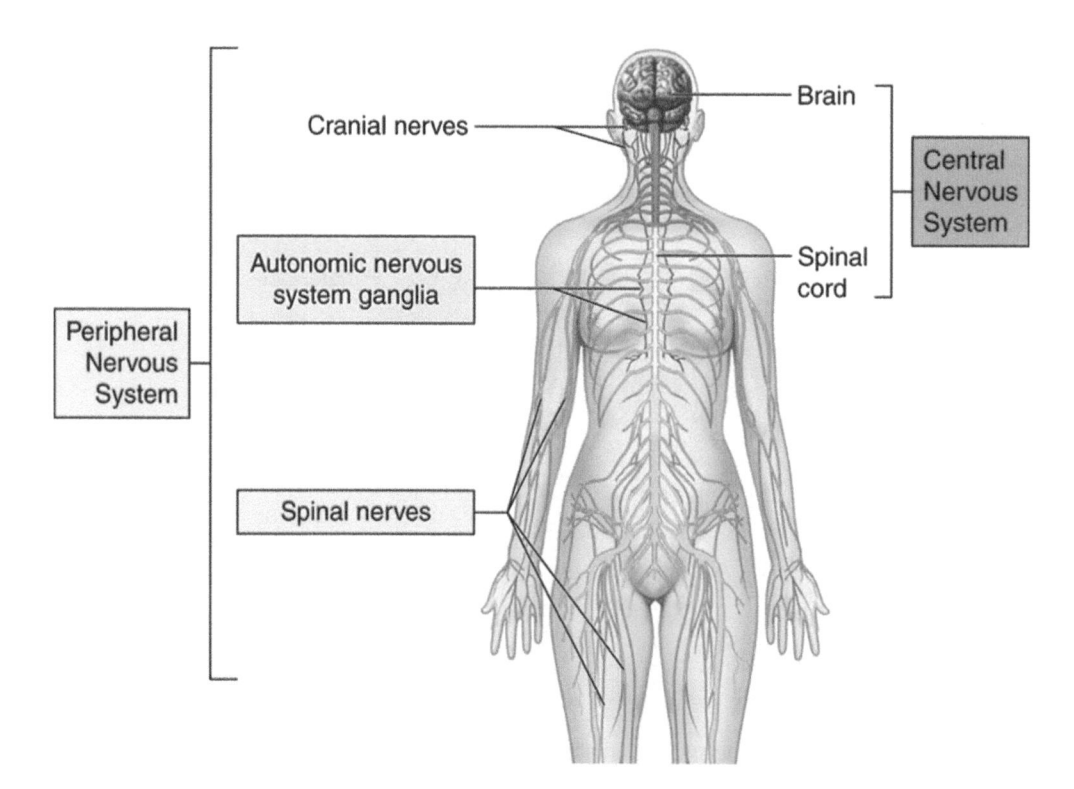

Figure 4.9 The nervous system: central nervous system and peripheral nervous system. *Image from* Cenveo, CC BY 3.0 US DEED as seen on neurotechedu.

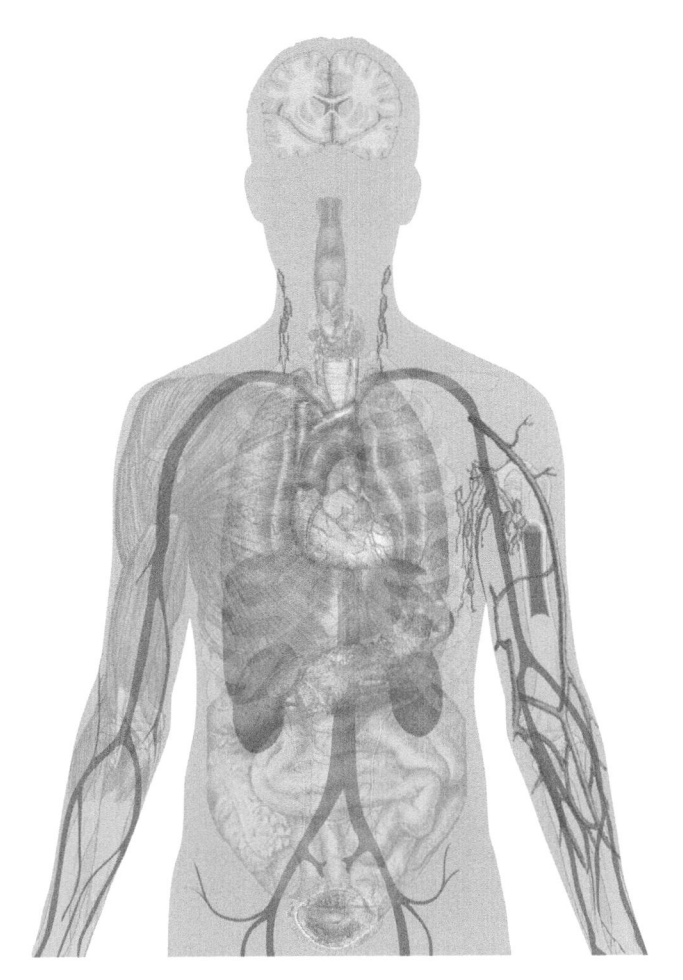

Figure 4.10 The major organs of the body's torso which the vagus nerve connects to. Rawpixel CC0 1.0 DEED.

The *CNS* is made up of more than a 100 billion nerve cells; it is this system that relays information from the brain to the body and back again.

One of the most important areas for this bi-directional communication is the *Vagus Nerve* in the PNS (it is the 10th cranial nerve which means it emerges from the brain and brainstem).

The vagus nerve

"Vaga" is Latin and means "to wander," an appropriate name for a nerve that wanders all around the body (Figure 4.10). This longest nerve connects all major organs with the brain, so it essentially controls all involuntary body processes (i.e., breathing, speech, swallowing, heart-beat, blood pressure, hearing, taste, circulation, digestion and gut health). The brain and body work together. This helps explain why there are physical symptoms associated with mental health.

The PNS is further sub-divided into the autonomic (automatic) and the somatic nervous systems.

The autonomic (automatic) and the somatic nervous systems

The autonomic nervous system is responsible for involuntary, automatic functions such as our breathing, heart-beat, blood pressure, pupils dilating and digestion. We do not have conscious control over these things. However, *the somatic nervous system* is the part that we are aware of and have control over, such as when we purposefully move, or when we use our eight senses (the main five – sight, smell, hearing, touch, taste – and the three other senses of – movement, balance and interoception).

The autonomic nervous system (Figure 4.11) is the part that we are interested in as it has a role in our fear response system. It is composed of both the *Sympathetic* and *Parasympathetic* nervous system.

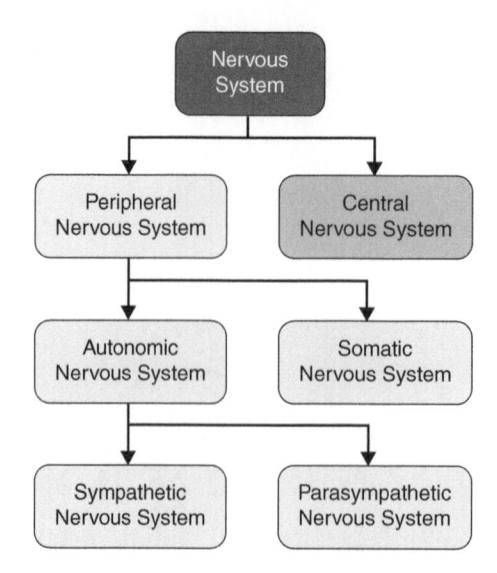

Figure 4.11 The nervous system: components of the peripheral nervous system. Taylor J. (2023), adapted from Components of the Nervous System, Jenna Fair (2013) CC BY-SA 3.0 via Wikimedia Commons.

The sympathetic and parasympathetic nervous system (Figure 4.12)

The sympathetic gears us up (fight and flight) and the parasympathetic calms us down (rest and digest) – their actions are autonomic (involuntary) and all work to regulate us (and achieve a balanced state of *homeostasis*). To keep us regulated, the brain tries to predict our requirements.

For the adaptive brain to be able to predict our future requirements and actions, it needs to receive information from our outside world, and from inside our body. This is called *neuroception* and consists of *exteroception* and *interoception* (Backman, 2022).

Exteroception and interoception

Exteroception (*outside*): it is the process of automatically gaining and internalising information through our *senses. There are an abundant number of things which we see, hear, smell, taste, touch, and sense from our body's position, balance and movement and these all bring a reaction in us.* We perceive, interpret and react to the *external* world around us by experiencing bodily sensations. We may love something we taste, dislike a smell or feel scared from hearing a certain noise. The sensations triggered by external stimuli (environment), and the linked internal pathways that these sensations impact, are known as **exteroception**.

Interoception (*inside*): it is the sense of the internal state of our body, through sensations which are triggered by *internal* stimuli related to the body's physiological state. We may perceive "butterflies in our stomach," "feel discombobulated," "are too hot," "have goosebumps" where our "hairs stand on end," "feel too sick (with anger or worry) to eat," "shaking like a leaf," "are broken-hearted," "feel tense" or *so elated we "could burst."* We have many creative expressions to describe these perceptions; so many of them are tied into our emotional state too. How we receive information from our body, and how we interpret it is largely automatic, and so we know if we are thirsty, hungry, in pain, sleepy, unwell or feeling anxious.

Interoception is key to regulating our nervous system following chronic and traumatic stress. So, following a shocking event, the body works to return itself to "normal" heart rate, breathing and functioning; it aims to regulate and maintain stable internal body conditions – this is *homeostasis.*

The brain constantly scans and assimilates the information received from our exteroceptive and interoceptive stimuli; it infers the information input from these sources and responds appropriately (in most cases). This reflects our adaptive capability, as we act in response to environmental changes. The fMRI research *supports* these findings.

REST and DIGEST (Parasympathetic)	FIGHT or FLIGHT (Sympathetic)

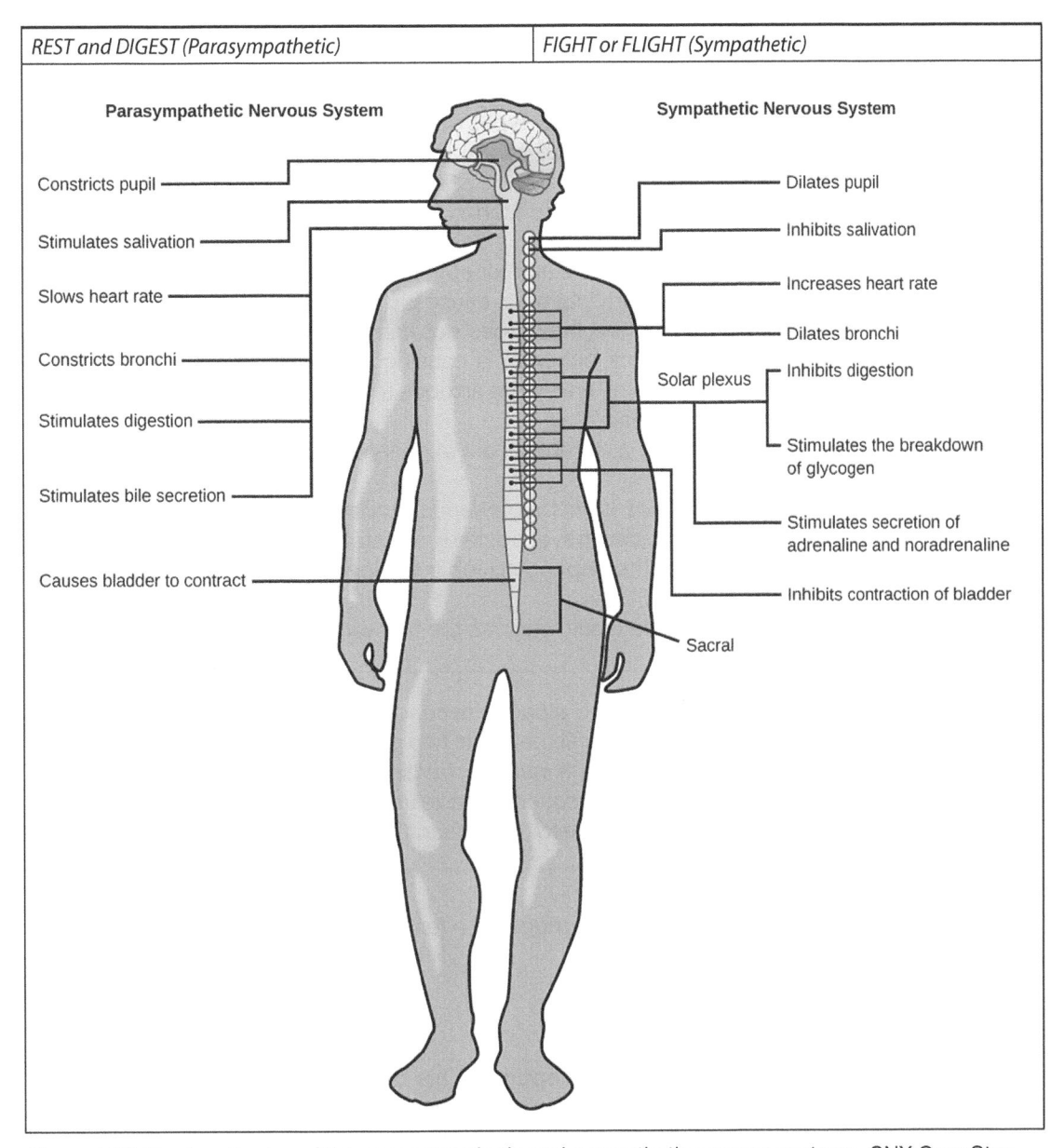

Figure 4.12 The functioning of the parasympathetic and sympathetic nervous systems. CNX OpenStax, CC BY 4.0 via Wikimedia Commons.

In a study (Araujo et al., 2015), participants were given tasks to perform which related to either exteroceptive or interoceptive activities. Their brains were scanned (fMRI) whilst doing so. It was discovered that different parts of the brain were used to interpret this information, with some brain areas activating in response to activities pertaining to exteroception and other brain areas responding significantly to tasks relating to interoception. The image can be viewed here: https://www.researchgate.net/figure/Interoception-versus-exteroception-The-red-yellow-color-scale-shows-brain-regions-with_fig5_283959707

Highly noteworthy to our *support* of children, the study indicated that the **prefrontal cortex** is a region where *interoception* occurs. That is, internal information is sifted and considered. If this is the cognitive reasoning, planning part of our brain then it leads us to presume that it works to interpret the state of our body during any emotional reaction. However, it is one of the last brain areas to fully develop, as we will read later.

To surmise, we receive, assimilate and utilise information that has been gained externally and internally – and act accordingly. This has been backed up by fMRI studies.

Interpreting and inferring information

A key point here is that the brain has two distinct types of sensory input flowing upwards towards it: *sensations from the outside world and sensations from the body itself*. These signals feel physical.

No matter what we are consciously paying attention to at any given moment, our brain is always receiving information from our senses about what is going on in the world and what is happening in our body. These internal bodily sensations (interoception) may be experienced as moods, or *gut-feelings*. They feel real but have many potential causes.

The problem is a reverse inference, the brain does not know the cause – it only senses the outcomes (Barrett, 2021). It has to work out what is causing these changes or feelings in our body and answer questions such as "why have I got anxious feelings in my stomach?" "Why am I shaking?" "Why have I got physical pain?"

So, to solve this puzzle, the brain re-assembles past experiences that are *similar* in some way to the present.

Hence, our brain asks itself, *"what is this experience similar to?"* and links it with a situation that has gone before. This can have positive results such as linking a stomach-churning sensation to concerns for the impending job interview, resulting in preparation and route-planning.

However, it can also have a negative result, such as the following example:

At a previous school, a pupil I taught had a bad experience. He heard a noise in a corridor and was inadvertently caught up in a scuffle between two pupils. Since that time, whenever he hears a noise in a school corridor, he is instantly transported back to the bodily sensations from the last time he heard such a sound. As a result, upon hearing any sounds in a corridor, or in school, he is filled with a dread and a fear that immobilises him.

In this example, this traumatic experience triggered a *fear response.*

Perception

Accordingly, in this example, it was his **perception** of his body's internal state (interoception) and his perception and processing of environmental sensory stimuli (exteroception) that acted together to control his adaptive behaviour (as in that human aim, to survive).

Exactly how we respond to trauma or ACEs is a result of our perceptions about that experience (rooted in our early attachment experiences). Often though, to aid our survival, our brain gears us up a notch.

One way the brain gears us up, **or adapts,** *is to lurch into a* **stress response** *– as in the example of the pupil on hearing a noise in a school corridor.*

A stressful situation can activate the whole of the sympathetic nervous system, producing an immediate widespread response. Originally called the *fight-flight response* (Cannon, 1915), it has more recently been added to and become known as the *fight-flight-fawn-freeze-flop-flock response.* The purpose of this response is to avoid, decrease, limit or end the danger.

The fight-flight-fawn-freeze-flop-flock response

- Fight: the reaction of fighting something off (verbally or physically) to increase our chance of surviving.
- Flight: the urge to run away from danger (literally or metaphorically) rather than stay in that situation.
- Freeze: frozen with fear or shock and unable to move. We may feel numb or dread.
- Flop: we become physically or mentally unresponsive and may faint. In freeze and flop states, the response to traumatic stress is "feeling numb," where we disassociate from any feelings

or sensations and block out an internal awareness; our body is exhausted emotionally, it "cannot feel anything" and it brings a reduced ability to feel signals from our body. Here there is less activity in the insula.

- Fawn – if fight or flight does not work, then "fawn" is often the next step when we say things to please the other person; this may be to our detriment but used to diffuse a situation and return us to feeling safe.
- Friend/flock – we turn to others to bond, for social communication, or to discover what to do or how we should act. We look for non-verbal communication cues; knowing we cannot act alone, we turn to others for *support*.

This response occurs through the *sympathetic nervous system* – it activates the hypothalamus in the brain, which communicates with the rest of the body so that we have the energy to fight or flee, for example.

At this point, it is worth mentioning **Polyvagal Theory** as I have heard it used in education training and resources. Porges first developed the theory in 1992 (Porges, 2009) and, putting aside the contested evolutionary links and peripheral aspects to the theory, he asserted that as we (through our vagus nerve) detect various factors present in our environment, we can enter one of three physiological responses states:

- *Mobilisation* – fight-flight-fawn response.
- *Immobilisation* –freeze-flop-flock response.
- *Social communication* – rest and digest, where we can chat and function as we feel safe.

Recapping the above: part of our nervous system is the autonomic nervous system (which controls our body automatically, without conscious thought) and this is divided into the sympathetic and parasympathetic nervous systems.

The *sympathetic nervous system* gears us up and controls the *fight-flight-fawn-freeze-flop-flock response* to stress when we perceive danger [through stimuli detected internally (interoception) and externally (exteroception)].

The *parasympathetic nervous system* does the opposite: it calms us down, working to bring our body back into a stable state of homeostasis, which allows us to recover and heal. The *vagus nerve* is the main neural component of the parasympathetic nervous system. It automatically controls *parasympathetic* functions of the major organs which it connects – the heart, lungs and digestive system, for example. It therefore has a role in calming us down to stimulate the "rest and digest" functions of these organs.

Theoretically, it is our ability to regulate our stress response system that allows us to engage socially and learn.

This essentially can be summarised as:

To participate with others and learn effectively, we need to feel safe in our relationships and environments (Gilbert et al., 2021; Porges, 2009, 2022; Siegel and Bryson, 2011).

In a sense, at this point, the theory aligns with *attachment theory* (chapter 3). Attachment theory also suggests that when we feel safe and secure, we can engage more effectively with others and our environments; we can practise problem-solving and, educationally, we can learn new information.

The overall sense from neuroscientific research is that attachment theory, emotional self-regulation research and neuroimaging studies explain the concept more precisely than polyvagal theory does.

Nevertheless, the vagus nerve exists, it has a role, and polyvagal theory's appeal may be the fact that it provides a simplified model. It also highlights the impact of a stress response on the major organs that it connects and controls:

- It connects – heart, lungs, digestive system, liver, gallbladder, spleen, pancreas and kidneys.
- It controls – skeletal muscles of the mouth, pharynx and larynx, allowing us to swallow our food safely and speak.

It gives a picture of how under stress, each of these body components can be affected – we may sense a fast heart-beat, rapid and shallow breathing, stomach-lurching, a need to visit the bathroom, pain internally, a dry mouth so we cannot speak and "feel unable to eat." A prolonged response to stress can cause damage to our physical health, as can be seen in Table 4.1 which shows the impact that sustained stress has on the human body.

The **SUPPORT** strategies in chapters 5–8 address the importance of returning our body back into a stable state; relaxation, mindfulness, grounding and breathing techniques help our physiology by *passing on the message* that our body is calm; returning it to a more peaceful "rest and digest" state can help us overcome debilitating stress. This is why these techniques in school can be essential for a pupil who has undergone trauma.

Trauma changes the accuracy of interoception

Since interoception is our ability to *notice* and *understand* our internal sensations, in the corridor situation (described in the box above), the pupil's interoception gave a false message. Based on his previous trauma (when embroiled in a scuffle), it told him that danger was impending. Therefore, the pupil *physically* felt the changes that the *increased stress*, *anxiety or panic attacks* brought on – the rapid-breathing, stomach-churning, high-alert response. Since the *vagus nerve* connects all the areas that respond to stress, it communicates information to the brain about the internal state of our body, and vice versa. Information received about our constantly-changing-bodily-state arrives in the insula in the brain. The *insula* within the brain is a key component in this process of sifting and sorting information.

Sorting and sifting "danger" information

Under conditions of stress – such as a looming homework deadline, a persistent worry or something environmental, such as when facing danger – the stress response begins in the brain. When the eyes or ears (or both) send the information to the *amygdala*, an area of the brain that contributes to emotional processing, the amygdala interprets the images and sounds. When it perceives danger, it instantly sends a distress signal to the *hypothalamus* **[see "The stress response system" diagram below]** (LeDoux and Pine, 2016).

PART 1. Command centre – the first response (see Figure 4.14)

The *hypothalamus* functions like a command centre, communicating with the rest of the body through the *autonomic nervous system* so that the person has an *energy burst* to react to survive, such as fight or flee.

The *hypothalamus* (in the brain) gives this *energy burst* by sending signals through the autonomic nerves to the *adrenal glands* (on the kidneys).

The *adrenal gland* is a small gland that makes steroid hormones, adrenaline and noradrenaline. These hormones help control heart rate, blood pressure and other important body functions. There are two adrenal glands, one on top of each kidney (also known as suprarenal glands).

These glands respond by pumping the hormone adrenaline (also known as epinephrine) into the bloodstream. Adrenaline activates the sympathetic nervous system to gear us up and brings on the physiological changes described in the table below (Table 4.1).

All of this is *"normal stress"* and occurs in *mere milliseconds* – such as when we react by *jumping out of the way.*

PART 2. What happens next – the second response (see Figure 4.14)

As the initial surge of adrenalin *subsides*, the hypothalamus activates the *second stage* of the stress response system – known as the *HPA axis*. This network consists of the hypothalamus and the pituitary glands (both in the brain), and the adrenal glands (next to the kidneys), as shown in the below "stress response system" diagram (Figure 4.13).

Table 4.1 Table to show – as adrenalin circulates through the body, it brings on several physiological changes – all with a purposeful (automatic) function

A table to describe physiological changes caused by the autonomic nervous system.	
What happens	*Why*
The heart beats faster than normal	Pushing blood to the muscles, heart and other vital organs – in order to react quickly. Therefore blood vessels in the skin *constrict*.
Blood vessels at the skin *constrict*	To lessen blood loss *if injured*.
Sweating may occur	As a response to an increase in temperature that has been brought on by this bursting into action. Sweating is the body's means of regulating temperature.
Pulse rate and blood pressure go up	The person starts to breathe more rapidly. Small airways in the lungs open wide, to intake as much oxygen as possible. An increase in cardio output is preparation for fleeing or fighting; we may feel faint or nauseous, but it is actually rare to faint in a panic attack.
Extra oxygen is sent to the brain	Increasing alertness.
Pupils dilate	Thus sight, hearing and other senses become sharper.
We feel tense	Because it causes muscles in the neck, shoulders and back to "constrict."
We feel we cannot eat when stressed	As the digestive system shuts down, to conserve glucose needed for energy to run or fight.
Energy is supplied to all parts of the body	Adrenaline triggers the release of blood sugar (glucose) and fats from temporary storage sites in the body. These nutrients flood into the bloodstream.

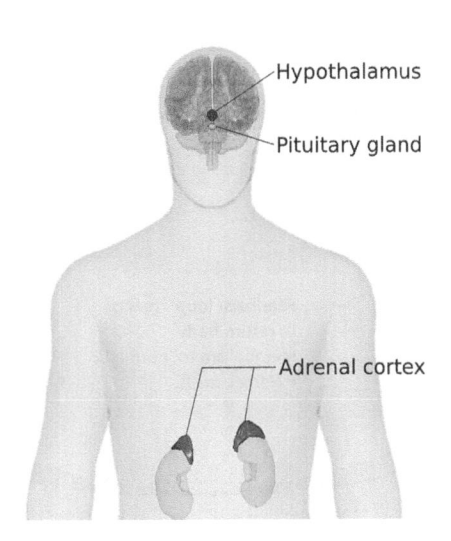

Hypothalamus

Pituitary gland

Adrenal cortex

Figure 4.13 The HPA axis of the stress response system. Anatomography (2015) CC BY-SA 2.1 JP DEED, via Wikimedia Commons.

The HPA axis relies on hormonal signals to keep the sympathetic nervous system, the *gas pedal*, pressed down. If the brain continues to perceive something as dangerous, the hypothalamus releases a (corticotropin-releasing) hormone (CRH), which travels to the pituitary gland, triggering the release of another (adrenocorticotropic) hormone (ACTH). This hormone travels to the adrenal glands, which induces them to release **cortisol**. The body thus stays revved up and on high alert. When the threat passes, cortisol levels fall (Harvard Health, 2020).

The *parasympathetic nervous system*, the *brake*, should then dampen the stress response, to calm our body system down, regulate it and return it to a normal, stable condition. Sometimes we shake, or our fingers involuntarily tremble as this happens; the danger has passed, but the traumatic ordeal has taken its toll on our body.

PART 3. A long-term response (see Figure 4.14)

PART 3. However, prolonged traumatic experiences or "loss" may cause chronic low-level stress that keeps the HPA axis activated. Trauma or loss prevents the brakes being put on stress (described further below on p. 52), see *Figure 4.14*.

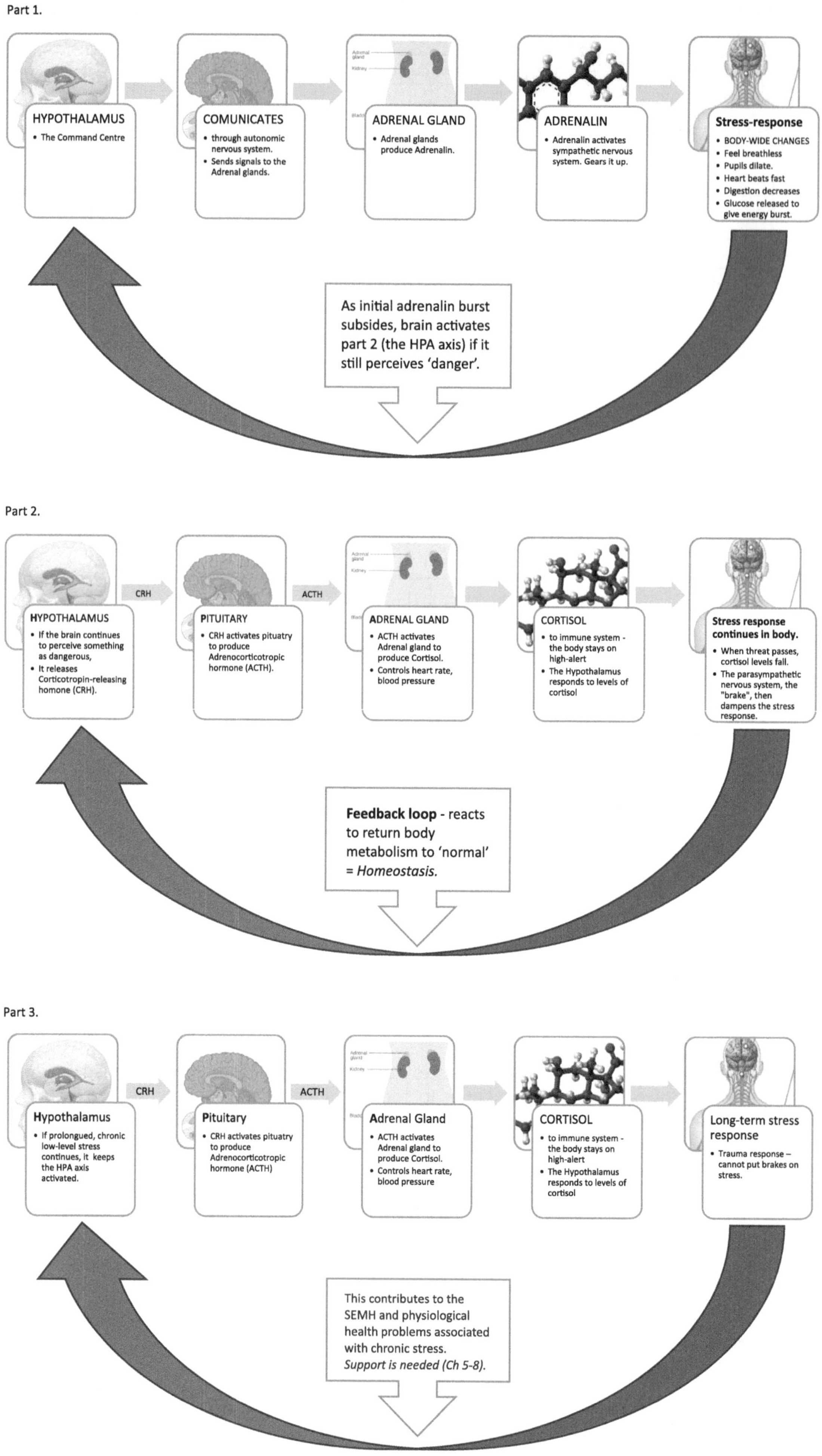

Part 1.

HYPOTHALAMUS
- The Command Centre

COMUNICATES
- through autonomic nervous system.
- Sends signals to the Adrenal glands.

ADRENAL GLAND
- Adrenal glands produce Adrenalin.

ADRENALIN
- Adrenalin activates sympathetic nervous system. Gears it up.

Stress-response
- BODY-WIDE CHANGES
- Feel breathless
- Pupils dilate.
- Heart beats fast
- Digestion decreases
- Glucose released to give energy burst.

As initial adrenalin burst subsides, brain activates part 2 (the HPA axis) if it still perceives 'danger'.

Part 2.

HYPOTHALAMUS
- If the brain continues to perceive something as dangerous,
- It releases Corticotropin-releasing homone (CRH).

CRH →

PITUITARY
- CRH activates pituatry to produce Adrenocorticotropic hormone (ACTH).

ACTH →

ADRENAL GLAND
- ACTH activates Adrenal gland to produce Cortisol.
- Controls heart rate, blood pressure

CORTISOL
- to immune system - the body stays on high-alert
- The Hypothalamus responds to levels of cortisol

Stress response continues in body.
- When threat passes, cortisol levels fall.
- The parasympathetic nervous system, the "brake", then dampens the stress response.

Feedback loop - reacts to return body metabolism to 'normal' = *Homeostasis.*

Part 3.

Hypothalamus
- If prolonged, chronic low-level stress continues, it keeps the HPA axis activated.

CRH →

Pituitary
- CRH activates pituatry to produce Adrenocorticotropic hormone (ACTH)

ACTH →

Adrenal Gland
- ACTH activates Adrenal gland to produce Cortisol.
- Controls heart rate, blood pressure

CORTISOL
- to immune system - the body stays on high-alert
- The Hypothalamus responds to levels of cortisol

Long-term stress response
- Trauma response – cannot put brakes on stress.

This contributes to the SEMH and physiological health problems associated with chronic stress.
Support is needed (Ch 5-8).

Figure 4.14 The stress response system. Diagram by Taylor J. (2023).

Hormones and neurotransmitters

Two key components discussed in the previous section are adrenalin and cortisol. They help the body respond to stress.

- Adrenaline: this hormone is produced by the adrenal glands on the kidneys and is responsible for the *fight-flight-fawn-freeze-flop-flock* response. Adrenaline increases heart rate, blood pressure and the release of glucose into the bloodstream to provide the body with energy. It also prepares the muscles for physical activity.
- Cortisol: this hormone is produced by the adrenal glands and is involved in the stress response by increasing blood sugar levels, suppressing the immune system and influencing other systems in the body to help the individual cope with stress. Cortisol helps the body respond to stress by providing a burst of energy. Cortisol can be a good thing, as it is what helps us get out of bed in the morning; it can give us that energy burst when we need it. However, too much prolonged cortisol is physically damaging to our brains and bodies, as the next illustration, Figure 4.15, shows.

Hormones and neurotransmitters influence our thoughts and motivations, as well as our ability to learn and concentrate. However, *to briefly clear up differences between hormones and neurotransmitters, there are* two different types of chemicals that carry signals from one part of the body to another. They control a variety of physical and psychological functions, including our mood, our eating patterns, our ability to learn and our sleep cycles.

Neurotransmitters' actions are short-lived and can affect both voluntary actions (eating, bathing, walking) and involuntary actions (breathing, blinking). The *nervous system uses neurotransmitters for its chemical signals,* released into the synapse in the brain and transmitted across the synaptic cleft. Neurotransmitters work locally (in the brain) and their actions are very fast.

Hormones act for longer periods of time; the *endocrine system uses hormones for its chemical signals*. They are transmitted through blood and are long-lasting as they can act on distant cells. They always work involuntarily.

> *If hormones take a while to respond and neurotransmitters act rapidly, then when a child, or a teenager, goes 'whoosh,' it is their brain, not their hormones that caused it!*

Both systems work together to maintain homeostasis. They are both forms of a chemical signal.

Growing research suggests that chemical signals can act as a neurotransmitter in the brain while serving as a hormone elsewhere to impact emotions, wellbeing and mental health. These include a-e:

a. Dopamine: involved in the regulation of mood, motivation and reward. It helps to regulate feelings of pleasure, satisfaction and happiness. Low levels of dopamine can be associated with depression.
b. Serotonin: regulates mood, appetite and sleep – it makes you happy. Low levels of serotonin can be associated with depression.
c. Oxytocin: often referred to as the "love hormone," this is involved in social bonding, trust and positive emotional experiences.
d. Endorphins: released in the brain in response to pain or stress and act as natural pain-relieving hormones and mood enhancers that are involved in feelings of pleasure and happiness. They create a general feeling of good wellbeing.
e. GABA: a neurotransmitter that helps to regulate anxiety and calm the nervous system.

These interact and influence each other; imbalances in their levels can contribute to conditions such as anxiety, depression and other mental health disorders. Maintaining a healthy balance of hormones and neurotransmitters brings good mental wellbeing. However, trauma may bring an inability to "rest and digest" and instead may lead to rising panic or a prolonged traumatic response. If a pupil cannot calm themselves, then we need to calm and *support* them by using strategies at the appropriate stage of the "5-S Scaffold" described within chapters 5–8.

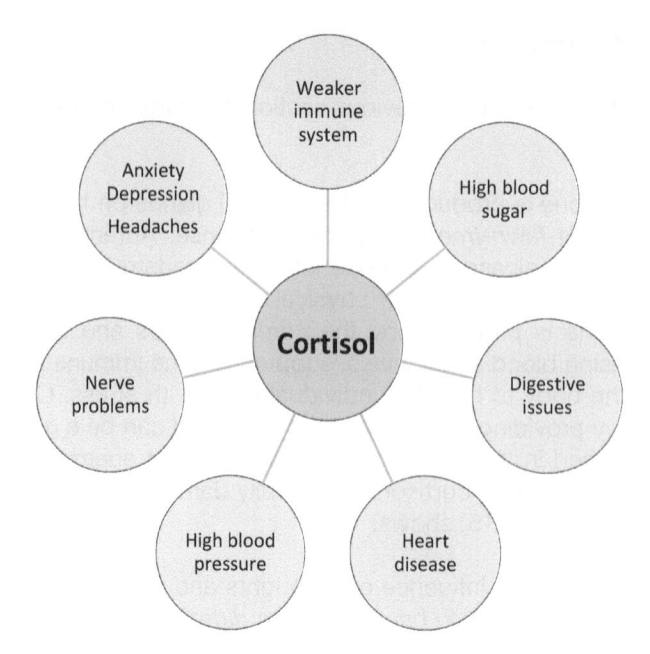

Figure 4.15 Diagram showing the impact of sustained stress on the human body.
Image: Taylor, J. (2023).

Trauma brings an inability to put the brakes on stress

Many people are unable to find a way to put the brakes on stress, that is, to engage the parasympathetic nervous system. In *Figure 4.14, part 3*, the dark grey arrow indicates the feedback loop; a raised cortisol level sends a message to the hippocampus that it is on *high alert* and needs to stay in that mode.

Chronic low-level stress keeps the HPA axis activated, much like a motor that is idling too high for too long. After a while, this has an effect on the body and contributes to the health problems associated with chronic stress (Harvard Health, 2020) as in Figure 4.15 above.

Unfortunately, the body can also overreact to *stressors* that are not life-threatening, such as not only traffic jams, work pressure and family difficulties, but also past traumas.

Sometimes these emotions match what has happened, and sometimes they do not. When "triggered" by a seemingly fearful situation, the pupil may, in fact, be safe – such as with the corridor noise, in the earlier example.

In these situations, the brain is responding to a perceived threat: it has utilised its fast-acting threat-detection circuits (including the amygdala and hypothalamus) rather than applying rational thought. It utilised:

- Learning from a previous experience (there was a noise in school and boys had a fight).
- Memory (I remember being scared when the fight happened near me and I got caught up in it).
- Language and culture (I don't like fights; I should not fight).

These additional ingredients are also added to the mix to create conscious feelings of fear and anxiety (McKay, 2020). The pupil was unable to regulate himself and logically assume, "there's a noise in school, but it's probably a class coming out to break," rather than "it means there are boys who want to fight me." It is the job of those teachers and carers around the dysregulated child to *support* them to become regulated again (LeDoux and Pine, 2016).

Too much *stress or* too little *stimulation can be damaging to the brain*

Conversely, having no extra stimulation (via interoception or exteroception) is damaging too; this can be seen in cases of **neglect**, just one of the many ACEs impacting brain development and functioning.

A Positron Emission Tomography (PET) scan of a "neglected, abused brain" compared with a "healthy brain" reveals this impact. At birth, only basic structures such as the brain stem are fully functional. Regions of the brain that are wired through early childhood experiences, such as the temporal lobes, are significantly more developed in the healthy brain. By contrast, the temporal lobes, which regulate emotions and receive input from the senses, are almost inactive in the brain scan of a Romanian orphan, institutionalised shortly after birth. Such children suffer emotional and cognitive problems. The image can be seen at https://simplyfosteringconsultancy. co.uk/impact-neglect-developing-brain/.

In the late 1990s, brain researcher Charles Nelson discovered that Romanian, state-run orphanages provided basic needs (food and shelter) but provided virtually no social-emotional or physical stimulation (Wade et al., 2022). Compared to other children, these orphans smiled and laughed less, had poorer language skills, exhibited lower intelligence, had higher rates of mental illness and showed less brain activity. In 2001, Nelson and his colleagues began **The Bucharest Early Intervention Project** (Wade et al., 2022) designed to remove children from these orphanages and place them in foster families. When comparing children, those with foster families have made greater gains in language, intelligence, social skills and most aspects of mental health. Thus, this demonstrates the brain's **plasticity**, or ability to be repaired, we will return to this later, but first, a brief recap to set the scene.

Returning to our pupil

So, when the pupil experienced rapid breathing, a racing heart and churning-stomach, the sensations laid the foundations for his emotions; he experienced high anxiety. This anxiety made him aware of his bodily sensations, but these were misread by the (insula in the) brain as they signalled a much bigger danger than was present. Any corridor noise produced overwhelming feelings; these prevented him functioning, from thinking and applying logic. His "survival state" was usually in the form of action, resembling *the fight-flight responses*. However, occasionally his dysregulation took the form of a *freeze-flop response* where he clenched his fists, tensed his shoulders, curled his toes over and put his chin on his chest to stare into space. Occasionally he would say he was light-headed and felt unwell too.

His previous life experience had altered the accuracy of his interoception

Research shows after chronic, traumatic stress our sense of panic can be amplified because of the increased connectivity between the insula and several regions of brain's fear-circuitry (Barrett, 2021; Kosner, 2019, 2021).

Our body responds with physiological changes which are autonomic (i.e., automatic) such as heart rate, nausea and stomach pains; a debilitating impact of stress or trauma, as we read on the table above (Table 4.1). To illustrate this, we will think about phobias.

Phobia: an example of a stress response

One example of being "triggered" (trigger-alert regarding phobias), meaning a situation seems to be far more fearful than it really is (there may be a logic to it in some cases, or there may not), is with phobias.

Just take a few seconds to think of something you are scared of, have a phobia or fear of:

Flying	Snakes	Sudden noises	Heights
Wasps	Water	Crowds	Spiders
The dark	Dogs	Clowns	Public speaking

Then imagine:

- That thing is an image on paper. Consider what you think of and feel.
- Now imagine that "thing" is on the other side of your window. What do you sense then? An element of relative safety may combine with impending concern.
- Now imagine you are face-to-face with "it." What would you feel? What would you be doing? How would you act? What are your bodily sensations?
- Now consider that last example; you are panicked and extra vigilant, you are on high alert and your heart is racing – but you have to sit still in class and learn!

Clearly, in a hyper-anxious state of arousal, you cannot concentrate if that "thing" is present or is lurking nearby. You would constantly be in threat mode.

You aim to seek control, act randomly, attempt to avoid whatever the threat is, you are hyper-vigilant and lack concentration on any task at hand.

That is how a child or young person/pupil under stress will feel. When they are in that state of body and mind, they cannot participate, function nor learn! Their cognitive, reasoning part of their brain cannot be engaged whilst they are on alert – similar to the earlier hand-brain-fist model of "flipping your lid" (Siegel and Bryson, 2011).

Our supportive strategies and our interventions are, therefore, key.

Learning is impossible *when a child or young person is in a state of trauma, is experiencing sensations linked with a past trauma or has just experienced a moment of real fear or a shock.*

The "Escalation Cycle" chart below (Figure 4.16) shows the pattern before, during and after a "meltdown."

In the chart, the trigger-point could be phobias, stressful situations, trauma-linked memories or increased anxiety.

The graph reminds of the length of time that, as neuroscience has determined, a recovery period can take. If the lower horizontal line represents the pupil functioning calmly, regulated and rational (age-determined), then we estimate that it takes 25–30 mins for their adrenalin level to return to near normal.

Time from the trigger-event to de-escalation potentially represents an hour when the pupil was unable to learn or function well. That may constitute one whole lesson out of a school day. During this time, the pupil would have felt and experienced many physical changes that *anxiety, panic attacks* or *increased stress* can bring (Table 4.1), caused by changes in our autonomic nervous system.

To give substance to this theory, researchers from Yale School of Medicine made discoveries about how the brain communicates with the body and its major organs (Backman, 2022; Zhao et al., 2022).

They confirmed that our brain detects *signals* transmitted to it from various parts of our body. By discovering the DNA coding of a **neuron** in the vagus nerve pathway, researchers knew exactly which body part the *neuron* had travelled from. This was conclusive evidence that the vagus nerve communicates different signals to the brain; the brain can very precisely discriminate which signal is from which part of the body.

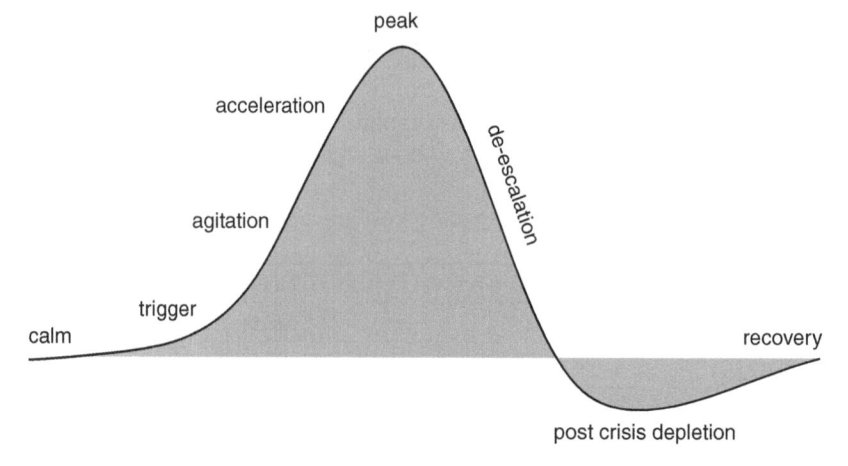

Figure 4.16 The "Escalation Cycle." Adapted from The Escalation Cycle, hes-extraordinary.com.

Knowing which **neurons** are involved with specific bodily functions suggests that bespoke *support* or treatments can target specific signal neuron pathways. This gives insight that a supportive intervention can transmit information which positively impacts the brain and thus makes the *support* effective.

The next section considers *neurons* and *synapses* in the brain, to explore brain plasticity.

Neurons and synapses

Moving into the minute detail of how the brain senses these bodily and environmental changes (changes essential for survival), we will look closer at how the brain is wired.

Neurons and synapses form the wiring of the brain. Neurons are specialised nerve cells that make up a network. Messages are passed between neurons at connections called synapses, a microscopic gap, as the neurons do not actually touch (Sumners, 2018). There are sometimes tens of thousands of synaptic connections between neurons.

Synapses join neurons in the brain to neurons elsewhere in the body. They connect our sensory organs, such as the ones that detect pain and touch.

The brain sends and receives electrical and chemical signals through this network to transmit information between the brain and other parts of the CNS. These messages are the physical basis of learning and memory.

The growth and strength of these connections change over time and vary throughout childhood and into adulthood (Sumners, 2018).

Brain development: early childhood synaptic growth – and pruning

These very early synaptic connections are largely genetically determined. Prior to birth, a great deal of brain development happens. At birth, the brain is proportionately the largest part of its body, weighing about 25% of its adult weight; yet, at birth, it already has *all* of the neurons it will ever have.

Compared to the rest of the newborn's body, the brain is very heavy. Whilst the average newborn weighs about 5% of adult size (7½ lbs), its brain doubles in size in the first year. It weighs about 75% of its adult size at age two, and 90% by age five. This brain increase is due to gaining *connections* between these neurons; this is known as *synaptic growth* (Urban Child Institute, 2023).

In a young brain (from conception to age three years), synapses are multiplying like crazy. Early overproduction is determined by genes, whereas later overproduction is due to the many new experiences within the first few years of life. Synapses are formed at a faster rate during these years than at any other time. In fact, the brain creates many more of them than it needs: at age two or three, the brain has up to twice as many synapses as it will have in adulthood (see Figure 4.17). These surplus connections are gradually eliminated (being pruned and killed off) throughout childhood and adolescence – a process sometimes referred to as *blooming and pruning* (Van der Kolk, 2015).

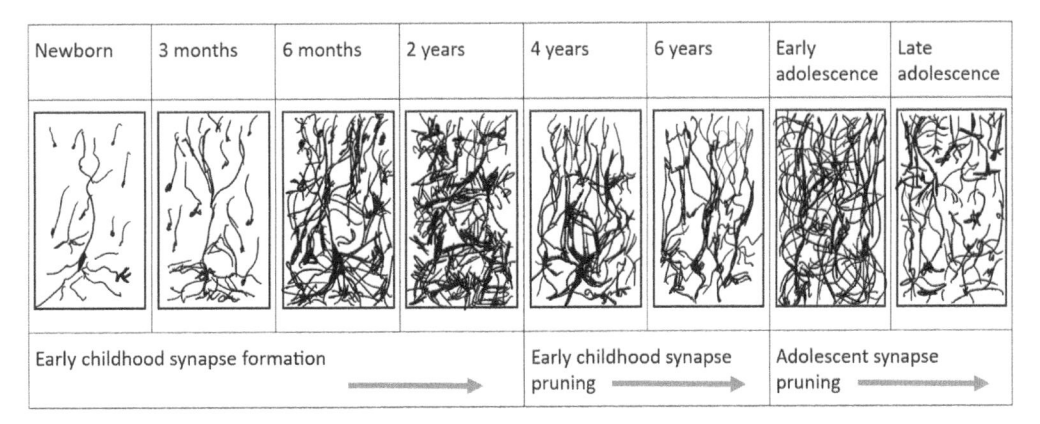

Newborn	3 months	6 months	2 years	4 years	6 years	Early adolescence	Late adolescence

Early childhood synapse formation ⟶   Early childhood synapse pruning ⟶   Adolescent synapse pruning ⟶

Figure 4.17 Synapse Formation in children and young people. Taylor J (2023) adapted from Video Source: https://youtu.be/r3OH0hT-gBoHoxby(2022)TheForkintheRoad:Adolescence,Education,Economic Fatalism, and Populism with Caroline Hoxby. Lecture.

Which synapses survive and which die off are determined by what situation the child lives in and what activities they like to be involved with. Growth and pruning allow the child's brain to invest in and *strengthen* the neurons and synapses that are most used, due to being completely necessary and important to them and their situations. This is similar to deleting old Apps off a mobile phone in order to maximise the running efficiency of the Apps we still use.

Plasticity

Synaptic pruning is due to our experiences, therefore constant stimulation of certain synaptic connections, due to a hobby or speaking two languages from an early age, causes this wiring to grow strong and remain permanent (Blakemore, 2019). Conversely, those connections that are not used much are weakened or "pruned," and so they waste away and disappear. *Neural plasticity* is the term used to explain that neural connections can be altered through experience; it is the *"use-it-or-lose-it"* principle, or alternatively we can say *"those that are used together, fuse together"* or *"neurons that fire together, wire together"* (Hebb, 1949).

The brain develops and re-wires itself in response to the environment around it throughout its life. Therefore, we say the brain is malleable and has *plasticity* (in both cognitive development and emotional development), including during adolescence and into adulthood. Plasticity, first proposed in 1949 by Canadian psychologist Donald Hebb (QBI, 2023), refers to flexibility. "Plasticity" describes how the brain can change in form and function, proven from MRI scans (Giedd et al., 1999, cited in Feinstein, 2009) who discovered the overproduction of "grey matter" during adolescence.

For example, the brain at birth is wired to hear every phonemic sound in every human language. If children hear sounds from only one language, the pathways for the phonemes in that language are strengthened, but pathways for other phonemic sounds are lost. So, an adult who was raised hearing only English will have difficulty hearing phonemes unique to Japanese or Russian because those neural connections were never stimulated and were lost. Moreover, that adult will hear a second language through the filter of his or her first language. This is why most adults who learn a second language speak it with an accent (Shelley and Beins, 2012).

Experience dependent

This refinement, *blooming and pruning*, of synaptic connections is dependent on experience gained through sensory input and interaction with the environment (the *interoception* and *exteroception* previously discussed). Therefore, this refinement occurs most profoundly during critical or sensitive periods of development; our earliest memories are often something out of the ordinary (chapter 1).

The adults who matter to the young child have the greatest impact on what the brain feels, what emotions are evoked and what sense they have of the situation they are in, whether they feel fear, confusion, safety, calmness or joy, for example. At birth, brains are very much *under construction*, babies must be completely looked after which makes them vulnerable, but they become uniquely wired to the circumstances they are born into.

ATTACHMENT revisited in the neuroscience context

Ultimately babies need complete care, physically and emotionally, and children need to sense comfort and warmth from the adults caring for them. As we read in chapter 3, those youngsters who were protected and kept safe were those who were most likely to survive. We call this "attachment." Natural bonding, security and joy occur in positive shared experiences which bring contentment and happiness. Play or activities together *strengthen* the two-way connection, the reciprocal bond, between infant and caregiver (Colley and Cooper, 2017). This also *strengthen*s the synaptic connections responsible for healthy emotional growth and bonding.

When these happy, playful, calm times change, when the infant is crying or in pain, it is the adult parental-figure who acts to *support* the infant, alter the situation, relieve distress and bring comfort. Co-regulation develops the ability for self-regulation, this brings positive synaptic connections; since they are *used together, they will fuse together*, thus imparting effective emotional development and resilience.

Adolescents also need guidance and *support*; the next section considers how their *brain changes* impact their actions and what is often referred to as "typical teenage behaviour." A deeper understanding brings a greater ability to empathise and intervene appropriately.

Adolescents and their myriad of neurological developments

Adolescence is described as the time of life that starts with the physical, biological and hormonal changes of puberty and ends when the individual has a stable and independent role in society (Blakemore, 2012).

An adolescent has that desire to venture out and experience life! So, what is happening in those teenage years, what can neuroscience tell us?

In brief, researchers have confirmed that neurological developmental milestones take place but rather than leave childhood and enter adolescence with a fully formed and calmly functional brain, adolescents have to struggle with a changing brain, one that is destroying old neural connections and building new ones (Feinstein, 2009). *Brain plasticity continues! Understanding more about the brain which teenagers are navigating helps with interpreting their behaviour, and thus our response to it.*

Recent scientific research explains what is physically happening inside their brains (Bethlehem et al., 2022; Durston and Casey, 2006; Fairchild et al., 2016; Giedd, 2008; Giedd et al., 1999). MRI scans have revealed that rather than leaving childhood with a brain ready to take on the responsibilities of young adulthood, the brains of teenagers are in the middle of some major transformations.

MRI images (found here: https://www.pacesconnection.com/blog/the-developing-brain-and-adverse-childhood-experiences-aces) reveal the brain's bursts in activity, causing a growth spurt that results in less dense synapses; this occurs throughout adolescence from ages 12 to 20. It is now understood that the brain continues developmental changes through to age 22 on average for women and 24 on average for men.

The incredible growing and shrinking brain: imaging technology

In a separate ongoing study, an international research team created brain charts spanning our entire lifespan, from a 15-week-old foetus to a 100-year-old adult. It shows brain changes throughout our life (Bethlehem et al., 2022).

The charts are the result of a research project spanning 6 continents (and a few decades) and bringing together possibly the largest ever MRI datasets ever aggregated, almost 125,000 brain scans from over 100 different studies. Although not currently for clinical use, the team hopes that the charts will become routinely used in a similar way that standardised, paediatric growth-charts are used; potentially, any world-wide MRI brain scan can be compared with the chart to shed light on any "differences" that exist and, therefore, allow more accurate understanding, *support* or course of action (Bethlehem et al., 2022).

The brain charts have allowed the researchers to confirm developmental milestones that were formerly only the subject of hypothesis (Figure 4.18). Among the key milestones observed by the team were:

- *The volume of grey matter (brain cells) increases rapidly from mid-gestation onwards, peaking just before we are six years old. It then begins to decrease slowly.*
- *The volume of white matter (brain connections) also increases rapidly from mid-gestation through early childhood, and this peaks just before we are 29 years old.*
- *The decline in white matter volume begins to accelerate after 50 years.*
- *Grey matter volume in the prefrontal cortex peaks in adolescence* (more on this next).

It is imaging technologies that have produced an explosion in such research, enabling experts to visibly see how the brain develops. This contributes to the pool of knowledge in both describing the physical changes throughout adolescence and in helping explain why exposure to **ACEs** *greatly alters a young person's brain* and thus impacts their physical health, emotional health and, potentially, the quality of life across their lifespan. These will be considered next by describing the process intrinsic to a teenager's brain circuits becoming wired.

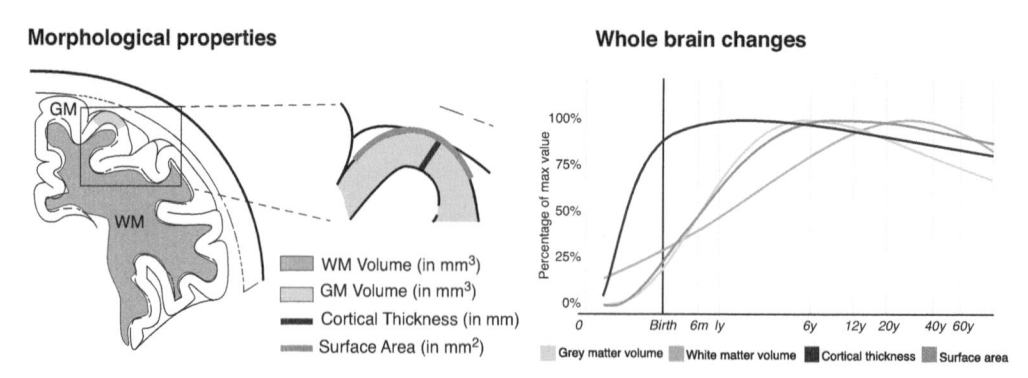

Figure 4.18 Adapted from Brain Charts for the Human Lifespan, R. A. I. Bethlehem et al. (2022).

What is physically happening in their brain during these teenage years?

A greater understanding of how a teenager's brain is wired is gained from knowledge of how their brain is structured.

If we consider that adults have hormones in their bodies too yet manage to function, remain calm, apply logic and persevere. Hence, if an adolescent has trouble sitting still in school, concentrating on their work or has the occasional reactive behaviour or "slip of the tongue," it is not their hormones but is because their brains are not yet finished! (Barrett, 2021; Gilbert et al., 2021).

MRI scans revealed that rather than leaving childhood with a brain ready to take on the responsibilities of adulthood, teens have to contend with a shifting brain that is destroying old neural connections and building new ones (Brierley, 2022). It is equivalent to navigating a storm at sea having lost direction.

The diagram (Figure 4.18) shows that between ages 12 and 19 years, the brain is physically undergoing an incredible amount of change. In terms of the percentage of actual maximum brain volume:

- The average cortical thickness and surface area are both decreasing.
- The grey matter is proportionally decreasing in volume, as it has since approximately age 6.
- The white matter (connections of neurons and synapses) is, overall, increasing in volume (combined with the growth, comes pruning).

This is all illustrated by the overlapping of lines on the chart at around age 12–13 years (Figure 4.18).

Interestingly, a relationship has been discovered, in preadolescent children, between the cortical thinning and language ability improving. The changes of cortex thinning, white matter volume increasing and grey matter decreasing are all simultaneous (Durston and Casey, 2006). These changes have a tremendous impact on the preadolescent and teenage brain; the language area and cognitive functioning is rapidly developing (teens do often "find their voice") but not yet fully formed. Their brain is also continuing its "blooming and pruning" based on their interests and life experiences.

ADOLESCENCE and synaptic pruning (a golden opportunity)

Synaptic pruning continues through adolescence; it stops in the early 20s, eventually the total number of synapses stabilises. Incidentally, some pruning and increases in synaptic density continue throughout life; our brain constantly modifies in response to information, challenges and changes in the environment (Blakemore, 2019).

The neural connections a teenager makes endure a lifetime and unused connections are lost forever. If they are not reading, doing science or solving maths problems, the synapses for those activities will be pruned. It is hypothesised that pruning at this age permits the adolescent brain to organise its circuitry and refine its thinking processes (Thompson et al., 2000). It is a golden opportunity to build a better brain; it is also a window in which the brain's potential can instead be wasted (Feinstein, 2009).

A young child's thinking is only in the concrete, the here and now, but the brain continues to grow and change and is at its largest size as children reach puberty (biologically around 14 years in boys, and 11 years in girls). Whilst it is (in a sense) fully grown, the brain continues to transform and develop. Hence, a teenager's brain is a work-in-progress, it is "under construction"; these brain changes directly cause, what is regarded as, *typical teenage behaviours*. We have likely experienced teenagers' emotions quickly reaching a combustible point; many regard the influx of *hormones* (blamed during puberty) as being responsible for these outbursts. However, to reiterate, it is their brains not their hormones that cause high emotions and behavioural fluctuations (Hohnen et al., 2019).

During this time-period, the brain changes, adapts and responds to its environment. These responses all help make the brain what it becomes.

The brain is "finished" around our mid-20s, consequently the teenage brain reacts differently to how an adult brain would. Hence, it also responds to stress differently, and it can be around this vulnerable time that stress, anxiety or related mental health disorders begin to emerge. An adult brain can calmly respond to think things through logically, it can consider the impact of any here-and-now decision and remain reasonable when discussing conflicting ideas. Whereas young people, during adolescence, tend to make decisions based on the moment they are in without considering the consequences; these run-the-risk of these being a "poor" decision. Two separate neuroimaging studies (Sowell et al., 1999; Yurgelun-Todd et al., 2002) helped discover why this is:

> Until the frontal lobes, the seat of language and reason, are completely formed, teens rely [too] much on their **amygdala**— the seat of emotion. Not only do the wild emotions get first say about what teens will do next, their ability to negotiate their way out of a tense moment by using carefully chosen, diplomatic language is fledgling at best. Fortunately, the adults and adult brains that are often at the receiving end of adolescent outbursts can understand what is happening and de-escalate confrontations when they do occur.
>
> (Feinstein, 2009, p. 14)

The amygdala also gains pleasure from reward-seeking or risk-taking behaviours, things we typically see in adolescents. Since it is involved with emotion-processing and reward-processing, it is what gives us the kick out of doing fun things or taking risks, riding rollercoasters as an example; in adolescents, this part of the limbic system is hypersensitive to that rewarding feeling from risk-taking, compared with most adults, and so it seeks, or even craves, that *feel-good sensation*. The most-likely reason is because the part of the brain that stops us taking excessive risks, that helps us make levelled decisions, the prefrontal cortex, is still underdeveloped in adolescents. So "being reasonable" is not always possible for them.

Parts of the brain that we need *to understand another person's point of view* are not fully developed until adulthood (Blakemore, 2012). Grasping other people's perceptions is something we need to do daily to guide our behaviour, to understand how people are feeling and gain an understanding of their take on the world they live in. However, as we have seen, during adolescence the brain network required in still under construction, they quite literally cannot clearly see someone else's perspective.

Why does the amygdala get first say?

At this stage, the amygdala is the boss, this "emotional control centre" gets first say in how the teenager reacts. The main reason for this is the adolescent's prefrontal cortex is not yet fully developed so the amygdala goes unchallenged.

The prefrontal cortex is one of the regions that has the most drastic changes in it over the time-period known as adolescence. It is involved in a whole host of high-level important cognitive functioning:

- Decision-making.
- Planning (for that evening, the next day, next week or next year).
- Social interactions (understanding other people and self-awareness).
- Inhibiting inappropriate behaviour (stopping yourself saying something rude or acting aggressively, for example).

Grey matter volume increases throughout childhood and peaks in early adolescence (Figure 4.18) which means that it is decreasing throughout adolescence (Blakemore, 2012). This significant

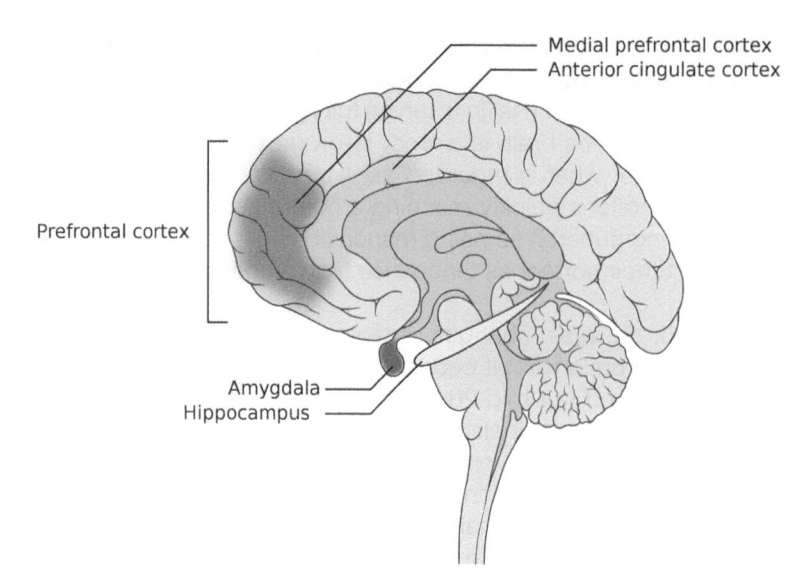

Figure 4.19 Diagram showing the prefrontal cortex and the amygdala location. Patrick J. Lynch, medical illustrator, C. Carl Jaffe, MD, cardiologist, Fvasconcellos Whidou, CC BY-SA 4.0, via Wikimedia Commons.

decline in grey matter volume in the prefrontal cortex is thought to correspond to synaptic pruning (described earlier). Which means the brain is getting rid of unwanted connections and strengthening the ones that matter. It has been likened to pruning old apple-tree branches to make the important ones grow stronger and produce fruit. This is what effectively fine-tunes the running of the brain. However, it is dependent upon the young person's environment; this includes their circumstances, any world-events impacting them, their friendships and their family culture and values.

The environment, including teaching and its social-emotional *support*, helps shape a young person's brain. This therefore directly assures us that *how* we educate, guide, *support* and encourage our children and young people impacts and shapes their developing brain. It helps it get wired or re-wired correctly (thanks to plasticity), at a time in their life where the brain is particularly open to change, it is adaptable and malleable (Barrett, 2021).

What this tells us is that our interventions make a difference!

It is therefore a ripe time for learning and creativity, for enjoyment in building relationships and an opportunity to help children and young people heal from past *loss* or develop resilience and strength within any global traumatic situations they find themselves living in.

Why our *support* helps?

When pupils are in a state of high alert, it is the amygdala that has jumped into action; responsible for our fight-flight-freeze-fawn-flop-flock response, it regulates the emotional brain of the adolescent. The reason our children and young people bounce between such intense emotions is that their logical, reasoning thought is controlled by a not-yet-fully-developed prefrontal cortex within it.

Hence, the impact of the amygdala and the frontal lobe, working together or independently, will cause the next action or response in a pupil. The emotional amygdala can be quick to respond when the pupil feels they have heard criticism or feels unvalidated or misunderstood. The brain cannot yet organise this mass of information, so we need to organise it for them.

Teenagers *feel* things BEFORE they can *understand* them. They get an immediate sense of an emotion but cannot put it into words, they may rage or hit out. Insults require less brain processing compared with a calm, rational response. A highly emotive retort, from teacher or parent, might provoke a situation to escalate and become explosive. For the young person to de-escalate, a safe and predictable adult is essential. Ways of achieving this calm, trusted approach are described in chapters 5, 6 and 8.

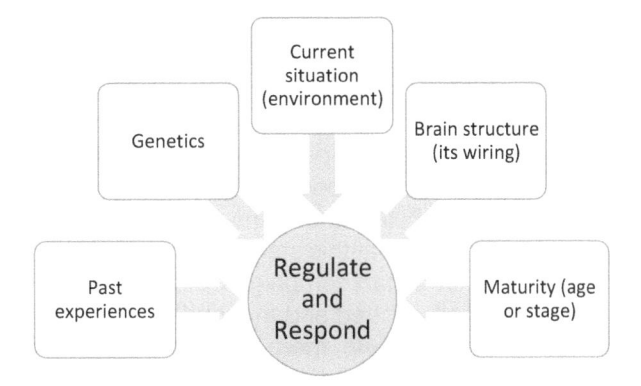

Figure 4.20 A diagram showing factors that influence and alter the behavioural response (impact). Diagram by Taylor, J. (2023).

When this knowledge is combined with a consideration of the many physical brain structure changes within a teenager's brain, it is apparent that the combination requires careful understanding and handling. Our children and young people need to feel that we, as caring adults, can help them feel safe.

Assessing safety and ACEs

When we feel safe, our thinking and our behaviour is driven by integrated functioning in the brain; we can logically *reason* and rationally act accordingly. We constantly, and mostly unconsciously, assess our safety and monitor threat levels (Porges, 2009). We learn to predict the safety of a situation – our knowledge is gained by our learning through trial and error, through copying and practice (modelling and mirroring), through watching and waiting and by repeating events (Shonkoff, 2010). Our prediction of an outcome of an event leads us to either suppress or activate our defence mechanisms.

Hence, our prediction ability diminishes when life-situations are out-of-the-ordinary and are unexpected or shocking in some way. We no longer have that ability to predict, life is uncertain, our world feels unstable. When that ability to accurately predict has vanished, it can lead to vulnerability and traumatic stress. The child or young person is amid an "ACE".

This impacts our brain structures. The pathways alerting to danger may be strengthened; we may see the impact of this over-alertness in children and young people who we meet in our professional roles.

These behavioural responses reflect an active three-way relationship between our setting (exteroception), our body's physiological changes (interoception) and our brain (psychological factors) (Clark, 2019). As Figure 4.20 shows, these interrelate because of a combination of our brain's wiring, environment, past experiences, genetics and our *age or stage* (our maturity). These components result in variations in how we individually regulate our emotions and how we respond (Barrett, 2018; Siegel and Bryson, 2011; Van der Kolk, 2015).

This is what wires the brains of our young people and, importantly, is why we are all unique and individual!

Adolescents: wired by social experience

How do teenager's brains get wired? They are wired by their real social experiences. Teenagers may spend a long time working out who they are and what role they fit into; as they change their "look," their hobbies, try to fit in- or stand out, work out their music tastes and dating choices, they form an identity as they define themselves. Their social grouping can set the tone for them understanding who they are. Their brain-wiring instructions happen from the words and actions of other people (Feinstein, 2009).

Their physical workings inside the brain occur alongside a teenager's gradual realisation of others around them (others with thoughts and opinions); this plus their ability to imagine what these other teenagers may be thinking and feeling towards them, can all give rise to angst, and a desire to "fit in and conform." The validation of their peers is highly important in helping form their identity.

Teenagers are in a tug-of-war with themselves, with their brains and with the world. They are exploring who they are and what they believe in, influenced by developing views on the world around them, but they remain emotionally dependant on supportive parents and peers who accept them (Feinstein, 2009). Previous childhood brain development level and the corresponding, naturally expected egocentricity (Shelley and Beins, 2012) may have prevented this type of thinking from occurring sooner. Hence, it is at this stage of adolescence that teenagers can often feel that they can take on the world (and start campaigns, or fund-raising, as examples) contesting the myth that all teenagers are self-centred and thoughtless.

Therefore, it is their emotions that rule them, rather than reason. The influence and control that parents, teachers and other key adults had over the toddler or child are reducing. Parental-figures are needed to set boundaries, to help the teenager's changing brain develop into a thinking adult. Boundaries give the teenager something to push against at a time when they are not able to make reasonable, well-judged, fore-thought decisions, as they simply do not have a developed prefrontal cortex to use for this purpose. Simultaneously, the teenager (guided more by the amygdala than the reasoning prefrontal cortex) may act in rebellion. Incidentally *rebellion* can be a positive quality, since it is a form of "active protest" (chapter 3). So, the recipe for a teenager is a developing emotional brain coupled with a striving for independence. However, they need *support* more than they realise – *helping them make good choices* is what *strengthens* their neural networks in the process of synaptic pruning. They cannot do this without adults, this is because they seek pleasure or take risks when their amygdala over-rules their not-fully-developed reasoning and decision-making centre (their prefrontal cortex). This is reassuring to parental-figures too to know that they are not being over-authoritative whilst maintaining balanced input into their adolescent's life choices.

Consequently, there is a tug-of-war happening as the teenagers strive for autonomy and being-their-own-person yet rely on parental-figures for emotional guidance, *support* and affirmation. The parental-figure making time and talking through these issues, with active-listening and validation (chapters 3 and 7), is often the best way to navigate through complex or delicate situations; this requires an intuitive balancing act (Blakemore, 2019). Rather than facing this situation head-on and watching it escalate (or erupt), the adolescent needs guidance from adults in a calm, understanding and validating manner rather than a heavy-handed, scolding, dictatorial approach.

However, if the young person feels safe and emotionally secure, and if school is a safe place to them, then it offers a strong position for the pupil to explore their identity and comprehend a complex world.

An adolescent's identity, their hard-wiring, happens through the culture they are living in and through the words and actions of other people, from parents and caregivers early on, to neighbours, teachers, schoolmates and eventually the people they choose to surround themselves with as an adult (Barrett, 2021).

What is so powerful about our families, communities and cultures is that they teach us concepts before we are even aware that they are doing it. Concepts, like anger, pride, bias or unconscious bias, will seem intuitive and natural to us and hard to break away from. As our cultural concepts feel natural to us, we intuitively assume they do for others as well. This can lead not only to prejudice, but also to cooperation.

Differences in people's beliefs can substantially impact their interpretation of a series of events. In an fMRI study, subjects' beliefs were manipulated by feeding them a truthful or invented backstory to the situation they were asked to judge (Abramson, 2023). This led to the two groups of subjects interpreting the same narrative in different ways. MRI studies of these groups found that brain functional responses tended to be similar among people who shared the same interpretation, but different from those of people with an opposing interpretation. This study demonstrated that brain responses to the same event tend to cluster together among people who share the same views.

This is grounds to refrain from harshly or negatively judging a young person, in their absence, whilst in a group conversation with other adults (social groups or professionals); the assertion is that if the adult brain responses *cluster*, then the child or pupil will perceive negative responses towards them. A child needs to feel secure. This is solid grounds for turning this situation around and using a "solution-circle" positive conversation style among the adult supporters, to prevent the escalation of negative body language.

Table 4.2 Symptoms of childhood trauma. Diagram by Taylor (2023)

Symptoms of childhood trauma		
Physical symptoms	**Behavioural symptoms**	**Emotional symptoms**
• Poor concentration • Shaking • Nightmares or night terrors • Lack of energy • Physical illness • Sleep disturbance	• Compulsions • Eating disorders • Impulsiveness • Isolation • Numbness or callousness • Refusal	• Anger • Unresponsiveness • Emotional outbursts • Depression or anxiety • Panic attacks • Afraid or in shock

Trauma, displacement, post-traumatic stress disorder

If the young person does not feel safe or emotionally secure, or if their culture (or sub-culture) feels scary or school seems unsafe, then the consequence is an absence of a safe, strong base from which to explore their identity and comprehend a complex world (Geddes, 2006). Rather, they and their whole world are thrown up in the air and they are desperately seeking a safe landing place. Many symptoms can occur; even if the child cannot put their feelings into words, they may give us visible cues, as seen in the diagram (Table 4.2) above.

With the case of the upheaval caused by a pandemic or displacement, such as fleeing a war-torn region, it may take time for school (or home) to feel consistently stable and secure. Creation of a "safe space" can help as a **SUPPORT** strategy. When they are in a place of safety and not on "high alert," then their brains can cognitively reason and sieve through new information (chapters 6 and 7).

However, when they are in a state of stressful trauma, their brain undergoes changes, such as can be seen in PET images showing scans in an individual with post-traumatic stress disorder (PTSD) versus a healthy comparison participant, found here: https://news.yale.edu/sites/default/files/styles/horizontal_image/public/ptsd_0.jpg?itok=0EClM8Vy&c=8acb728 cf74d3ff47d07477352e09341

The study (led by Yale University) also shows increased levels of a *receptor* in the brain which is associated with fear and stress-related behaviours; this study may have implications for the treatment of PTSD if medication that reduces this receptor also reduces the stress-related symptoms. Additionally, the study is the first to link PTSD symptoms with brain chemistry changes (Holmes et al., 2017) which is evidence that:

- Trauma impacts the brain to cause physical chemical brain changes.
- A changed brain requires an intervention (whether that is medication or **SUPPORT** strategies) to help it.

Adverse childhood experiences

As the study and our experience shows, ACEs impact the child's or young person's *brain structures – the pathways alerting to danger may be strengthened. We can see the impact of this over-alertness in youngsters who we meet in our professional roles. The pupil may be over-alert or over-anxious because they have emerged from a traumatic situation in which they felt unsafe because they were unable to predict.* Their ability to predict outcomes results in children activating, or suppressing, their defence mechanisms. We saw this too with "attachment styles" (chapter 3) if the child cannot predict, it can lead to trauma.

Encouragingly, since the teacher-pupil attachment relationship develops independently to the family-community one, we are able to build relationship and our **SUPPORT** strategies can positively alter the child's brain structures due to its innate plasticity. Over time these interventions, described in *Part Two*, can have a positive impact.

Summary

	Neuroscience in action summary table
1.	**The brain's main role is to predict our needs before they arise, to maintain stability and keep us alive.** The brain actively makes predictions using data gathered from our external surroundings (exteroception) and from the internal information it receives (interoception) to maintain stability (homeostasis) within the internal workings of our body by controlling our physiological processes and our behaviour. "Thinking" is a by-product of this need to stay alive, since thoughts and emotions inform *complex cognitive processes* such as decision-making. The brain also plays a crucial role in social interaction, learning and memory, all towards the ultimate aim of continuing our existence (Clark, 2019).
2.	The parent, or attachment-figure, has an important role in early childhood, not only for safety and protection (for survival), but also in guiding and modelling behaviours. Games and routines act as a **scaffold for the *thinking* prefrontal cortex.** Games build resilience (encouraged through "wait times") and develop self-control. However, this brain region is not fully developed until mid-20s; therefore, in childhood and adolescence, the "thinking" prefrontal cortex (upstairs brain) can be quickly taken over by the "emotional, impulsive" limbic system (downstairs brain) which is quicker to respond to a perceived threat. *Emotions occur faster than thoughts.* The *hand-brain* and upstairs-downstairs *house-brain* theories (Siegel and Bryson, 2011) consider that only when a child's brain is effectively functioning, can it carry out highly *important self-regulation tasks* and will *regulate their emotions, consider consequences, think before acting* and *consider how others feel*. This translates as the important skill of *making good decisions in a high-emotion situation.* The brain develops its skill set originally through the relationship with those around us. Neuroscience and attachment theory (chapter 3) interlink here, as through the attachment figure's co-regulation we develop our ability to self-regulate and learn and practise these *important self-regulation tasks.*
3.	**Importantly**, we are not passive, we receive sensory information, so **we actively construct our emotions** (Blakemore, 2019; LeDoux, 1996). We construct our emotions from a whole range of information. The *ingredients* are: • Sensory input and bodily sensations. • Previous life experiences, and our expectations of if "X" happens, I will feel "Y." • The people we are with. • The situation we are in. • What occurred moments before we felt that emotion (usually obvious, but sometimes the link is irrational). • Learning, memory, language and culture; these can give us priorities and a belief system. These *ingredients* (sometimes unconsciously) combine to **make the emotion** that we feel in that moment. Our brain interprets, constructs meaning and recommends a course of action. However, when under traumatic stress, the emotional *limbic system* rules, with the purpose of keeping us safe and alive (Hill and Dahlitz, 2022). In some situations, this is displayed as: heightened emotion, a reactional outburst or a distress level which alerts others. An adult can often assess any "threat" (fear, stress or anxiety) they may feel and apply rational thinking using the *ingredients* above. However, a child or young person does not have their fully developed "thinking" prefrontal cortex; their response to these feelings is a reaction designed to help them survive.
4.	**INTERPRETING and INFERRING INFORMATION** The brain receives *sensations from the outside world (exteroception) and sensations from the body itself (interoception)*. These signals feel physical; the brain does not know the cause, it only senses the outcomes (Barrett, 2021). It must work out what is causing these bodily feelings. So, it re-assembles previous experiences that are *similar* in some way to the present. Thus, linking it with a past situation can have positive results or arouse negative feelings. Exactly how we respond to trauma or Adverse Childhood Experiences is a result of our **perceptions** about that experience (rooted in early attachment experiences). Often though, to aid our survival, our brain gears us up a notch by *lurching into a* **stress response.** A stressful situation can activate the sympathetic nervous system, producing an immediate widespread **fight-flight-fawn-freeze-flop-flock response**. The purpose of this response is to avoid, decrease, limit or end the danger. The *sympathetic nervous system (fight-flight)* gears us up, while the *parasympathetic* nervous system takes us down (*rest and digest*). These work together towards achieving stability (**homeostasis**) in our body systems.

(Continued)

	Neuroscience in action summary table
	Theoretically, it is our ability to regulate our stress response system that allows us to engage socially and learn. *To participate with others and learn effectively, we need to feel safe in our relationships and environments* (Gilbert et al., 2021; Porges, 2009, 2022; Siegel and Bryson, 2011). However, trauma changes the accuracy of our interoception.
5.	In a trauma-stress response, the system in our body misinterprets information and **can overreact to *stressors* that are not life-threatening.** If we have been "triggered," a safe situation may bring involuntary fear. Some noise, smell or sensation may have inadvertently connected with feelings from a past trauma. **In these situations, the brain is responding to a perceived threat** – it has utilised its fast-acting threat-detection circuits (including the amygdala and hypothalamus) rather than applying rational thought. Hence • learning from a previous experience • memory • language and culture all impact how we respond to trauma and loss. Trauma brings an inability to put the brakes on stress.
6.	Over time, trauma and loss physically change the **brain** structure and its wiring; *the pathways alerting to danger may be strengthened.* A child or young person responds to stress using the most frequently used "trauma" pathways in their brain; so, they remain over-alert and overreact to typical daily events or to relationship interactions. Over-alertness occurs *after a traumatic situation, as when feeling unsafe they are unable to predict.* Their ability to predict outcomes results in children activating, or suppressing, their defence mechanisms. The brain, responding to a *perceived* threat, keeps the trauma-response system activated and physiological changes occur (e.g., increased heart rate, shortness of breath). However, the brain is malleable and has plasticity, and plasticity gives hope. Since the brain is adaptive, those "trauma" pathways (synaptic connections) can be positively altered through using supportive interventions. With the *use-it-or-lose-it* principle, the synaptic connections that are *used together, fuse together*, therefore strategies can alter the brain over time, to re-wire it; this should diminish an active fear response system and help reduce the harmful impact of perpetually raised cortisol levels. ***Part Two*** (chapters 5–8) describes strategies to *support* a pupil's responses to trauma or loss. *Brain plasticity is the good news in that our supportive strategies and interventions can have an impact.*
7.	When children feel safe, their unconscious and automatic threat-monitoring, that assesses their safety, will be allowed to relax (Porges, 2022). They will be receptive to *support* when they feel safest and relaxed. Calm, stable adults bring a positive, secure relationship experience. This has the added benefit of producing positive hormones and neurotransmitters that positively influence their thoughts and motivations. However, the *amygdala versus the prefrontal cortex* plays the central role in the lives of adolescents.
8.	Adolescents face many challenges: • Media expectations, exposure to and scrutiny from social media, threats from cyber bullying, internet access to some less desirable areas of life and pressures to succeed. • Poor employment prospects, unstable economic crisis and inadequate access to basic needs (shelter, food and warmth). • Education, health and social care services are stretched, particularly during global events. • Possibly early trauma, grief or loss. The current climate and personal circumstances may bring a difficult and frightening time for young people, requiring targeted *support* to help them navigate challenges. While their situation brings intense vulnerability, it also offers many opportunities; because of brain plasticity, change is possible.

(*Continued*)

	Neuroscience in action summary table
	Young people need a specific type of adult input whilst striving towards independence and discovering who they are. Their adolescent brain enjoys excitement and risk (drawn towards music, noise, socialising and physical challenge) but cannot accurately assess situations to keep themselves safe. Adults are needed to contain their experiences and set boundaries – this brings security and gives the teenagers something to push against to forge their own identity. However, adults need to be flexible to allow adolescents to develop responsibility when facing consequences of any choices they make. Therefore, just as the young infants need a secure base, from which to explore the world and return for *support* and guidance, so does the adolescent. A child or young person who is overwhelmed is not in a place to learn, and this chapter showed the range of neurological factors at play. The overriding message is that brain plasticity brings hope and the knowledge that **SUPPORT** strategies can, and will, have a positive impact. The following chapters in **Part Two** will describe simple, practical hands-on **SUPPORT** strategies. Easy to put into practice, these strategies, and the theory underpinning them, will help lessen the serious impact of the loss, grief or trauma children and young people are facing.

The 5-S *Scaffold*

A practical 5-layered supportive approach

INTRODUCTION TO PART TWO AND THE 5-S SCAFFOLD

Part One (chapters 1–4) has addressed the theory that underpins Part Two.
Part Two consists of the practical *SUBSIDE–SOOTHE–SUPPORT–STRENGTHEN–SELF-CARE* scaffolding presented from chapters 5–9.

The theory provides the foundation for understanding the suggested practical strategies. When the underlying principles are recognised, we can begin to see how our *physiological processes* are a natural response to trauma. Thus, gaining that knowledge enables us to have increased empathy. To *understand* rather than *judge* allows the *support* we offer to be more effective; we have insight that it will not be a "quick fix," and compassion brings patience and kindness in our approach to the children and young people we *support*.

Some key components of chapters 1–4:

- Trauma, grief and loss (including collective trauma) were defined.
- Various grief models were described to discover the commonality among them regarding emotional impacts from trauma and loss.
- To better understand the range of emotional reactions to the same event, child development *protective* factors and *risk* factors were considered; secure and insecure attachments to the primary caregiver were expounded to describe the base that the child is operating from and better understand the "back-story" to their responses.
- Children on *"high alert"* are unable to learn as their focus is directed towards the source of their anxiety, fear or phobia. This produces externalising responses (observable behaviour) because of what is happening internally in their brains and bodies.
- Neuroscience has added to our understanding of these adaptations, and the impacts upon our brain and body during a traumatic response. Many complex processes work together to produce a physiological reaction. Both the biological, internal response and the external stimuli affect us, so we may feel physical symptoms and our brains become wired to respond in a certain way. Additionally, age-related brain growth impacts how we react at certain stages of life.
- *Brain Plasticity* is the good news. *Support* can re-wire the brains of our children and young people. Rather than remain in a cycle of distress, with negative emotions and on high alert, effective strategies and interventions can help *halt* an emotional outburst, *soothe* and then *support*. This strengthens the resilience of our young people and offers a more optimistic outlook for the future.

Armed with this theoretical understanding, Part two seeks to suggest hands-on practical approaches and strategies which can be implemented to *support* the children and young people who have encountered trauma, grief or loss.

These chapters are each represented by one of the segments in the 5-Scaffold graphic:

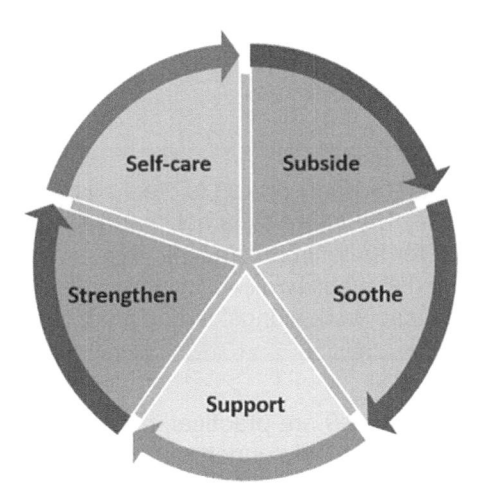

A graphic (repeats throughout book) to depict components of the 5-S Scaffold (Taylor, 2023).

DOI: 10.4324/9781003275268-7

The 5-S Scaffold: a 5 layered supportive approach

The scaffold provides a framework for the range of *support* offered. The following chapter order will be used; however, our response to the child or young person can start at any point within this scaffold:

A table to depict components of the 5-S Scaffold (Taylor, 2023).

Chapter	Interventions
5.	*SUBSIDE: a* "natural break" activity to de-escalate or halt a rising emotional situation. The child may feel overwhelmed, distressed, or have had a sudden "outburst," but not be ready to be *"soothed"* or receive *"support."*
6.	*SOOTHE:* Experiences which encourage self-regulation and teach self-soothing bring the child or young person to a place of calm; teaching self-soothing allows it to be learnt and used in the future.
7.	*SUPPORT:* Practical strategies to *support* each of the emotional states of: shock and denial, anger, guilt and shame (bargaining), depression and anxiety, and acceptance. A pupil may be exhibiting all, or any, of these after experiencing grief, trauma or loss.
8.	*STRENGTHEN:* when at the "acceptance" stage or within a peaceful phase, a child can address some of those "big emotions"; it is a time for conversation with pupils, an opportunity to build positive relationships, a chance for them to talk about their feelings and reflect on *how* they feel and *why*.
	It is also a time for giving hope and looking to the future. This should not be viewed as a "final" stage, but one that is passed through; at any point in time a pupil may feel overwhelmed or enraged, and interventions from any of the *SUBSIDE–SOOTHE–SUPPORT–STRENGTHEN* strategies may be re-visited.
9.	*SELF-CARE:* for those doing the caring. It is recognised that there can be an emotional or physical cost on those adults who are caring for vulnerable children and young people. This chapter highlights the stress inherent within teaching and strategies to reduce "compassion fatigue" or "burnout." These include: school ethos, considerations for a school's senior leadership team, sources of teacher *support* and practical *self-care* suggestions.
Online	Practical resources can be downloaded for printing by following the access instructions at the front of this book.

Tiia Monto, CC BY-SA 3.0, via Wikimedia Commons

> These *support* suggestions can be hand-picked to create a bespoke interventions package for any child or young person. The intention is not that they are all used but that *support* offered can be personalised for their *circumstances, needs* and *neurodiversity*. This book is congruent with a social model of ability/disability where we adapt the situation and environment to fit the child, but it can work alongside any medical and specialist *support*.

While the main thrust of chapters 5–9 are practical, hands-on interventions that anyone can use, there is some interwoven theory to help understand how and why the strategies fit.

A common concern, that I have heard raised by educators or senior leaders, is the worry that "something they *do*" will cause more harm than good or will interfere with any specialist medical *support*. If other mental health professionals are involved with the child or young person, their advice and suggestions should be sought. However, these supportive options in chapters 5–9 are designed to work *with* the child and not *against* them. Talk to the pupil, ask what they would like or hold a meeting with the pupil and their family to discuss strategies together. This book can form a base for those conversations.

Interventions such as: adapting a timetabled school day, providing a named adult for a start-of-day one-to-one meet, discovering interests or hobbies that can enthuse a young person, providing their own "safe space" to sit when overwhelmed by emotion, creating an "SOS bag" to carry around, filling a "happy memory box" (chapter 7) to bring out when the "going gets tough" or finding new ways to connect and build joyful relationship, should all be positive experiences which help a child or young person feel noticed, valued and listened to; this will hopefully reap rewards in the form of a young person strengthened to face a future with some optimism.

A summary "Top Tips" table at the end of the following five chapters will list some main strategies or takeaways.

5 *SUBSIDE*
A natural break to calm, de-escalate and regulate

Chapter overview

- A child who is overwhelmed by emotion may be livid, rigidly silent or may be completely distraught. When they are exhibiting a traumatic stress response, or showing resistance, before offering supportive means, it may be necessary to "do something" to de-escalate or halt the rising emotion. This can act as a natural break, thereby breaking the cycle of rising emotion and returning them to a calmer state.
- These practical interventions to calm, are strategies that can be applied in a classroom or at home.
- The importance of remaining a calm and kind self-regulated adult, using words carefully and taking appropriate practical actions, are given below.
- Hands-on ideas of how to provide space in the form of a non-threatening natural break include: having "time out," a cup of tea and a biscuit, a quick shared board game or physical activity (a game, watching a video, listening to music), a walk or ball game, use of a weighted blanket/cushion or cuddly toy.
- The explanation of how and why these "calm" will be given; the importance of voice tone and approach in de-escalation will add supportive and practical theory.

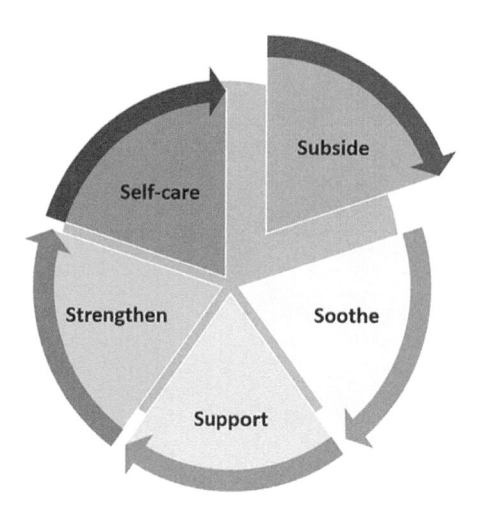

Chapter 4 described the role of the amygdala in the brain, and how it responds to threat, overruling the developing thinking part of the brain (the prefrontal cortex) and causing a state of high alert to continue. These overwhelming emotions may be a response to loss, trauma or to change which is beyond their control (chapters 1 and 2). A child or young person may "see red," be quickly infuriated or overcome with emotion. The state of being overwhelmed may cause a child or young person to involuntary act using their *fight-flight-fawn-freeze-flop-flock* system (as described in chapter 4).

In a dysregulated emotional state, the child at home, or pupil in school, is not in a place where they can think, reason or learn. They are unable to self-soothe (chapter 6) or calm themselves. We are unable to engage in conversation with them, and any direct communication may only serve to enrage or engulf them further.

DOI: 10.4324/9781003275268-8

As an aside, within a parent-child scenario, often these situations can cause us to feel uncertain about what to do, especially if it is in a public setting and there are onlookers. A top tip is to consider that these observers do not know why your child is having a meltdown, therefore by scooping the child up in a gentle cuddle and speaking soft words such as "let's help you feel better, I can see you're upset" may help prevent that adult rising panic; as a parent, you can sometimes feel judged when a child is publicly having a tantrum. It is also helpful to remember that all parents have been in a similar situation at some point. It is *what we do in response that matters*.

"It's unrealistic to expect them always to be rational, regulate their emotions, make good decisions, think before acting and be empathetic – all of the things a *developed* upstairs brain helps them do" (Siegel and Bryson, 2011, p. 44). As with the case of an upset toddler, they are literally unable to control their body or emotions they cannot consider consequences, solve problems or consider the feelings of others. They have "flipped their lid" (Figure 4.7, chapter 4).

At these times, de-escalation can be achieved by the "**SUBSIDE**" technique where a "natural break" activity can help their body, which in turn helps their brain. This works in the way that a breathing, relaxation or grounding exercise does; with the body acting in a relaxed state, it tricks the brain into thinking it is relaxed and therefore has a positive impact on the body's parasympathetic ("rest and digest") nervous system. The "**SUBSIDE**" approach is similar to the first stage of Siegal's "*Connect then Re-direct*" communication tool (Siegel and Bryson, 2011) as it places emphasis on both *how* you speak (voice tone and eye contact, and so on) and *what* you say or do next.

The "*how you speak*" element involves being an adult who is calm, self-contained and therefore self-regulated; if we feel calm, then we are able to respond in a controlled manner at a time when the child or young person lacks control of themselves and of their own emotional response.

The two components to the "*SUBSIDE*" technique are:

1. **Being a self-regulated adult:**
    a. non-verbal communication,
    b. verbal communication.
2. **Taking action:**
    a. Know your child and know when/how to de-escalate.
    b. Distraction techniques.
    c. Using words and phrases that de-escalate.
    d. Some things to avoid saying/doing.
    e. Praise personal *qualities.*

These are important components to the strategy "**SUBSIDE**." When used by the teacher or parental-figure to help a child's big emotions *diminish*, these components of 1a and 1b may also form an effective "self-check" list for anyone, young or old, involved in any form of communication; whether it is teacher-to-pupil or staff-to-staff communication, *how* we communicate affects others. Pupils pick up on the atmosphere within a school setting and overhear *how*, for example, senior leaders speak to their staff, it is only right that the adults model the very behaviour that they wish pupils to emulate.

The components of remaining self-regulated fall under the headings of *non-verbal* or *verbal* communication:

1. **Tips to remain a self-regulated adult.**
    This consists of the key adult keeping themselves contained, to prevent them externalising negative reactions to a dysregulated child or young person.
    a. **Non-verbal communication.**
        i.) ***Deciding* to have patience and stay calm. Self-regulate.**
            Since the child or young person is unable to remain calm and rational, we need to remain calm for them. By doing this, we are demonstrating how they should, or could, be behaving. However, staying calm is a skill; we should remain **professionally detached** in order to respond calmly when a challenging emotion surfaces in the pupil. Sometimes remaining detached requires every bit of the adult's self-control, or sometimes it is as simple as *making a decision and sticking to it*.

> A friend once said to me, "*I have long journeys every day now, I simply decided that I would not have road rage as it wasn't good for me and changes nothing except makes me an angry person.*" This struck a chord, as she recognised the personal cost to her if she allowed herself to become irate daily.

We may not know what we are going to do or how we are going to react, but we can keep in our heads what we are *not* going to do. When the child has least control, it is time for the teacher or parent-figure to have the most control over themselves. Otherwise, a cycle can result where the child or young person makes us angry. If the child can make us as angry as they are, then it is like giving them *permission* to be angry; the child is vindicated for being angry. As a result, we can become embroiled in a situation where we feed off each other's anger, the situation escalates and the child becomes even more dysregulated. Not only do our rising emotions cause the situation to feel out of control to the child (causing further upset), but also the very behaviour we are trying to reduce will have heightened.

Creating a combustible combination achieves nothing.

However, *de-escalation* isn't easy, it is an attempt to reverse their natural *fight-flight-fawn-freeze-flop-flock* reflexes at a time when they are at their highest. In de-escalation, we are aiming to reduce their level of distress to achieve the next stage of *soothing* or better still, *supporting* – and, consequently, achieve a better outcome. This outcome is achieved when we reach the "*strengthen*" stage of the **5-S** scaffold and can have a calm conversation or encourage a pupil's next ventures.

Self-regulating ourselves will act as a model to the child of how to control their emotions. The adult (parent-figure or teacher) will *co-regulate* to develop the child's ability to *self-regulate* (chapter 6).

To self-regulate, we may need to engage in breathing exercises, think calm thoughts or practise active decision-making to stay calm, as these may help us remain peaceful as we help the child or young person.

It is helpful to have an awareness that our own childhood, previous experiences and our belief system about emotions will impact on our thought and feelings. All of us, at times, feel overwhelmed and doubt ourselves; whether we are a parent-figure or a teacher, it may help to talk things through with a trusted friend, join a local *support* group, seek out an organisation such as the National Childbirth Trust or the local toddler group, for example. If your feelings persist and it all feels too difficult, then seek professional help; a counselling service, GP or a mental health professional can *support* you in identifying personal issues that may hinder you from reacting in a calm and loving manner (chapter 9).

ii.) **Communicate that you are calm through body language.**

We should communicate calm to the child, as *calm* can be just as contagious as *fear.* In any human interaction, only 7% of what we communicate is through our words, whereas 38% is through our tone of voice and around 55% is through our physiology, our body language (Mehrabian, 1972).

Our body language is formed by our body position, movements, posture and our gestures. Check that it is not too sudden, harsh or overbearing. It should not communicate disapproval or nonchalance.

Meeting a child's rising emotion with a reprimand, sharply worded threat, an order to "stop it" or a hand gesture to signify "no" will only cause the situation to escalate. The child will be unable to reason and think, "*oh, the adult is communicating that I should calm down and should stop displaying my emotion;*" they will be unable to apply their thinking part of their brain and reason. Giving a threat feeds fuel to their emotional state and exacerbates it. The outcome is the opposite of what we set out to achieve.

iii.) **Maintain a peaceful facial expression and use appropriate eye contact to communicate *calm*.**

Image by Dorricott S. (2023) original artwork, and with permission from illustrator, to reproduce in this book.

Very often our faces give away our emotions, whether it is the look in our eye, the angle of our head, the scowl on our forehead, the tilt of our mouth, the smirk on our lips, a quick glance at someone else or the movement of our eyebrows. All expressions together, or separately, can indicate anger, shock, fear, nonchalance, disapproval or surprise.

I had a colleague who, when asked by Ofsted what her classroom management technique was, replied, "*My eyebrows!*" the class knew her thoughts by her silent expression, and she used it to her advantage. It is an example of how our faces give clues about our reactions.

When we are alongside a distressed child, it is essential to maintain a calm expression and not give away our emotion with any "tell-tale" signs. We should silently check ourselves for signs of agitation, such as having gritted teeth, a curled lip, raised eyebrows, clenched fists, eye-rolling, frowning or scowling.

Other natural reactions we might have, besides feeling angry or out of control, are to laugh or smirk; this too needs to be controlled. If we are not sure about how we react, then asking a supportive adult peer to notice our response and constructively feed back to us can raise our self-awareness.

iv.) **Be aware of your breathing.**

Another natural reaction is to sigh in exasperation, or anger, when we are ourselves overwhelmed by the child's outburst.

The child may have rapid and shallow breathing in among their distress. If we are consciously trying to maintain our calm, this will be helped by taking slower, deeper breaths (rhythmically counting breaths in and out can help by counting in our heads). Automatically the child may synchronise their breathing with ours. It can be effective for us to match the child's breathing pattern and then gradually slow it down. The second step, where sometimes breaths are deliberately audible, may be harder to implement as it can sound unusual and disconcerting to a distressed child, unless breathing exercises are part of the normal daily routine or a familiar supportive technique. It helps to prepare and talk through your aim, so that the pupil will understand your audible breathing.

v.) **Consider space (including personal space and physical contact).**

Look for a safe space which may help the high emotions "*subside*" and the child or young person calm more readily. It may be that a teacher has a pre-organised safe place in the corner of a classroom or has made use of a small, enclosed area that looks comfortable and friendly (maybe with cushions or a bubble lamp, items that do not suggest punishment). A child moving around the school could carry a personalised "SOS bag" containing items to calm; this could include a blanket to fetch out anywhere and sit on as their own "safe space."

Importantly, the child may need space so take care not to enter their *personal space*, if possible, limit the amount of people around them. When in a classroom (or, for example, a mental health centre waiting room), consider advanced planning, or policies, if a child has a meltdown or angry outburst. The safety of the child themselves and the safety of others around them are paramount when deciding the best use of space. This helps prevent harm from a flaying or aggressive child (who may hit out or throw something), keeps the distressed pupil safe and may benefit from the "**SUBSIDE**" stage or *"natural break" activity*.

> A teenage pupil I taught had previously barricaded themselves in an empty classroom and roughly placed a circle of chairs around themselves. He was highly distressed and so upset that he could not speak, explain or function. He was not misbehaving or mistreating property, rather he had created his own safe space, away from all people, with the protection of a circle of chairs. Some adults had misunderstood the event; only days later when the young man could explain were the adults able to comprehend his level of distress and over-stimulation. Being unable to find words to explain this, he displayed severe signs of irritation and discomfort.

In this example and in any volatile situation, staying aware of the pupil's location is always important rather than abandoning or turning away from them.

Conversely, touch and physical contact (a pat on the back, a hug or placing a hand on an arm) improves our ability to cope with stress, when it is absent, may be the times when we need it the most. An adult attuned to the needs of the child or young person can judge whether they need to give the child "space" or whether the child needs some reassuring appropriate human contact.

b. **Verbal approaches.**

If we have consciously maintained our composure, remained calm and are aware of how our body is responding, it is important to continue this peaceful approach vocally too.

i.) **Paralinguistic communication: keep your tone of voice calm and your volume on quiet.**

Tone of voice is one aspect of "**paralanguage.**" It is not *what* we say, but *the way* that we say it. Our speed, pitch, intonation and volume all convey meaning too. When excited, we may speak quickly, with a high-pitch and be animated. When sad, our tone may sound melancholy and voice may lack energy. When we are angry, the intonation and harsh inflexions we place on our words may convey the fact that we are seething or "about to lose it"; a raised volume often follows.

It is helpful to pay extra attention to our voice tone in our communications. Responding with a loud voice that sounds irritated or angry will only raise the tempo, and the child may respond back in a voice that equals or is louder to our own. Instead, if a pupil is shouting and we respond in a more peaceful manner, it will help the situation to "*subside*" rather than add to the heightened tension. It is also harder for the pupil or young person to continue an argument with someone who is not arguing.

ii.) **Communicate *acceptance*.**

If the child has had a response to a traumatic event that required using "**SUBSIDE**" techniques, hopefully this enables them to enter the being "**SOOTHED**" phase. They cannot control what they feel and (referring to chapter 4 on brain development), they may be unable to reason or respond logically. We should recognise that for the child, their own emotions are valid.

Speaking sternly or reprimanding them, shouting at them (words such as "stop crying" or "because I said so") can aggravate or intensify a tricky situation. It also demonstrates that their emotions are not understood, not valid and therefore not accepted. They have not experienced the caring *support* of co-regulation (chapters 3 and 6) at a time when they were feeling dysregulated. It can cause greater harm to punish these emotions. A lack of co-regulation in the child's early years will hinder the child's emotional growth and ability for self-regulation (Eisenberg et al., 1996), as we read in chapter 3.

iii.) **Validate emotions.**

Validate their emotions by naming them. By expressing "I can see you feel cross, how can I help you?" you show acceptance. Ignoring the child, "not speaking to them" or dismissing them, feels like rejection. Social-emotional difficulties and psychological distress can arise from a child's continued feelings of invalidation (Krause et al., 2003). Invalidating ("you can't possibly feel that bad"; "you're really lucky"), dismissing or rejecting children's emotional states only serve to hurt their feelings and make them feel as if it requires too much effort to "be heard" (Gilbert et al., 2021), energy which they simply may not have.

2. **Action: de-escalation and distraction.**

This consists of the positive actions we can take, that is the things we can "do" (or not do) to introduce an effective "natural break" activity to halt behaviour linked with a rising negative emotion.

a) **Know your child/pupil, and know when and how to de-escalate.**

If possible, be alert so that you are ready to step in and de-escalate *before* the critical explosion occurs. This applies to the emotion of "anger" as well as to crying or anguish.

Know the pupil, to know the pupil's signs of distress. Early signs of agitation may include:

- clenched fists,
- fidgeting,
- pacing up and down,
- shaking,
- staring at or scowling at another child,
- thrusting the jaw out,
- clenched teeth,
- change of stance or posture and
- speech becoming more rapid or high-pitched.

Signs of becoming over-stimulated:

- putting their hands over their ears,
- bolting from the room,
- hiding under a table or creating their own "safe space,"
- an increase in self-stimulating, self-soothing or repetitive behaviours such as rocking, tapping, humming, flapping hands, "la"ing, head banging or hitting themselves and
- a verbal shout.

b) **Distraction techniques.**

If all the ideas and suggestions described in this chapter so far do not come naturally, then jump to this stage, because by engaging this approach as your foremost **SUBSIDE** technique, all the previous suggestions should more easily follow.

As we read in chapter 4, when a child is distressed and is responding with their own *fight or flight, freeze or flop* instincts, then they are unable to reason and think about their actions. Using a distraction or diversion approach may engage the "thinking brain" (chapter 4) just enough to cause the distressed state to "**SUBSIDE**," even if only momentarily. Carrying out a physical activity complements the mode they are operating in – *doing* rather than *thinking*. A physical task may decrease their innate desire to physically lash out and may gradually engage their thinking brain. The physical task is also a distraction and can normalise a heightened situation, bringing it back to a situation where care, comfort and relationship are the main ingredients.

We can help calm or divert attention by:

- *Acknowledging the child's feelings:* it shows we have listened that we understand their extreme emotions. Validating their feelings can be crucial when we are trying to diffuse a situation. Words such as "'I can see that you are very upset/distressed. It must be really difficult for you, thank you for letting me know" show you accept the child and recognise their emotion.
- *Giving positive choices*, repeating them over (and over) if necessary, shows we can remain calm and unmoved by the screaming (for example) that we are witnessing. Repeating the positive choice also prevents us from being drawn into an angry exchange.
- Any of the following options can be offered to help the child make a positive choice such as *"would you like to listen to some music or blow bubbles?"* or if the child is unable to make a choice, then the adult could choose one and begin it, with the

hope of the child or young person joining in, to help their big emotions *subside*. Ideas include:

- Get a drink, or a tea and biscuit.
- A quick shared game or activity: e.g., blow bubbles, get out Lego, throw a small ball or quick doodle art.
- Play ball from a rolled-up piece of paper thrown across a table.
- Use a "sensory" room.
- Watch a video.
- A walk or ball game.
- Settle in a comfy chair or bean bag (consider buying one for a classroom).
- Use of a weighted blanket or weighted cushion or cuddly toy – a physical comforting object can help *soothe*.
- Play music (on a phone, a radio) or encourage the pupil to mess around on the class guitar or keyboard.
- Knock the tin of pencils on the floor (accidentally on purpose) and ask the pupil to help pick them up... thereby you distract and can also praise their helpfulness/appreciate their help (Brammer, 2023).
- Draw a pattern or picture together or provide the pupil with paper to draw or doodle; a pattern can be repetitive which is a soothing action.
- Play a game. However, the pupil may not want to play their favourite game, it may be far too taxing to "think."
- Comment on something they have done or are wearing, that is, "noticing" something positive.
- Give choices, do an activity they like or open a book and read a story out loud (have good choices of books handy); a poetry book has the added advantage of being soothingly rhythmical (see chapter 6).
- Repeat the options given-as when in a state of high alert, the child may be unable to listen.
- Talk about something you watched on television or something outside the window.
- Acknowledge how the pupil might be feeling; demonstrate that you have listened to them.

c) **When suggesting or starting any of the activities listed above, use words and phrases that de-escalate** (Smith, 2016) such as:
- I wonder if...
- Let's try...
- It seems like...
- Maybe we can...
- Tell the child what you want them to do rather than what you do not want them to do; for example, "I want you to sit down" rather than "stop arguing with me."
- Give the child take-up time following any direction and avoid backing them into a corner, either verbally or physically.

d) **There are some things to be avoided:**

Trust and distrust are key factors in any conflict negotiation. Joint decision-making is particularly effective. Framing and re-framing the issue or the question allows a choice to be made (Milburn, 1998), therefore some things are best avoided:
- Do not make "you will" statements such as "you will do x because I said so."
- Do not make threats you cannot carry through, such as threatening to exclude the child from school, or stop playtimes for a week, or (if at home) to have no television for five days.
- Do not be defensive or take it personally. What is being said may seem insulting and directed at you, but this level of aggression is usually through anger and not about us, in the heat of the moment.
- Do not use humour unless you are both sure it will help, and you have a very good relationship with the child. Humour can seem as if you are "poking fun" and be hurtful at a time when the child (despite all appearances) is vulnerable and hurting.
- Do not use sarcasm or humiliate the child; sarcasm is too difficult a concept to understand.
- Do not stand aggressively: do not "square-up" to the child, tower over them or invade personal space inappropriately or untimely. Do not maintain solid eye contact, as this can feel uncomfortable.

Being familiar with any individual "child support plan" is needed to be aware of any pre-planned personalised strategies and interventions to meet the child's needs. This may include an "Individual Education Plan" or "Education, Health and Care Plan" written by school staff, parent and/or other professionals. However, sometimes, no matter how carefully and skilfully we try to de-escalate a situation, it may still reach crisis point. It is important to know school systems for summoning help and moving bystanders to safety.

After any outburst or incident, always make time to chat, debrief, *repair and rebuild*, or the relationship may *rupture* for a while (chapter 6), and deteriorate. Problem-solve the situation and teach new behaviours where needed. Resolve any conflicts through negotiation and discussion, aiming to be fair. Being fair or ensuring equality does not mean doing the exact same thing for each child; rather it means that the personalised plan is followed for a particular child which equalises their opportunities and gives them access to the most appropriate, bespoke *support* for them. All children may need to be made aware that an intervention allowed for one pupil may not be permitted for another; a teaching point can inform all children that they are uniquely valued as individuals. A strict adherence to school policy or "sanctions" can often be detrimental. If the pupil has Social, Emotional and Mental Health difficulties, permanently exclusion only serves to bring trauma, increasing their vulnerability and isolation.

Hence, ensure any sanctions are appropriate to what has happened and act to challenge the pupil's behaviour, as this is more important than "being right" or "having your way" with the final outcome. Avoid zero-tolerance school policies. Take time to discover what caused the child's emotions to escalate, consider underlying factors and make reasonable adjustments. Resolving conflicts is one of the most important skills to model (Milburn, 1998).

When the child or young person is responding and acting appropriately, it is important to remember to give praise and use these opportunities to build a positive relationship. Sadly, it is so much easier to notice when things are going wrong, rather than when things are going right.

e) **Praise personal qualities:** look for any action, thoughtfulness or any small gesture they do that you can praise – if they are trying to explain their feelings, praise that… a simple "well done for trying to explain to me" or "that was kind of you to pick that up which you'd dropped." Use any positive words or encouragement that show affirmation and that you accept them. This can also serve to disarm and de-escalate. Similarly, "noticing" something about what they are wearing, or remembering something they told you a while ago, and commenting/asking out loud can also help them feel "noticed" and valued.

The "natural break," calming and *SUPPORT* techniques include many physical and sensory strategies. These are especially important for those whose *speech, language and communication difficulties* make it difficult for them to make sense of language or understand how to communicate effectively and appropriately with others.

This may make providing *support* more challenging, requiring it to be bespoke for that child or young person.

How do we do this… know your audience! Relationship is key; know your child or young person well, talk to someone who does (maybe include their family and *support* network), or seek help from other professionals. It can be helpful for a teacher to spend some time consciously reflecting on their relationship with each of their pupils. By simply considering who they like best, who they feel at ease with (or not) or whose company they do/not enjoy, they will gain awareness of which pupils they need to build a greater connection with and why. Self-reflection can be a useful and positive tool.

Summary

	Top tips for "SUBSIDE" technique (chapter 5)
1.	In a dysregulated emotional state, the child at home, or pupil in school, is not in a place where they can think, reason or learn. They are unable to self-soothe (chapter 6) or calm themselves. We are unable to engage in conversation with them, and any direct communication may only serve to enrage or engulf them further.
2.	**Be a self-regulated adult: non-verbal communication:** • *Decide* to have patience and stay calm. Self-regulate. • Communicate that you are calm through body language. • Communicate "calm": maintain a peaceful facial expression and use appropriate eye contact. • Be aware of your breathing. • Consider space (including personal space and physical contact).
3.	**Be a self-regulated adult: verbal communication:** • Paralinguistic communication: keep your tone of voice calm and your volume on quiet. • Communicate *acceptance*. • Validate emotions.
4.	**Taking action: know your child and know when/how to de-escalate:** be alert so that you are ready to step in and de-escalate before the critical explosion occurs (this applies to the emotion of "anger" as well as to crying or anguish) by knowing the pupil, to know the pupil's signs of distress. Be aware too of their own "tell-tale" signs that they are becoming over-stimulated.
5.	**Taking action: distraction techniques:** carrying out a physical activity complements the mode they are operating in – *doing* rather than *thinking*. A physical task may decrease their innate desire to physically lash out and gradually engage their thinking brain. The physical task is also a distraction and can normalise a heightened situation, bringing it back to a situation where care, comfort and relationship are the main ingredients. **We can help calm or divert attention by:** • Acknowledging the child's feelings: it shows we have listened, that we understand their extreme emotions. Validating their feelings can be crucial when we are trying to diffuse a situation. Words such as "I can see that you are very upset/distressed. It must be really difficult for you, thank you for letting me know" show you accept the child and recognise their emotion. • Calmly offer positive choices of a practical activity.
6.	**Taking action: using words and phrases that de-escalate:** I wonder if…let's try…it seems like…maybe we can…
7.	**Taking action: some things to avoid saying/doing:** Do not make "you will" statements such as "you will do x because I said so." Do not make threats you cannot carry through. Do not be defensive or take it personally. Do not use humour or sarcasm unless you are sure it will help, and you have a very good relationship with the child. Do not humiliate the child. Do not posture or stand aggressively.
8.	**Taking action: praise personal qualities:** look for any action, thoughtfulness or any small gesture they do that you can praise; or "notice" or remember something about them; positive words or encouragement show affirmation and that you accept them. This can also serve to disarm and de-escalate.

6 *SOOTHE*

Co-regulation, self-regulation and *soothing*

Chapter overview

- Long term, the aim is to enable a child or pupil to self-regulate their emotions.
- This chapter will give practical strategies and describe methods for co-regulation and *soothing* that encourage *self-soothing* and self-regulation. A range of accessible ideas and activities will be presented.
- A brief consideration of any prior repetitive calming experiences (e.g., rhythmic rocking, cradling) will help explain the link to activities that encourage *self-soothing*. Examples of activities include practical actions, physical activity, mindfulness Apps, doodling or colouring, talking, hobbies, music and fidget toys.
- A child is then armed with these essential skills when a trauma or loss occurs. During a trauma, a child may revert to having needs, or wanting to feel secure, in ways that were used years earlier.
- During enforced separation, shared gesture is an alternative to direct contact e.g., blowing a kiss, an air high-five or placing a hand on your heart; during a traumatic event, it maintains a social identity and has a positive physiological impact.

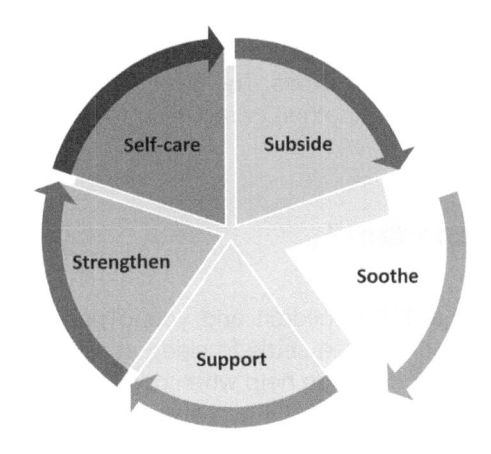

Introduction

The previous chapter included signs to be aware of that may signal a child or young person is in distress or has rapidly rising (negative) emotions. It described how a *natural break activity*, when accompanied with the verbal and non-verbal approaches described, could help the heightened emotions *subside*.

After an emotional outburst, *soothing*, or *self-soothing*, may need to occur to help the child de-escalate and begin to function again, whether they are in school or at home. A child being *soothed* involves an appropriate adult calming the child to allay fears or pain, whereas *self-soothing* is a self-reliant, internal process (Gračanin et al., 2014). If we are feeling negative emotions, distressed or "out of sorts," then by allowing ourselves to be *soothed*, or by *self-soothing*, we can calm and comfort ourselves to reduce anxiety and stress and therefore feel better.

Since touch and physical contact (cradling/rocking a baby, a pat on the back, a hug, a fist-pump or placing a hand on an arm) improves our ability to cope with stress, being in sync physically can help us be in sync emotionally (and vice versa). Joy and connection results in relaxed breathing,

DOI: 10.4324/9781003275268-9

a steady heartbeat and a low level of stress hormones (chapters 3 and 4); when the body is calm, so are the emotions (Van der Kolk, 2015). Hence, *physical contact* helps with emotional regulation, yet the times when it is absent may be the very times when it is needed the most. In situations such as the COVID-19 pandemic, displacement due to war, or encountering a natural disaster, a caregiver's *soothing* touch may be unavailable, feel uncomfortable or considered to be unsafe. It is at these times of traumatic stress that *self-soothing* offers a way to reduce anxiety. Shared gestures such as blowing a kiss, an air high-five or placing a hand on your heart offer a shared social identity which may bring an element of *self-soothing* (Dreisoerner et al., 2021; Häusser et al., 2012, 2020).

This chapter will explore what *self-soothing* is, how it all begins in infancy and how it can be developed. Practical aspects such as stages to teaching *self-soothing*, and groundwork preparation needed to be *the comforter*, are described to practically help with applying the techniques.

There are three main parts to this chapter:

- **What** *soothing* and *self-soothing* are, and how we teach it.
- **How** we use the verbal, non-verbal and action strategies.
- **Why** we know it has a positive effect – an evidence base.

WHAT soothing and self-soothing are?

What is soothing and self-soothing?

Being *soothed* initially relies upon a parent-figure to bring calm, whereas *self-soothing* refers to the ability of babies, children and young people to calm themselves down and regulate their own emotions (Gračanin et al., 2014); this act of comfort reduces anxiety and stress, it helps them feel better. Rather than address the emotions *before* they arise (as prevention), *self-soothing* practices regulate the distressing emotions after they begin (Gross, 1998).

Soothing or *self-soothing* is a focused response in that moment, and to that emotion. Both involve an internal process which monitors the level of arousal (chapter 4). When a need is noticed, *soothing* or *self-soothing* may positively alter the emotional reaction. Therefore, this should act to bring composure to the distress. The level of arousal is "regulated" and stabilised by either directed (as with "*soothing*" another) or self-directed (as with *self-soothing*) behaviours and internal processes.

Why is self-soothing important?

Self-soothing is an important skill for children and young people to develop as it has many benefits: it can help toddlers and children settle to sleep at night, it can help calm a distressed toddler in a tantrum, and importantly, it can help when coping with stress and difficult emotions throughout childhood; this helps later in life. It can also promote feelings of security and independence, which benefit overall emotional and mental wellbeing (Ainsworth et al., 1991) since it aids self-regulation and builds resilience. *Self-soothing* helps prevent children from developing *maladaptive coping methods* (such as internalising or supressing "boxed" emotions or acting as if it happened to someone else) which can damage their future wellbeing and mental health. These factors are particularly relevant during times of trauma or loss; a well-developed self-regulation and *self-soothing* ability is like having your own *first aid kit* to help equip your emotional responses; it can help emotionally and physiologically to keep us calmer.

Self-soothing behaviours will vary depending upon the age of the child and become more complex as the child grows older; a baby may suck on a dummy/pacifier, a young child may stroke a soft toy or rock themselves, an older child or teenager may choose a weighted blanket, fidget toy, rhythmic drumming or repetitive doodling.

What precedes the ability to soothe and self-soothe?

Soothing, or rather the experience of being *soothed*, begins in infancy. In chapter 3, we read how a baby's emotional regulation system is not well developed at birth, but (to encourage their survival) they are able to signal their distress or discomfort to their primary caregiver(s). This is achieved by noises such as crying, or actions such as clinging to a parent. These behaviours, and the adult's response to them, help form attachments.

Attachments can be "secure" or "insecure" depending upon how reliable and consistently the baby's needs are met (and therefore how *safe* the baby feels). We previously read about the impact of inconsistent or absent parental *support*, which consequently leads to insecure attachments forming, thus impacting the "behaviour" in the developing child; behaviour is their form of communication. Hence, *early parental practices develop the child's ability to be soothed and to self-soothe.* Families who find natural attachment bonds difficult to establish (ostensibly because of their own upbringing) may need *support* to develop and grow compassion; other professional roles, such as a health visitor, may be key in teaching and nurturing these essential skills.

However, teacher-attachment develops independently of the parent-attachment. Therefore, if a child has a home-based "insecure attachment," the pupil is able to develop a secure attachment in the school environment. This is positive, with regard to a child or young person needing to feel safe and secure, for *SUPPORT* strategies (chapters 5–8) to have a positive effect.

Soothing – the groundwork for developing self-soothing

A baby cannot invent *self-soothing*, they must experience it to know what it is. Therefore, *self-soothing* cannot be acquired alone, a baby left to cry cannot comfort itself, it cannot invent a **SELF-SOOTHING** technique in isolation, it needs to be taught (Herbers et al., 2014). This *experience* can be initially gained by a parent-figure meeting the baby's needs, so when uncomfortable or distressed they are responded to and brought relief; these are acts which comfort and *soothe*.

Since *self-soothing* needs to be experienced to know what it feels like, a positive relationship is needed for a baby to internalise this knowledge. A good relationship brings with it good techniques. Within a secure attachment, *soothing* paves the way for co-regulation, and *co-regulating* is the forerunner of *self-soothing*.

Hence, the parent-figure and infant need to *co-regulate before the infant can self-regulate* (see below).

Teaching self-soothing

In brief, teaching *self-soothing* involves the following hierarchical stages:

I. *Soothing:* the adult *provides the opportunity* for the infant, child or young person to experience being *soothed*, using a suitable "stage, not age" approach; experiencing it is essential.
II. *Co-regulation* with a parent or parent-figure occurs. The parent co-regulates by creating a warm and receptive interaction with their child. Or a teacher may model a positive emotional state with a pupil. It is necessary to **co-regulate** to enable a child to **self-regulate**; co-regulation acts as a supportive coaching experience which creates positive emotions within the infant or child. Bowlby (1973, p. 202) established the term "*availability*" to represent the parent-figure's important qualities of *accessibility* and *responsiveness*.
III. *Self-regulation*: a baby or child needs to have someone oversee their initial attempts at self-regulation in order to learn how to self-regulate. This is when the child's emotions can be spoken back to the child to explain what they are feeling (chapter 3).
IV. *Self-soothing*: potentially, an older child can utilise the **SELF-SOOTHING** techniques acquired through innate learning that accompanies the experience of being *soothed* as a baby, toddler or young child.

To expand further:

i. *Soothing*: **low level and high level.**
   A baby is unable to deal with a challenging situation themselves and needs a safe and reliable adult to guide and *support* their emotions as they grow and develop. As a child grows from newborn through to adolescent, commonly, parents naturally move from using *high-level* **SOOTHING** strategies through to more frequently using *low-level* **SOOTHING** strategies (Adams et al., 2022). *Low-level* input is less invasive, more passive and requires less *active* parental participation. This can be seen in the natural and gradual move from:
   • feeding or rocking until the baby falls asleep (high level infant) to

- rubbing the infants back whilst in bed or putting back in bed whilst awake, or comforting verbally (low-level infant),
- bedtime bath and story routine for a toddler (higher level adult strategy) to
- saying goodnight and walking out of a primary school child's bedroom (low-level input) and
- the teenager who may walk up their room themselves and enjoy some "me time" (lowest level input).

Parents effectively applying a greater proportion of *low-level* **SOOTHING** strategies can lead to the infant's increased ability to *soothe* themselves back to sleep, rather than wake their parent(s). Whilst parenting style is a very individual and personal decision, a study suggests that gradually moving from high- to low-level sleep-related parenting practices (above) actively encourages *self-soothing* behaviours, thus benefitting both infant's and parent's/carer's social-emotional health. The research confirms the importance of teaching *self-soothing* (Adams et al., 2022) and that early parental practices develop the infant and child's ability to *self-soothe*.

ii. **Co-regulation, leading to self-regulation.**

Co-regulation is required for babies and children to learn self-regulation. Co-regulation occurs when the parents and baby aim to match their emotions; they subtly change the pattern of the communications and actions between them to create and maintain a positive emotional state (Feldman, 2003). If, for example, a parent is holding a baby and the baby gives a small cry to indicate that something is not quite right, the parent (assuming their baby is bored) may begin to interact and play with them. However, the baby may be communicating tiredness, and the last thing they require is over-stimulation; the parent's attempts to *soothe* did not match the baby's need and this is called a *mismatch* in co-regulation. A *mismatch* or even a *rupture* can be *repaired* (made good again) by the adult adjusting their response to match the real need (Tronick, 1989, 2017). The adult responding with "oh you are feeling sleepy" and gently singing, whilst calmly rocking the baby successfully, changes their interactions, after picking up on cues. Co-regulation can also be seen in an exchange in which a parent chats to a disinterested baby and the baby responds, the parent lightens their tone, and the baby giggles, the parent repeats the words, gesture or game of peek-a-boo and the baby responds gleefully.

During times of acute distress (as may occur in a pandemic, times of unrest or economic or political turmoil), a baby may show increased signs of unrest as they pick up on the emotional state of their parents. Their interaction with their caregiver conveys to the infant exactly what is safe, and what is dangerous (Van der Kolk, 2015). If the parents are not feeling "warm and responsive" themselves, then the co-regulation may be *mismatched* (not aligned) or *ruptured* (cracked, and in need of repair). If the connection "goes wrong," such as if the baby's signals are misinterpreted and needs are not correctly met the first time, then a wait time may occur before the parent-figure alters their response; this adjustment leads to the infant and carer being aligned or "matched" in their interactions once again.

Hence, babies being *soothed* learn to *self-soothe* through this process of *co-regulation* with their primary caregiver. Research has shown that the emotional regulation provided by a primary caregiver, also known as an *attachment figure*, plays an important role in helping babies learn to *self-soothe* (Bowlby, 1988) as they can provide reassurance to comfort an upset baby.

Reassurance can take many forms: (see 5a in Table 6.1 below.)
- physical comforting touch,
- vocal *soothing* (noises or phrases), chatting and singing,
- rocking or patting,
- distracting,
- offering a favourite (cuddly) toy,
- feeding or giving a dummy/pacifier,
- emotional *support*,
- wrapping up,
- cooling down,
- changing position and
- meeting needs – feeding or a nappy change.

iii. **Learning self-regulation.**

A baby learns to associate comforting, *soothing*, reassuring behaviours with feelings of a sense of safety and security.

Since they cannot self-regulate when upset, they wholly rely on their parent-figure "attuning" to their needs to bring comfort and calm. *Attunement* plays a big part in developing early secure attachment (chapter 3); it gives babies the feeling that their needs are met, and that they are understood. Attunement can encompass the whole sequence of interactions between adult and infant: the "coo-ing," game of "peep-o," responding to what they respond to, mimicking each other or joining together in mock-dismay (Tronick, 2017). Van der Kolk (2015, p. 132) refers to this as "The Dance of Attunement." This *"attunement,"* and experiences of *co-regulation*, helps the infant learn how to best communicate and navigate their emotions. They take cues from their parent's response to any distress displayed. As they associate their communications with feeling safe and receiving comfort, so they are likely to use the response again in the future; this becomes the child's "go-to" behaviours, and thus their ability to *self-regulate* grows (Feldman, 2003; Herbers et al., 2014).

Ultimately, it is the original emotional regulation and co-regulation that develops *self-soothing* behaviours. Modelling *self-soothing* behaviours, such as singing, rocking or repeating a rhythmic nursery rhyme, help the baby learn these behaviours too.

In those early days of having a baby, my husband and I would go through our mental checklist to understand why they were distressed; sometimes we got it right first time, at other times our guessing (attuning and co-regulating) went on longer. My own supportive mother had a saying that I embraced through my own stages of early motherhood, which was:

"You don't teach them, they teach you," which sums up our co-regulating attempts.

Followed by *"A baby can't be 'naughty,"* all words to encourage the parent to remain calm and not get fraught by a crying baby.

Other early *self-soothing* activities may include being rocked, cuddled or held, as well as listening to *soothing* music or white noise (Feinstein, 2009). They may also find comfort in having a dummy/pacifier or a soft blanket nearby.

The distress caused to an infant by an unresponsive parent can be witnessed in *"Still Face Experiment"* (Tronick, 1975, in Tronick, 1989, 2017) and by an absent parent or one displaying unpredictable behaviour in "The Strange Situation" test (Ainsworth et al., 1979). Both videos can be found with a search on YouTube.

The ability to effectively self-regulate forms the basis of a child's social and emotional growth and development. The external framework of co-regulation has formed the building blocks which point to the healthy ways a child should manage their own emotions. Without this *support*, unhealthy dysregulated emotions could manifest outwardly, such as with aggression or flare-ups, or internally, such as with quiet, retreating behaviour where supressing emotions can lead to internalising issues and depression.

iv. **Self-soothing.**

A baby can *self-soothe* by, for example, sucking their thumb, sucking a dummy or the label of a cuddly toy, clinging to a soft toy, clasping their hands or toes, even fiddling with their own hair.

According to research, *self-soothing* behaviours begin when infants within their first few months **instinctively** start to use their hands and fingers to explore and *soothe* themselves. Known as "self-regulation" (Greenspan and Shanker, 2004), it is a process of trial and error, as babies experiment with different methods of calming themselves down. Later, they will begin to use other *self-soothing* behaviours such as sucking on a dummy/pacifier or thumb, rocking or stroking a soft toy (Ainsworth et al., 1991). As children grow older, *self-soothing* behaviours become more complex and can include activities such as listening to music, reading a book or engaging in a hobby; even hanging out with friends becomes an activity that can *soothe* if positive relationships bring predictability, security and comfort.

Babies also learn to *self-soothe* through the process of **habituation**, which means they learn to become accustomed to certain stimuli over time. For example, if a baby is exposed to a loud noise repeatedly, they will eventually stop reacting to it and will instead learn to *self-soothe* in the presence of that noise (Field, 2013). This can also have a negative impact, such as a house where there is a lot of shouting or unmet needs become normalised to the infant, and *self-soothing* practices (to comfort or to gain control over stress) may not be wholesome coping mechanisms.

As part of developing self-regulation, chapter 3 described how a parental role of actively describing the emotions back to the young child helps develop their emotional intelligence, resilience and understanding; thereby *"**connecting**"* with the toddler and assisting with their growing emotional regulation.

Most importantly, babies learn *self-soothing* through the **emotional regulation** (the *soothing*) that they receive from their main caregivers, known as their *attachment figures*; they provide a safe and secure environment for the infant to explore and experiment with their own *self-soothing* behaviours (Bowlby, 1988). It helps them cope with stress and difficult emotions (Ainsworth et al., 1991).

This coping ability is especially needed during times when their mental wellbeing is challenged, such as throughout any traumatic stressful event. During unpredictable, uncertain and unexpected incidents, a well-developed *self-soothing* ability is needed the most. This is when the adult's groundwork, in helping the child develop resilience, pays off. Similarly, during times of enforced separation (i.e., covid pandemic lockdowns, or displacement), *self-soothing* touch can have a positive impact at lowering cortisol levels to reduce one's own stress (Dreisoerner et al., 2021). See Table 6.2 (below) describing remote comfort tactics.

HOW we use the verbal, non-verbal and action strategies to *soothe*

The last chapter described:

- The reasons for remaining calm.
- The importance of knowing the child or pupil and the cues that may indicate a rising emotion.
- Ways to communicate that we are calm, and vocalisations to avoid.
- Phrases that de-escalate.

This was particularly important when using the "**SUBSIDE**" *techniques* within a situation where the child or young person's emotions seem out of control, and they are very upset or angry. Within this "**Soothe**" chapter, and chapters following, we still need to be mindful of the need to remain patient, calm and responsive.

Techniques to soothe and co-regulate, which encourage self-soothing and self-regulation

There are important components to help towards the success of *soothing* and co-regulation, they are applicable to education staff, parents or other main caregivers:

1. **Remaining consistently calm and kind** are essential elements (chapter 5). This caring approach is needed not only during the times of trauma and immediately post-traumatic event, but calm understanding is needed in all general interactions too. Chapter 3 emphasised how this gives a secure attachment which helps with emotional regulation. A positive relationship builds trust, and good conversation can happen where children are more likely to express their worries; a positive response to the trusted adult means "change" may happen where they adapt their behaviour or their communications. **SUPPORT** strategies (chapter 7) then have the opportunity to be far more effective. Remaining a consistently calm adult is essential to keep that trust.
2. **Pick up on a child's cues** that they have a need, something is going wrong for them or that they are becoming agitated, to prevent growing distress and an outburst erupting. Modelling emotional regulation will help the child both understand and express their feelings, as the secure situation helps them internalise the emotional regulation strategies which they experienced – and *potentially* apply them to other situations in the future; this includes situations outside of the parent-child relationship (Brumariu, 2015).
3. **Use age-appropriate co-regulation strategies:** as a child moves through different ages or stages of development, their co-regulated experiences develop their skills, thus their capacity for self-regulation builds. These internal resources provide a scaffold for a child's emotional experience and guidance towards higher order emotional regulation and resilience.
4. **Remember the most effective strategies:** it is important to remember that **SELF-SOOTHING** techniques may vary depending on the individual and what works best for them. It may take some experimentation to find the most effective strategies for each person. Here, the teacher is the researcher who is looking to see what made the biggest difference. Ponder who you gave help to in the last year, and how.

5. **Be tuned into trauma throughout the "normal days":** after a traumatic event, some situations may spark a severe reaction in the child; knowing this is key, as we are able to reduce its impact or even prevent it happening.

> *For example, after an incident, a child I knew could not watch any medical-related television programmes, having once been a huge fan of the television drama "Casualty" – anything medically related caused too much distress. Hence, these were then purposefully avoided.*

This boxed example is an illustration of something that can often be prevented. If it is unpreventable, then observing and remembering past instances helps the correct *support* be there at the time it is needed. It is helpful to show empathy and be consistent, as something that worked "the last time" could also work again.

6. **Help them practice, to develop their resilience:** instances where the child or young person is distressed, and displaying a range of emotions can occur at any time (as we read in chapter 3). These instances can be used positively by the parent-figure or teacher by encouraging and scaffolding a response appropriate to their stage of development (see Tables 6.1 and 6.2). This *support* helps a child as they calm themselves and practice the skill of *self-soothing*. This also helps children learn to cope when the teacher, parent or carer are not present.
7. **Have patience and do not yield to demands:** the previous chapter described how, with our words, tone and body language, we communicate that we are calm and have patience. Maintaining that exterior will help a distressed child remember their coping techniques – it is likely that the child or young person makes angry demands or gets upset because they "can't have something" or "wants things to be different from what they are." If the teacher or parent-figure yields to the demands or suddenly produces that item, then the child or pupil will not have opportunity to learn coping strategies. It is important to remain patient and continue to *support* children to remember their coping techniques, to help them regulate their emotions. As Tables 6.1 and 6.2 show, this can help the child master skills to *independently self-soothe*.
8. **Be a good role model:** a dysregulated child requires a regulated parent who they can learn alongside. Co-regulation leads to a child's self-regulation. Therefore, the parental-figure or the professional should role model how to manage strong emotions healthily. When we, as adults, are overwhelmed or angry, the child(ren) will look to us as the example of how to cope well. Remaining calm, and using a considered approach is critical.

Table 6.1 describes stage/age-appropriate *soothing*, co-regulation and **SELF-SOOTHING** strategies – and what they physically achieve.

PANDEMIC OR TRAUMA: attachment in babies

During times of acute distress, as may occur in a pandemic, times of unrest, continued poverty, economic or political turmoil (all regularly in the news), a baby may show increased signs of unrest as they pick up on the emotional state of their parents. It is no easy task for an adult (parent or teacher) to self-regulate before supporting the child or young person; indeed, they will have concerns, worries or traumas of their own. At these times, the parents co-regulating with their children using warm, responsive interaction may be "putting on a front." It is important to act calm; however, if older children detect worries in their trusted adult, then sometimes it is best to be honest and open and, in a measured way, talk your worries and resolution through. This not only "models" how to deal with a concern, but it also prevents the child's imagination running riot by knowing that *something* is the matter but not *what* it is; sometimes gaining a sense of a situation can help alleviate the feeling that they are not trusted or "not in-the-know."

Clearly, it all needs carefully gauging, and knowledge of the child is needed to do so. Parents or teachers may find that they can still *support*, coach and model to co-create a positive emotional situation state with the child or young person; in turn, the child may gain self-worth from

Table 6.1 A table to describe stage/age-appropriate *soothing*, leading to **SELF-SOOTHING** techniques

Stage/age-appropriate soothing, leading to SELF-SOOTHING techniques.
Practical *SELF-SOOTHING* strategies to *soothe*, during co-regulation.

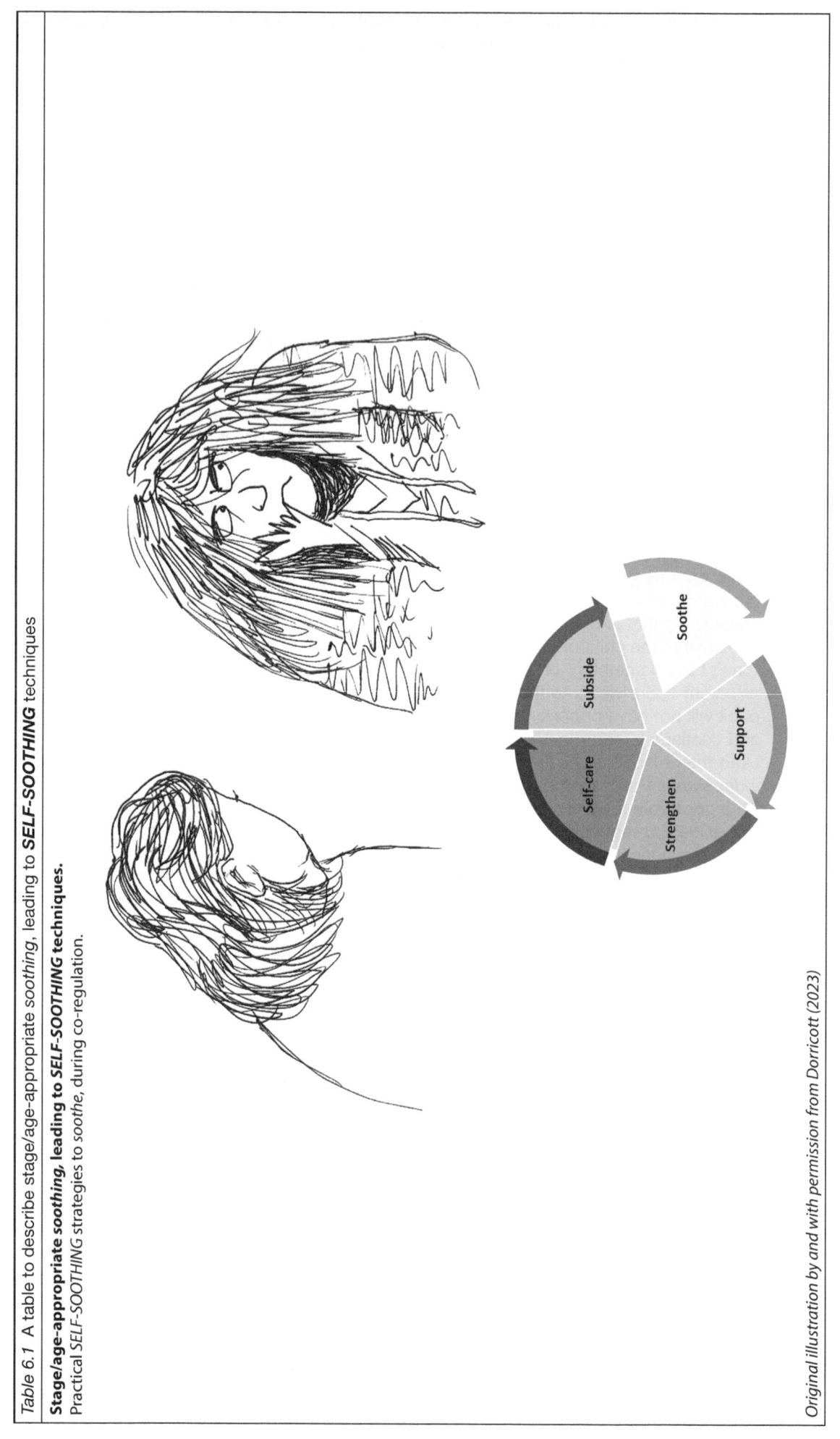

Original illustration by and with permission from Dorricott (2023)

(Continued)

Table 6.1 (Continued)

Age or stage	Infant to toddler	Child	Young person
1. First self-regulate	Self-regulate		
2. Checklist of "do nots"	Do not punish or threaten – they can't help their emotions at whatever their age (chapter 4 helped explain this). Do not invalidate their emotions; do not ignore, dismiss or reject negative emotions.		
3. Do: cues from the individual	Pay close attention, be responsive. Be patient and consistent. Respond quickly to the cues children send.		
4. Consider: environment or emotional environment	Modify the environment (is it too loud, too bright, too cold or hot, too busy or too boring) or personal space. Check the baby, child's or young person's personal needs (e.g., nappy, hunger, warmth, sleep, do they need to change position). Are they bored or feel that a life-situation is too challenging and are stressed?		
5. Co-regulate (see below)	Co-regulate by responding to the cues they give and offering physical and emotional comfort; suggestions for this co-regulation leading to self-regulation and *self-soothing* are in the sections below.		
a. Physical comfort and reassurance. Physical touch.	• Physical comforting touch helps a baby stabilise. • Holding, patting or rocking are "contact comforts" which teach that *soothing* touch can ease distress. • Wrapping up or swaddling in a blanket. • Meeting needs – feeding or a nappy change. • Changing position. • Offering a dummy/pacifier.	• Hug. • Sit on lap or sit them tight in by your side on a sofa. • Read a story to them whilst holding a book together. • Sing nursery rhymes or action songs together. • Dance to music together.	• *Positive gesture:* high-fives, fist bumps (or knee, ankle or elbow bumps). Receiving massage. • Hugs are fine depending on relationship and location, for example, they may not want to hug in front of their friends, or they may request no hugs (but then return to them a few months later) a part of finding their place in a teenage world. • Listen to shared music sitting together. • Emotional *support*. • Take out for a small treat-time, walk, a visit or an ice cream. • Use a *mindfulness App*.
	• Vocal *soothing* (noises or phrases), chatting and singing. • Offering a favourite (cuddly) toy. • Cooling down (body temperature). • Distracting.		

(Continued)

Table 6.1 (Continued)

b. Verbal and emotional regulation – how to. Self-regulation. Emotional comfort and *support* (co-regulation). Comfort and reassurance.	Comfort the infant emotionally by speaking and chatting to give comfort and help them calm. An infant may give early cues to signal distress – in these early stages of arousal, a child's attention may be redirected with something to distract (distraction technique). Offer a favourite cuddly toy or blanket. The baby will associate being *soothed* with that object or toy – many infants form an attachment to a blanket or teddy bear, for example. **Emotion coaching skills** use one step at a time. Stages: 1. Tune in. 2. Intentionally view these emotional challenges as an opportunity that allows us to respond, connect and teach. 3. Listen. 4. Help them label their emotions. To begin with offer them a few *feelings* words to choose from. 5. Set limits whilst problem solving to resolve own adult-child or child-child conflict. See conversation framework in the downloadable resources.	Speak calmly or remove the child from a stressful situation. Teach them words to express and talk about their emotions. Model (that is do this yourself as a positive role model example) and teach self-regulating strategies such as taking a long mindful breath. **Emotion-coach** (Gottman, in Gilbert et al., 2021) them about their feelings, label and name their emotions and express with words. Teach simple problem solving skills by suggesting options (shall we do x or y, would you like to wear a or b, would you prefer that dinner is c or d). Teach strategies to resolve conflict – when they are calm, by referring to their own feelings, they can begin to understand the feelings in others. Explaining can help early sibling or friendship conflicts and teaches conflict-resolution strategies (Banaroya, 2023; Gottman, in Gilbert et al., 2021). Develop their "emotion management skills" such as how to reappraise the situation or see it from another's point of view. Engage in an alternate activity. "Connect then re-direct" (Siegel and Bryson, 2011).	Find a place and time to talk together. Or they may find comfort in talking to a friend, family member or counsellor/therapist. Teach problem solving, organisation, and time management skills to prevent problems. *Support* healthy stress management such as by encouraging exercising and meditating. Teach them critical thinking so they can make better decisions. Co-regulatory interactions will start to give rise to the young person's emerging self-regulation skills; they are taking on most of the regulating tasks. Now, the parent's or teacher's main role is to provide guidance for complex problems and emotional *support* in dealing with significant stressors. They are important as the young person's secure-base and safe-haven (Li, 2023).

(*Continued*)

Table 6.1 (Continued)

c. Reassurance in rhythm and predictability. Motion, rhythm and rocking.	Constant motion, rhythm or rocking: The arousal of a baby's stress response system can be reduced by continuous, monotonous, repetitive stimulation, such as • Rocking. • Swaddling. • White noise. • The human heartbeat. • Patting. • Stroking. • Baby massage. • Sucking on a pacifier/dummy. These are all rhythmical comforting actions. There is reassurance in repetition and predictability. Other examples are: • A rattle or shaker. • Game of repeating peek-a-boo. • A game of hand gestures such as clapping/ waving/in cycles. • A jack-in-the-box • Singing the same, familiar nursery rhyme or song (with or without actions).	These involve repetitive, predictable activities that bring comfort. Such as **Partner games:** • Bouncing a ball between you. • Throwing a cushion or bean bag/playing catch. • Clapping games. • Partner clapping, • Ball throwing/kicking • Copying games ("Simon Says…") • Read a familiar story, or rhyme – familiarity offers predictability and reassurance. • A story with "Rhyming Couplets" (such as Dr Seuss, Cat in the Hat or the Rupert the Bear series) offers a rhythm too. Singing nursery rhymes or action songs together. Playing music or a musical instrument (no matter how basic) this could be tapping a stick on a set of upturned tins or using a wind-chime. Or individual activities: fidget toys, skipping or "cats cradle."	• Doodling. • Zen-doodle. • Mindful colouring. • Drumming. Shared physical game or sports e.g., ball throwing, potting hoops, table tennis with rolled up magazines and a paper ball. *Support* independence and peer group activity. They may also benefit from practising mindfulness and meditation or engaging in physical activity such as running or yoga. Sport or dance. • Fidget toys. • Blue-tack: to create a picture on a table or have in their hands as a fidget-toy. • Knitting or crochet. • Weaving. • Listen to favourite music. Use a *mindfulness App, or other App that involves rhythm and predictability*.
d. Increasing independent *Self-soothing* activity.	A baby who is *soothed* by their primary caregiver will associate emotions and learn skills to *self-soothe*. As a baby becomes a toddler and gains independence, encourage time when they play alone, this not only develops imagination, and patience, but encourages self-reliance as a precursor to *self-soothing* and developing resilience (Bauer et al, 2021).	They begin to engage in independent, *self-soothing* activities which they instigate, such as: Listening to calming music, reading a favourite book, and calm activities such as art, colouring or playing with play dough. They may also benefit from taking deep breaths and blowing bubbles or engaging in gentle yoga or stretching exercises.	**For preteens and adolescents**, *self-soothing* activities may include journaling, writing poetry or fiction, or engaging in creative activities such as drawing or painting.
e. Long-distance *soothing*: shared gesture.	**See "remote comfort tactics" (Table 6.2).**		

Table 6.2 Remote comfort tactics.			
Soothing when apart *(see research)* *Making contact via a phone call or a screen.* *Whole body activity.*	• Have a key phrase or pet name. • Sing a familiar nursery rhyme or song or record yourself singing a rhyme or sending a message; hearing a familiar voice can bring comfort. • Wave.	• Both of you have the same cuddly toy or heart cushion. • Play a shared game – e.g., what object am I thinking of? • Record a bedtime story to be played at the child's bedtime if you are unable to make a call at that time.	• Placing a hand on the heart. • Invent a long-distance creative handshake. • Both of you wear the same item e.g., a cap, a scarf, a football shirt. • Blowing a kiss. • Compile a music playlist together.
Response to distress	Depending on the developmental stage, the duration and intensity of stimulation for your child must be adequate and long enough to interrupt or diminish distress.		

feeling that they are valued and respected. However, if the teacher or parent is not feeling "warm and responsive" themselves, then the co-regulation may be mismatched or ruptured (and in need of repair); similarly, a long-distance relationship can cause a feeling of separation; a traumatic event such as displacement, pandemic, natural hazard or illness may result in the main caregiver being physically apart.

When physically apart, receiving touch from others is not always available (when separated by distance or circumstance), or not advised (as in the COVID-19 pandemic), *soothing* self-touch gestures such as placing a hand on body parts like the heart or face may be an alternative way to improve stress responses, other ideas are Table 6.2 above.

Suggestions of ways to co-regulate, to comfort and *soothe* when not physically present are given.

Factors which may impact chosen *SUPPORT* strategies. Stage not age

A parent, or someone working within education, health or social care will be aware that babies, children and young people all have a varying ability to be *soothed* or to *self-soothe*. In addition to the severity of the traumatic event itself, these following factors are things to consider:

- The health and temperament of the baby, child or young person.
- Adverse Childhood Experiences (ACEs).
- Cultural practices and belief systems.
- Parental past experiences – physical and mental health and their own childhood.

These may impact not only this "**soothing**" component of the "**5-S Scaffold**," but also the other areas of *subside*, *support*, and *strengthen* (chapters 5, 7 and 8). To expand:

- **The health and temperament of the baby, child or young person**
  Different health conditions and differing temperaments affect how easy it is to *soothe* the individual and alter what their "triggers" may be. For some children with sensory sensitivity, loud noise, bright lights or uncomfortable clothing fabric can cause distress; autistic children may fall into this category, many also find "change" difficult. For some children, an unknown change of plan can evoke a strong response, they may react when a plan is cancelled or when they suddenly must visit somewhere unexpected. This requires groundwork (see **SUPPORT**, chapter 7), as transitions need preparation and planning.
  When *strong* reactions or emotions are involved, a baby or child can take longer to be *soothed* or to *self-soothe*. They may not calm as easy as a child whose attention can be re-directed (distraction technique). Additionally, the more intense the emotion, the longer they may take to *soothe*, as ever, patience and modelling calmness are key.

- **Prior ACEs**

  As we read in chapter 4, ACEs can alter a child or young person's levels of anxiety and responses to stimuli; their adaptations to cope with early adverse conditions or events may produce a maladaptive response to even "safe" events – due to how their stress response system has developed, and the "heightened alert" they have lived with. This can negatively impact their mental health, physical health and general wellbeing. Consequently, at times they may find *self-soothing* almost impossible and will also be harder to *soothe*.

- **Cultural practices and belief systems**

  Different communities or cultures have a variety of values or beliefs regarding topics such as carrying a baby, baby's bed and sleep routine and breastfeeding. These practices may impact how co-regulation occurs and how *self-soothing* is learnt. In recent years, there has been a move towards "attachment parenting" too, a style often advocated by the early "parenting classes" or "antenatal classes" (NHS, 2023). Keeping a baby close, carrying babies to help them feel safe and secure and breastfeeding on demand are all positive examples of what helps a baby learn to *self-soothe* and therefore have shorter crying times.

- **Parental past experiences – physical and mental health and their own childhood**

  A parent's upbringing, or their current health and wellbeing, can impact their understanding of and ability to *soothe* an infant.

  Chapter 3 described supportive parenting techniques to prevent a repeating negative cycle of parenting patterns. Views on discipline and punishment can also hinder a baby's opportunities to learn *self-soothing*. A parent who has been treated harshly or unkindly in their childhood may have embedded beliefs which are hard to shake. For example, calming or hugging a toddler in tantrum may not come naturally; the idea that the child is trying to communicate through their behaviour can be a difficult concept to understand. Some childhoods may have been filled with parental dominion over their offspring along with a desire to control. An upset tantrum could be incorrectly viewed as the child desiring to "disobey" and a parental-figure or professional might interpret this as a sign that they do not respect authority. However, these opinions and approaches can be reversed by receiving formal or informal *support* (Clarke and Dawson, 2009).

Attitudes of compassion

Attitudes within professions, including education, vary; generally, there is some movement towards compassion in education and an understanding of a supportive approach to wellbeing and mental health conditions. The level and type of *support* varies between institutions though (Sammons, 2019).

Mothers who have had a difficult pregnancy, experienced a traumatic birth, endured post-natal depression – or parents who suffer from a physical condition, endure pain or stress and anxiety, for example, may find themselves too unwell to always comfort their baby; as a result, the baby may cry more, leading to a cycle which is even harder to overcome. Mothers and parents need understanding *support* in these situations, from friends, family and professionals. Those circumstances are not "their fault," there should be no guilt nor blame attached, and their feelings should be validated. There are agencies to receive this *support* from or give advice (this book cannot do this topic justice). See "Mental Health problems and Pregnancy" in NHS, 2023.

Summary

In a traumatic stressful situation, the parental-figure(s) and the professionals are vital in validating the child's or young person's emotions by remaining a stable and reliably calm carer who can build a child's self-esteem by acknowledging those emotions, naming them and *soothing* appropriately. *Co-regulating* to teach *self-regulation* is a means of developing *self-soothing* abilities in the child or pupil. Approaching the child's emotions with annoyance or impatience does not show them that their feelings are respected or accepted. By showing them that their emotions have value, they will know self-worth.

Times of collective trauma are among the hardest situations in which it is genuinely difficult to remain calm and collected. However, *support* after the traumatic event can help repair the pain. Teaching *self-soothing* assists this process. Within *professional practice*, an evidence-informed approach to *support* the emotional regulation within children and young people is *"Emotion-Coaching"* (Gilbert et al., 2021). This aligns with content included in this book and is a suggestion for further reading.

WHY it works?

This section addresses the evidence-base for the theory underpinning this "*SOOTHING*" chapter; it offers further material to demonstrate that these techniques have a positive impact.

Adults will likely be aware that anxiety can be induced by psychosocial stressors; the cause may include home or workplace conflict, receiving criticism or a negative personal judgement. To an even greater extent, *traumatic stress* is caused through incidents of individual or **collective trauma***; the latter may occur because of events such as the COVID-19 pandemic, war, displacement due to war or being a refugee, experiencing a natural disaster or perpetual economic poverty.

At these times, being *soothed* and *self-soothing* are important. To understand the impact that a hug or *self-soothing* touch has on the stress response of young adults, a study was conducted (Dreisoerner et al., 2020). The investigation used three measures to determine if there was a difference in reactions between three groups of people:

- Those who received a hug.
- Those who could engage in *self-soothing* touch.
- Those who received no comfort.

In the investigation, the three measures were: an ECG heart-rate monitor, a social-emotional self-report measure and salivary cortisol samples (cortisol is a hormone released during times of stress, see chapter 4). In the study, a controlled stressor was applied to all the participants to study the impact. The result was that the stressor increased all three measures (cortisol production, heart rate and self-reported stress/anxiety), however, after noting this impact, participants in *Group A* received a hug, in *Group B self-soothing* touch was allowed and *Group C* was permitted no comfort (in the control group).

The impact witnessed was that the cortisol levels lowered in both *the receiving hugs* group (A) and the *self-soothing touch* group (B), however, they did not lower in the no-comfort *control* group (C). This demonstrates the *protective factor* that both hugs and *self-soothing* touch have on our physiological stress responses – and thus, on our social-emotional state. Therefore, it follows that receiving hugs or *self-soothing* touch, theoretically, brings a positive reaction which *supports* our response to a stressful event.

Interestingly, the self-reported social-emotional stress measure and heart rate did not return to "normal" as quickly as the cortisol level did. This shows that we may not psychologically be aware of or mentally feel the benefits of a hug, but our body's physiological responses (cortisol level) do – and our autonomic system reacts (described in chapter 4).

Admittedly, some level of cortisol is needed to operate efficiently, it is what causes us to be alert enough to get out of bed in the morning or perform optimally in certain situations (such as interview, or on stage). However, too much cortisol can be debilitating. Hence, strategies for coping with traumatic stress include giving/receiving hugs or actioning *self-soothing* touch.

Shared social identity

Other studies have confirmed that hugs or *soothing*-touch from a romantic partner have even greater cortisol-lowering benefits. Similarly, feeling part of a **group identity** also causes the individual to perceive the hug or touch as being freely and warmly given without judgement or "a hidden agenda" (Häusser et al., 2020).

Having that emotional connection with another human, or group of people, increases the positive effects of a hug or physical touch. This *social identity* is a significant factor that improves the impact of the hug. Supportive behaviours (nodding, smiling) have a stress-lowering impact only when they are from a person or group with whom we identify. Essentially, the more groups we belong to, and the stronger we feel we belong, the greater our health and ability to cope with stress (Häusser et al., 2012). This is because our identity also stems from the characteristic of *belonging* to our social groups (Social identity theory; Tajfel et al., 1979) or group with whom we identify. Consequently, within the case of a **collective trauma***, the other members of that same collective group will have an experience and have an identity with which we can associate. Consequently, this helps forge an unspoken bond; supportive behaviour (nods, smiles, a certain "look" or exchange of glances), supportive touch or a hug will all then have a greater stress-reducing effect. Why this is the case is examined next.

Why hugs and *self-soothing* touch have a positive effect?

Self-soothing touch and hugs (or pats on the back, for example) have a dual role, they calm when experiencing current stress and protect from known future stress (a protective factor), such as receiving *support* before an upcoming interview. We experience *social-emotional responses* and *physiological changes.*

Social-emotional responses

Physical contact from someone else – three reasons it makes a difference

- Generally, we experience affectionate, consolatory or compassionate "touch" from someone with whom we have a close relationship. It therefore communicates closeness and is an indicator of "safety"; it is usually interpreted as a sign of understanding (Eckstein et al., 2019).
- The magnitude of the effects of receiving a hug is directly related to the closeness or bond with which you feel with the "hugger." Whilst being physically comforted by a romantic partner is more effective than self-stroking, conversely it can also be viewed differently too; it is almost more "expected" rather than it be a deliberate act by someone who is less close or a relative stranger (Morrison, 2016).
- Research showed that receiving a hug or physical comfort was beneficial regardless of whether they had a shared social identity or not (Morrison, 2016). Hence, this evidences the benefits of massage therapy or animal therapy, for example, where stroking and touch are definitive elements.

Self-comfort-touch. Three reasons it helps!

- Similarly, *self-soothing* touch expresses *self-care.* It stems from having a compassionate attitude towards ourselves (Neff, 2003); this response of *being-kind-to-yourself* improves our ability to cope with stress whilst enduring a traumatic experience. Since it is often used *sub-consciously* (we put our hand to our mouth and hold our jaw, we may hug ourselves whilst drawing our knees to our chest), then it seems that when used *deliberately* it could also be a strategy to help us cope with a stressful situation. Our body's physiological mechanisms produce a positive impact, and it signals a sign of safety (Eckstein et al., 2019). Chapter 4 explained the reasons behind this in the *Exteroception and interoception* section; this is also relevant to the next bullet point.
- *Self-soothing* touch is freely available; it is risk-free and easily administered. Therefore, it can be relied upon as being available to meet the need to *protect ourselves* and signal *self-induced safety* (Eckstein et al., 2019). The result is we feel "content and safe" and receive a sense of being loved and cared for in moments of distress. Sometimes self-touch can be preferable to receiving a hug from someone else (and some people "don't do hugs"). Earlier in this chapter, a suggestion was to have an awareness of cues from a child's or young person's brief actions; witnessing the child using self-touch, grasping a cuddly toy or hugging their knees to their chest to comfort themselves could act as a predictor that the child or young person requires comfort or does not feel content or safe.
- Physical contact can give a social identity – this sense of belonging can increase the feeling of being comforted during times of stress. Additionally, some social groups have a distinctive and creative "handshake" or "high five."

Physiological responses

This is a brief consideration of a few physiological reactions (explained further in chapter 4) which are relevant to "SOOTHING" and "SELF-SOOTHING" as SUPPORT strategies.

Exposure to trauma leads to increased activity of the sympathetic nervous system and the hypothalamic–pituitary–adrenal (HPA)-axis (the adrenal glands being responsible for the release of adrenalin); this activates the stress response in the amygdala, causes raised cortisol levels (the "stress hormone") and an inability to "think clearly," sometimes referred to as "brain fog."

Hence, both cognitive abilities and memory become impaired (Morrison, 2016) (see previous diagram, chapter 4, Figure 4.15).

Some processes that cause comfort-touch to have a positive impact on our stress response system are:

- Oxytocin (the feel-good hormone) is triggered by and released during hugging/touching; this can activate the parasympathetic nervous system (chapter 4). Its effect is to increase feelings of trust, calmness and generosity whist reducing anxiety (Eckstein et al., 2019); simultaneously cortisol levels are reduced. Separate studies have shown that receiving a massage or hugging a human-shaped cushion may also bring this impact (Tang et al., 2020).
- Lowered blood pressure and reduced heart rate also occur through receiving affiliative touch, such as handholding or hugs (Tang et al., 2020).
- Cortisol (the stress hormone) measures recovered to "normal" faster in the *self-soothing* touch group (who were not in contact with another human) than in the control group (Dreisoerner et al., 2020, 2021). This suggests that self-touch has *stress-lowering effects* and therefore beneficial for individuals who are temporarily or permanently isolated from others or separated from loved ones.
- Receiving hugs leads to quicker recovery after having common cold virus infection, demonstrating a positive impact on our immune system (Dreisoerner et al., 2021).
- Skin-to-skin contact improves stress coping (in animals as well as in humans) (Tang et al., 2020). Applying this tactile pressure causes physiological response in the *vagus nerve* system; these are beneficial. Regarding the HPA-axis, the oxytocin is produced in the hypothalamus (the H) but stored and released by the pituitary gland (P), this means the adrenal glands (A) have lower activity and they produce less adrenalin, thus overall arousal is lower. Consequently, a weaker, or non-existent, fight-flight-freeze-flop response occurs. The tactile contact stimulates the vagus nerve and *parasympathetic stress response* to regulate our bodies i.e., heart rate, anxiety or breathing pattern may remain lowered (Field, 1998).
- However, (the non-tactile) psychological, *talking support* (including counselling) also offers benefits. Knowledge and security are gained from the proximity, social *support*, positive affiliation or feeling of belonging. Similarly *self-soothing* touch may invoke feelings of self-made safety (Eckstein et al., 2019) and mindfulness (being "present" and "grounded in the moment"). These all have benefits regarding the responses in children and young people around times of traumatic stress.

Conclusion

As humans, we need physical contact from the moment we are born to fulfil our need to feel content and safe (Gilbert, 2014). Life holds many challenges threatening this need, children and young people learn to *co-regulate*, within the realms of a *secure attachment*, before they can *self-regulate*. When comfort-touch from others is unavailable, *self-soothing* touch provides an alternative way to re-activate memories of *support* and compassion in the face of stress. This has relevance during traumatic stressful events which separate families. Displacement or the "lockdown" rules of a pandemic are examples; governments all over the world asked their citizens to keep physical distance from each other, sometimes issuing shelter-in-place orders (such as in March and April 2020). Thus, when we are prevented from meeting (and being touched and hugged by other people), *self-soothing touch* or *remote-comfort-tactics* may be effective options to reduce the effects of the stress resulting from a trauma and increased by enforced separation (Dreisoerner et al., 2020). Ironically, the physical health-improving benefits of *soothing* contact was therefore not present either, at a time when it could help recovery; this was a situation beyond the control of citizens but left long-lasting traumas concerning *not-being-there* at a time they knew they were needed. In chapter 7 (*SUPPORT*), we can read about the impact that a loss of control can have – and subsequent **SUPPORT** strategies that can be implemented.

Wellbeing and resilience in children and young people are now proven to be a requisite to educational attainment (Bloom et al., 2020; Feinstein et al., 2008; Feinstein 2009). Neurobiological evidence shows that learning, memory, decision-making, problem-solving and social functioning are impacted and largely ruled by emotion processing. This is of key importance to educators, as a child under stress will be unable to learn. It is essential to *support* the emotional regulation within children and young people.

Summary

	Top tips for "SOOTHE" technique (chapter 6)
1.	After an emotional outburst *soothing*, or *self-soothing*, may need to occur to help the child begin to function again, whether at school or at home. If we feel negative emotions, distressed or "out of sorts," then by allowing ourselves to be *soothed*, or by self-soothing, we can calm and comfort ourselves to reduce anxiety and stress and therefore feel better. *Self-soothing* is a self-reliant, internal process (Gračanin et al., 2014).
2.	**Soothing, or self-soothing,** is a focused response in that moment, and to that emotion. Both involve an internal process which monitors the level of arousal (chapter 4). When a *need* is noticed, *soothing* or *self-soothing* will aim to alter the emotional reaction. Therefore, this should act to bring calm to the distress. The level of arousal is "regulated" and stabilised by either directed (as with "*soothing*" another) or self-directed (as with *self-soothing*) behaviours and internal processes.
3.	**Soothing – the groundwork for developing self-soothing** A baby cannot invent *self-soothing*, they must experience it in order to know what it is. Therefore, a baby left to cry cannot comfort itself, it cannot invent a **SELF-SOOTHING** technique in isolation, it needs to be taught (Herbers et al., 2014). This *experience* can be initially gained by a parent-figure meeting the baby's needs, so when uncomfortable or distressed they are responded to and brought relief; these are acts which comfort and *soothe*.
4.	**Teaching self-soothing** In brief, teaching **self-soothing** involves the following hierarchical stages: I. *Soothing:* the adult *provides the opportunity* for the infant, child or young person to experience being *soothed*, using a suitable "stage, not age" approach; experiencing it is essential. II. Co-regulation *occurs when a parent/parent-figure creates a warm and receptive interaction with their child. Or a teacher may model a positive emotional state with a pupil. It is necessary to* **co-regulate** *to enable a child to* **self-regulate***. Co-regulation acts as a supportive coaching experience which creates positive emotions within the infant or child, when the primary-carer has* "availability" *i.e., the important qualities of* accessibility *and* responsiveness *(Bowlby, 1973, p. 202).* III. Self-regulation. *A baby/child needs someone to oversee their initial attempts at self-regulation to learn how to self-regulate; the child's emotions can be spoken back to the child to explain what they are feeling (chapter 3).* IV. *Self-soothing. Potentially, an older child can utilise the* **SELF-SOOTHING** *techniques acquired through innate learning that accompanies their early experience of being soothed.*
5.	1. **Remaining a consistently calm and kind** adult is essential to build and keep trust. 2. **Pick up on a child's cues** that they have *a need* to prevent growing distress and an outburst erupting. Model emotional regulation. 3. **Use age-appropriate co-regulation strategies:** these internal resources provide a scaffold for a child's emotional experience, to guide towards higher order emotional regulation and resilience. 4. **Remember the most effective strategies and** what works best for that child or young person. 5. **Be tuned into trauma throughout the "normal days":** some situations may spark a reaction. 6. **Help them practice to develop their resilience: times of distress** can be used positively to scaffold a response appropriate to their stage of development (see Tables 6.1 and 6.2). This also helps children learn to cope when the teacher, parent or carer are not present. 7. **Have patience and do not yield to demands:** if the teacher or parent-figure yields to the demands or suddenly produces that item, then the child or pupil will not have opportunity to learn coping strategies to independently *self-soothe*. 8. **Be a good role model:** a dysregulated child requires a regulated parent who they can learn alongside. Co-regulation leads to a child's self-regulation.

6.	**Stage/age-appropriate soothing, leading to SELF-SOOTHING techniques. See Tables 6.1 and 6.2** for a checklist of things to consider:
	
	1. First self-regulate.
	2. Checklist of "do-nots."
	3. Do: cues from the individual.
	4. Consider: environment or emotional environment.
	5. Co-regulate (see below):
	  a. Physical comfort and reassurance. Physical touch.
	  b. Verbal and emotional regulation. Self-regulation. Emotional comfort and *support* (co-regulation). Comfort and reassurance.
	  c. Reassurance in rhythm and predictability: motion, rhythm and rocking.
	  d. Increasing independent *self-soothing* activity.
	  e. Long-distance *soothing*: shared gesture.

7.	**Factors which may impact chosen SUPPORT strategies:**
	• The health and temperament of the baby, child or young person.
	• Adverse Childhood Experiences.
	• Cultural practices and belief systems.
	• Parental past experiences – physical and mental health and their own childhood.
	• A traumatic situation which causes enforced separation – the use of shared gesture is needed. Having that emotional connection with another human/group increases the positive effects of a hug or physical touch. This *social identity* is a significant factor that improves the impact of the hug; it is absent in a traumatic situation – but, shared long-distance, gesture has a positive impact.
8.	***Soothing/self-soothing* has a positive effect: studies have given an evidence base**
	Self-soothing touch and hugs (or pats on the back, for example) have a dual role – they calm when experiencing current stress and protect from known future stress (a protective factor). We experience *social-emotional responses* **and** *physiological changes*.
	In a traumatic stressful situation, the parental-figure(s) and the professionals are vital in validating the child's or young person's emotions; a stable and reliably calm carer can build a child's self-esteem by acknowledging those emotions, naming them and *soothing* appropriately. *Co-regulating* to teach *self-regulation* is a means of developing *self-soothing* abilities in the child or pupil. By showing them that their emotions have value, they will know self-worth – *support* after a traumatic event can help repair the pain. Teaching *self-soothing* assists this process.

7 *SUPPORT*
Practical strategies for each big emotion

Chapter overview

- Having described the theoretical and practical components of the *SUBSIDE* and *SOOTHE* stages, this chapter moves on to the hands-on *SUPPORT* we can offer for various emotional states (chapter 2). The techniques and suggestions described in chapters 5 and 6 therefore underpin our approach with children and young people as we *support* them through their range of "big emotions," evident after experiencing an individual or a collective traumatic event.
- For each emotional state of shock/denial/numbness, anger/distress, bargaining, depression, anxiety and acceptance/peace, there will be
  a. *descriptions of typical behaviours with reasons for these* and
  b. *the hands-on strategies/interventions to support a pupil exhibiting a particular emotion.*
- It will describe the variety of and variations in individual responses, and how children are not born with the ability to regulate their emotions, rather through their relationships and interactions they learn how to respond.

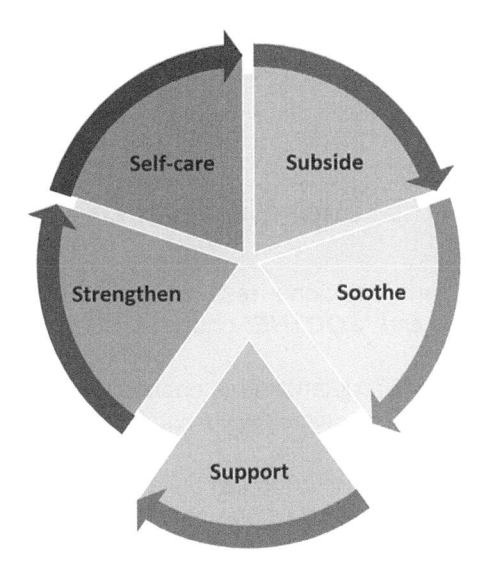

After experiencing a collective traumatic event, people seek comfort from those who have "been there" and therefore "understand" how they might feel; they also form initial comparisons by considering their experience to be "worse than" or "not as bad" as what happened to their friend, for example. Traumatic events often result in fear, change, grief, injury and loss, in all its forms (chapter 2). Their depth of response to the "stressor" depends mainly on three things: on the nature of the event, their assessment of what they experienced and their personality traits. To an extent, both these latter two are dependent on their *past life experience* (Horowitz, 2011).

A child's past life experiences include three areas: having their early needs met as they grow and develop, their type of attachment with their main caregiver (chapter 3) and any previous encounters with trauma or loss which impact later life events. How we feel, our stress response, our emotions, our wellbeing and our mental health *are inextricably linked to our biological responses to trauma.* Many physiological and brain-based processes impact our bodies in response to a stressor (chapter 4) and neuroscience can now demonstrate the

DOI: 10.4324/9781003275268-10

impact that trauma has on our brains. These chapters formed the foundation to understanding why the elements within this **5-S Scaffold** can *support* children and young people following trauma or loss.

A traumatic event can be a difficult experience for children and young people to process, particularly when it involves grief, loss, injury or other significant changes that directly affect them. Such events can lead to traumatic stress. A child or young person may instinctively know they are "feeling stressed," as so much happens "below the surface" – we feel it, it impacts us biologically and psychologically (as we read in chapter 4), yet it can be hidden from the outside world much of the time. It is often only when a child or young person demonstrably exhibits a strong emotional response (breaks down sobbing, reacts with rage, silently stares into space) that we may begin to understand something of what they are feeling.

An individual response to a group "event" can range from being completely numb to displaying extreme emotions. Chapter 2 described emotions that may arise from a traumatic experience, and why they occur. These included:

A. shock and denial (also called "numbing" or "avoidance"),
B. anger and distress – which can include separation anxiety,
C. bargaining: guilt and shame,
D. depression,
E. anxiety and
F. acceptance.

This "*SUPPORT*" chapter will address A–F in turn whilst re-iterating a key point from chapter 2, that:

The stages, the order and the intensity vary from person to person. The length of time an emotion may last is also individual, one emotional state may last fleetingly or many months, similarly many emotions may collide together. These are normal and expected reactions to trauma, to grief, loss and forced change, which can often be overwhelming to verbalise or make sense of. Children and young people need supportive adults.

The sections below will suggest *hands-on, everyday strategies*, accompanied with some *relevant, practical knowledge*, to aid understanding.

The key approach – that underpins all *SUPPORT* strategies

For ALL strategies and for any emotional response, it is important to remember three key approaches from "**SUBSIDE**" and "**SOOTHE**" chapters. This is:

- Maintain your own adult self-regulation (see chapter 5) to present a controlled, approachable self. Day-to-day calm consistency is vital to forge healthy, trusting child-adult relationships.
- Be tuned into trauma – even on the good days! Be vigilant in spotting early cues of distress, as after a traumatic event, some situations may spark a severe reaction in your child, or in the pupil; awareness and vigilance are key, as we are then able to reduce its impact or, potentially, prevent it happening. Observing and remembering past instances help the correct *support* be there at the time it is needed. It is helpful to show empathy and be consistent, as something that worked "the last time" could also work again.
- Create a positive and supportive home and/or classroom environment, where children feel safe and valued. This can be achieved through positive reinforcement and clear expectations, as well as providing opportunities for children to participate in home or classroom decision-making. However, there needs to be flexibility within this. Rather than rigidly stick to school-routine, rules, curriculum and timetabling, for example, an approach personalised for the pupil should include a level of adaptability. One positive hour in school daily can be built on and is a more positive experience than a devastating five hours that would result in pupil distress and, potentially, extended absence from school. Similarly, continuing to adhere rigidly to a school "Behaviour Policy" that includes punishing various minor demeanours can be detrimental; a neurodiverse pupil or one struggling emotionally can be subject to repeated "detentions" for example, which can harm their in-school relationships and bring more harm than good (chapter 9).

Other key means of gaining practical *support*:

- Use a search engine (such as Bing or Google) to discover age-appropriate resources that fit with the current situation, whether the trauma/loss is individual, or collective (see downloadable resources).
- Contact families who have experienced a serious event or bereavement, to acknowledge their loss and to express *support*. Compile condolences for bereaved children from their peers, collect messages to send or gather messages to form an electronic book to email to a family who have lost someone. A vigil, an assembly or a class lesson can address the situation sensitively too. Inform staff who need to know.
- Offer *verbal praise for pupil's patience or other coping mechanism which they instigated – particularly when there is a gap between the child having a need and the need being met.* This provides positive reinforcement of learnt ways to cope alone and develops resilience. Intervene, with *support*, as appropriate and help them practice, to develop their strengths and regulate escalating emotion.
- Depending upon the event, utilise any community or national *support* structures that may be in place.
- Set up channels for communication – such as via a school's or organisation's website, a direct-contact phone number or a Facebook or WhatsApp group. Community communication is practical to share news, gain updated information and feel a sense of belonging (Woodward, 2020).
- Prepare children for any practice or real government national text message that alerts citizens to a state of emergency (as was sent to UK citizens as a test at 3 pm on 23 April 2023). Preparation can avoid unnecessary anxiety for a young person receiving such an alert to their phone.
- Gather the *survivors' views* of their needs; these needs and emotional/psychological responses will change over time (chapters 1 and 2).

Support for each emotion

A. **SHOCK and DENIAL**: Also referred to as "denial and avoidance of loss" (Parkes, 1972).

After a traumatic event, it is common to experience a see-saw effect with our feelings – we may push our emotions away whilst, at the same time, having intrusive memories in the form of thoughts, dreams or "flashbacks" that unexpectedly invade our mind – we can be fully engaged in an activity when, suddenly, we are caught unaware as *something* sparks a memory. That *something* that sparked the memory could range from a smell, a sound, sight, an object, a date or a phrase overheard. These *intrusive repetitions* of the trauma and *acting in denial with emotional numbness* are at opposite ends of the emotional spectrum – but they can occur simultaneously (Center for Substance Abuse Treatment (US), 2014).

Individual responses may range from acting as if nothing has happened, "boxing our emotions" and carrying on as normal to avoid recalling the event, to responding instantly and openly. Whatever the individual's response, avoidance and denial are likely to occur; we may feel numb, be in shock or may even deny the event has impacted us. Alternatively, we may dwell on the past and talk about *the-good-old-days*. These are all types of *defence mechanisms*; we may not want to believe what is happening, or what has just taken place. This can occur immediately, or a long time after the event, and may show itself in different subtle ways that others notice, such as behaviour in our sleep, speed at which anger rises, use of coping mechanisms or personality changes which are "out of character." Supporting our pupils through the stage of shock and denial usually includes the need to *support* their feelings of anger (see "B. Anger").

Often, it is when we are doing nothing-in-particular, that intrusive, frightening thoughts or scary images occur the most; this can cause concern that things are out-of-control, bringing unwanted anxiety and initiating concerns for our own health or state of mind. Alternatively, we can become pre-occupied with the past and share fond memories of how things were or even talk through the event in a detached manner. Whether children and young people talk about and relive the event (as a means of processing and coming to terms with it) or act in denial (as if nothing has happened out-of-the-ordinary), our responses require sensitive *support*.

A. Practical *support* for SHOCK and DENIAL.

1.	Offer reassurance that (a) reactions are expected and (b) they are now safe.
2.	Allow more time for a pupil's response.
3.	Develop a safety plan for unwanted intrusions.
4.	Use resources to *support* the child (and peers/family) in understanding what is happening to them.
5.	Be "present" and listen empathetically.
6.	Allow task completion/random "safe" task-orientated behaviour.
7.	Be discrete and sensitive – especially with "accidents."
8.	Use analogies or cartoon drawings to name and describe all likely emotions.

1. **Offer reassurance** that:
   a. These reactions and emotions (or lack of) are common and usual responses to a traumatic event.
   b. They are now safe and/or out of danger.
2. **Allow more time for the pupil to respond.**
   Give them time to process conversation or instruction and allow them time to respond. Be aware that their perception and attention will alter; they may seem dazed, stare into space or act "in a world of their own," not even realising that they have *timed-out* and have missed the conversation, or the lesson. Knowing the child, and their usual response style helps the adult gauge their level of attention.
3. **Develop a safety plan for unwanted intrusions**.
   Immediately after a trauma, intrusive thoughts/images, flashbacks or nightmares may commonly occur.

   - *Intrusive thoughts* are threatening thoughts (or images in the mind) that occur uncontrollably, they may be about the trauma itself, or what could have happened/might happen in the future.
   - *Flashbacks* are when people involuntary relive a traumatic event in the form of images, smells or sounds; they feel as if they are back in the situation.
   - *Nightmares* involve the above or are dreams which can wake someone or cause them to respond vocally, or physically, whilst in their sleep.

Since these all can be visual (they see them), auditory (they hear them) or kinaesthetic (they feel them), any words, story, images, TV programme, external (unrelated) noise, words or music can bring a response similar to that felt during the original trauma (Van der Kolk, 2015). These sensations may seem very real to the child or young person since they have picked up on environmental cues and their brains have interpreted this information (see exteroception and interoception, in chapter 4). As a result, their response to new stimuli (such as a sound or a situation) may be inappropriate. They may also sense that everywhere feels different, such as walking down a street unaware of what is happening around them but experiencing the world as grey and lacking in colour. These events change their outlook on life.

A pupil who experiences any unwanted intrusions may find them scary and be frightened that they are going to occur. These symptoms can cause distress, anxiety or affect day-to-day functioning – systems in the brain are responding in a dysregulated manner due to trauma (chapter 4).

Support involves developing **a safety plan** for if or when they recur, such as:

- Write a plan in a handy format on a small, laminated sheet to keep in their bag, on the fridge or by their bed – this can be a list of what to do, reminders that they are safe and people to contact (outline example in downloadable resources).
- Creating a social story where the child's experiences are at the centre of the story which is used to describe their experiences and their *support* (example plan in downloadable resources).
- Encourage a drawing to illustrate their feelings or depict what they are seeing, thinking or experiencing.
- Use *grounding techniques*, or mindfulness techniques (see under 'Serenity and Calm' section within Table 8.2, chapter 8) to "centre" the pupil after unwanted, intrusive thoughts.

4. **Use resources to *support* the child (and peers/family) in understanding what is happening to them** within their signs of trauma or loss: books, articles, websites, YouTube video and/or grief *support* material help educate the pupil and those around them.

   They may have a changed outlook, react inappropriately to events or act differently towards their family, peers or social groups. So, supporting those who surround them is also key whilst offering reassurance that these symptoms should disappear over time. When educating the child or other peers/siblings, remember their developmental stage and use appropriate language and explanations that they can understand.

   Educate other teachers and staff about the child's situation and how they can provide *support* and understanding (Parkes, 2001).

5. **Be "present" and listen empathetically – use "active listening."**

   We each know how we like to be listened to and we know what we dislike. Often the dislikes are easier to spot (whether it is in a one-to-one chat or at a seated meeting) and these can include being talked over or continually interrupted. Not being listened to may cause us to feel disrespected; someone scrolling through their phone, shuffling papers or scribbling notes while we are speaking suggest that their attention is elsewhere. We would also be missing eye contact and an open, attentive body posture that says, "I am interested in what you have to say." Verbal responses such as a disparaging or sarcastic comment, a chuckle or a sweeping "don't worry, it will be alright" are likely to inhibit us sharing our thoughts in the future. As are yawns, eye rolls, regularly glancing at the time, staring outside or "into space" or averting our eyes.

   Generally, we appreciate being heard and understood, we like the person to "be present" and try to "get what we're talking about" or understand how we are feeling. This requires *active listening* or *"listening with intention"* which offers emotional validation and the potential for empathetic conversation. Our communication should be non-judgemental, and responses can check or indicate that we have heard what they are saying, enabling us to respond appropriately.

Active listening or "listening with intention"

One version (Souers and Hall, 2016) helps staff build relationship and listen for understanding. It involves these steps:

a. Listen: Focus on the child or young person. Listen with open body posture and appropriate eye contact. Hold the pupil's words in your mind, rather than plan what to next say, and without interrupting.

b. Reassure: Communicate your care for the pupil, no matter what happened. Find or remember something positive about them.

c. Validate: Acknowledge and affirm the emotions, needs and the meaning behind what the pupil has spoken about ("Tell me if I understand this correctly, you feel…because I…").

d. Respond: Reply by being appropriately open about something that is true of the situation – something honest about yourself, the relationship or the prior event – or where you could improve ("I'm not so good at …. I hadn't noticed…I find that difficult").

e. Repair: If a misunderstanding or hurt feelings occur, fix it ("I can see now that I made you feel…I'm sorry for…").

f. Resolve: End with a focus on how to make things better moving forward ("How about next time you/I try to…will that help…do you have an idea?").

   This is a strategy for creating a *trauma-sensitive classroom* – the child or young person will feel more encouraged to talk to us when we practice active listening – which means paying attention, with an open body language and ensuring, for example, that we don't continue an activity such as marking work.

   Incidentally, there are over 20 books on Amazon alone, with "active listening" in their title; for more information, do read further as this section only touches on the key points.

6. **Task completion:** If the child is acting "detached" or displaying an urgent approach to complete a task – either one that was started before the trauma or a new task (such as "I need to draw a picture for person x"), allow them to complete it. Getting alongside and completing it with them can *strengthen* relationship – even if remaining in silence or speaking gently.

7. **Be discrete and sensitive** – with "accidents." The child or young person may feel as if they have lost bodily control or have actually lost bodily control – for example, wetting-the-bed may re-start. Clear up any vomiting or accidental urinations discretely and *support* the child practically, such as with a clothing change. Shock can produce a drastic impact on our body.

8. **Use analogies or cartoon drawings to name and describe all likely emotions**. Use visual aids, or short videos, to teach about our many different emotions, what they are and why we have them. Give examples and validate the emotion by *naming it*; "I can see you feel numb/shocked/angry… take your time." Labelling feelings provides emotional *support* and helps the child or young person feel noticed and heard (see downloadable resources). Posters, hand-held cards or bought resource tins (that depict emotion-based images) may be useful at a "*Regulations Station*" (see below) or to aid an early-years pupil communicate how they feel.

   Visual resources, symbols or widgits (Widgit Online, 2023) can help create a communication keyring (small, laminated cards which each depict symbols, an expression or short phrase to help the child convey information, their emotions or their needs, and attached together with a keyring clip), visual weekly timetable, key events in the school year, gentle "rules," task-prompts or to signify use of space or expectations (Andrews, 2023).

> See *top five key characteristics and top five support suggestions for "shock and denial"* in end of chapter Summary Table.

As children and young people break through the painful barrier of denial and not accepting the loss, they may emerge to face the reality of the situation and into the state of anger at the "missed experience," missed person/people or missed community life, for example. Facing reality can give rise to feelings of anger (Grayson, 1970, in Horowitz, 2011).

B. ANGER and DISTRESS:

Anger is defined as "a natural response to feeling attacked, deceived, frustrated or treated unfairly" (Mind, 2016, p. 4). The complexity of this response means it affects how we think and subsequently act (Rae, 2012). Whilst there can be positives and negatives about anger (chapter 3), it constitutes an *active* response. However, children who feel fearful or who cannot communicate their exasperation are likely to show a more aggressive, frustrated response. School "behaviour management" policies and techniques can be adapted to *support* a distressed child; its design should not merely supress natural emotions but seek to help children and young people understand their feelings and interpret them (Rae, 2012). This prevents the pupils internalising or suppressing anger, which could cause them to seethe and anger to build. Higher order thinking skills, cognition and reasoning will not be functioning during an angry outburst (chapter 4) (Bloom et al., 2020; Gus and Wood, 2017) – commonly it can take 15–25 minutes for a child to de-escalate to achieve a calmer state, which is when "*SUBSIDE*" and "*SOOTHE*" techniques can be used (chapters 5 and 6).

Anger usually involves psychological pain and sometimes includes severe bouts of anxiety, separation anxiety, regression and/or acute physical pain. This usually becomes less frequent and less intense as time passes (Horowitz, 2011).

After a traumatic event, we may pick up on the pupil's body language or witness angry outbursts; reactions may not be age-appropriate and "*tantrums*" may be exhibited. It is necessary to work with a child at their emotional age, not their chronological age, in a "stage not age" approach.

Generally, the origin of the anger is themes or "issues" related to the event. Typically, a long-held personal belief system conflicts with a current concept (Horowitz, 2011); for example, their *safe world* now feels unsafe, or disbelief that close family cannot meet together. Anger may result from feelings about the unfairness of the situation, that it happened, were let down or experienced some type of loss – there may be multiple "reasons" to be angry all at the same time.

The adult may witness responses such as young people feeling angry with themselves (often this can be intermingled with irrational guilt) or angry with others. They may blame everyone; looking for someone to blame is a natural response. They may also ask "why me?", "where is God?" or aggressively state "it's not fair." This is linked to the need to find someone to blame, and anyone in the vicinity could be on the receiving end of an inner turmoil that spills over and turns into rage.

Sometimes *collective trauma* yields a *collective response* and to make sense of it or locate a figure to blame, a group response forms – whether it be a protest, a desire for "reform" of a system or a law or group action or lawsuit – the need to be appeased, along with the moral standing of "preventing it happening (in this way) again," naturally takes precedent.

Resentment can be aimed at:

- The person or people who are "*lost*" due to displacement, such as may be the case with families of refugees or asylum seekers, for example (International Rescue Committee, 2023).
- Other enforced separation (e.g., lockdown in the COVID-19 pandemic).
- Being resettled in a disaster.
- At the person(s) who has died; resentment here is due to feeling that they have been abandoned.

Resentment, coupled with anger or envy, can also be felt towards those who "have not lost someone"; even if the young person knows this is immoral or irrational, it may still be one of the many thoughts occupying them.

Conversely, **survivor guilt**, or shame associated with their own survival or successful escape, may bring conflicting emotions that bubble-up; relief coupled with feeling selfish are common emotions. This may cause the "survivor" to feel unable to share in the pain of loss; if they have lived, yet are surrounded by a troubled community, then they may feel unable to share in the community pain too (Anon, 2023). As social creatures, we feel an intrinsic need to share emotions at all levels.

A traumatic event can cause an individual or community to question the ethos on which they have built their personal views; a situation, or lifestyle taken for granted, may suddenly change in the-blink-of-an-eye. The child or young person may feel the disappearance of relative safety, or perhaps felt blindsided or naive, as if they were wrong to trust in the stability previously experienced. This is an emotional loss, as opposed to a real and physical loss, but equally as valid (Ratcliffe et al., 2014). All "loss" conflicts with our human desire for permanence and consequently brings difficulties that are inherent in experiencing "change."

Attempts to "regain control" may include *seeking information* by obsessing over news reports, the internet, social media or by messaging between friends in shared responses and a sharing of information/images. Scouring news is natural to intrinsically assess a potential or future threat. However, balance is needed as obsessive news watching, or internet/social media use is now possible with the move towards 24-hour television and internet availability. Usually, the aim of news items is to appeal to emotions, to get viewers hooked (McLaughlin et al., 2022) but devouring news endlessly can increase feelings of distress and being overwhelmed; it is commonly referred to as *doom-scrolling*, as it leads to increased poor mental health and physical ill-health (Taylor and Francis Group, 2022). Yet it may meet:

- The need to acquire recent information.
- The desire to seek control by understanding it.

The young person may express viewpoints based on the information and opinions they have been fed, these voicings may be hurtful, inaccurate or extreme. It helps to find sound, accurate and age-appropriate sources for information and resources, to help the pupils.

Levels of outward reaction vary, some may be silently "seething," whilst others scream, shout and punch the wall. Older children and young people may then "feel bad" for having been so angry that they lost control, or that they unfairly blamed someone, and this can also lead to feelings of guilt or shame over their own responses. The loss of control over one's own life may be the catalyst that causes the young person to *react*, thus enabling themselves to become "the one in the driving seat"; however, it can, in turn, lead to undesirable behaviour.

It is necessary to work with a child at their emotional age, not their chronological age, in order to *support* the range of feelings and reactions stemming from anger.

SUPPORTING ANGER and distress

Children need new skills to cope but they cannot know what new skills they need.

Importantly the *adult's own self-regulation techniques* and other suggested interventions in the **SUBSIDE** (chapter 5) and **SOOTHE** (chapter 6) chapters should be used initially, to first return the child to a place where these strategies may be more effective; distraction, *soothing* and *self-soothing* can be particularly helpful. Table 6.1 in chapter 6 suggests age-appropriate co-regulation, *soothing* and self-regulation interventions. For example, use the **pupil's chosen method for being *soothed* or *self-soothing***, whether that is listening to music, a weighted blanket, fidget toys, playing with blue-tack, doodling, colouring, skipping, a swing, bouncing a ball, playing catch, walking or counting objects, in fact anything that includes the relaxing qualities of *rocking*, *rhythm or repetition*. This all helps change their physiology for the better and reduces their sensory overload.

Responding to their needs may be repetitive, but caring and responsive interactions equip them for the future and aid the pupil's self-regulation abilities. Gaining understanding and compassion through what neuroscience teaches us (chapter 4) also helps our responses remain patient and empathetic.

Children who are experiencing grief, trauma or loss may be more prone to anger and may require additional *support* in the classroom. Supporting and calming a child who is angry can be challenging, but there are several strategies that can be effective.

B. Practical *support* for "ANGER".

1.	Pick up on child's cues and remember triggers and specific needs to help prevent an outburst.
2.	*Equip them with new skills to cope by using 3D objects as visual aids to describe anger.*
3.	Set up a *Regulation Station* or create a personalised SOS bag.
4.	Reduce sensory overload.
5.	Model and mirror.
6.	Use *distraction* to limit obsessional thinking. Predictability and structure, but with flexibility, are needed.
7.	Creative opportunities to *express* their emotions.
8.	One-to-one adult-pupil meet at start of school day.

1. **Pick up on the child's "early warning" cues – remember their specific needs** to help prevent an outburst. Be aware of their ***triggers***, their body language or other warning signs of rising anger – and intervene before the child becomes too upset – provide them with accommodations as necessary. This can be done through proactive strategies such as positive reinforcement ("I can see this is difficult, you're doing really well to communicate this with us; would it help if [offers options]"); knowing the child and being aware of their environment is vital.

   For example, a child who has experienced a traumatic event may need additional *support* and understanding when dealing with loud noises or certain smells (Van der Kolk, 2015). Preventing a situation is preferable.

   Be aware practically, this may include ideas such as suggesting staff/adults communicate in advance when there is going to be known building work, for example, or avoiding certain trigger topics in lessons.

2. **Equip them with new skills by using 3D objects to visually explain anger.** Children need new skills to cope but they cannot know what new skills they need. We should offer *validation*, naming it with words such as "I can see you're upset and feeling cross." It is important to actively listen to the child (see section above) and acknowledge their feelings, rather than dismissing or invalidating them (Gilbert et al., 2021). Similarly avoid yielding to their demands.

   With some thought and creativity, any 3D object may produce an analogy for anger, distress or high emotion. Helping the child identify and **label their emotions** aids their ability to regulate and manage them.
   - An expanding mechanical ball toy or wooden "Russian" dolls can describe how emotions may be small and hidden away, or expand and get bigger, but could still be hiding numerous feelings that we have underneath (Brammer, 2023).
   - The hand-brain model (Siegel and Bryson, 2011) explains what happens inside our brains.
   - A volcano experiment or shaken fizzy pop describes how things happen that may cause us to "explode."

3. **Set up a *Regulation Station* or create a personalised *SOS bag*** to help prevent angry outbursts peaking. A ***Regulation Station*** is a permanent feature in a classroom for anyone to approach, sit at and use. If pupils move around a school building, they

could carry a personalised **SOS bag** which will contain items at easy reach for the child/young person, or which the adult can positively instigate as *support*, should the child start to become dysregulated. Items could include a blanket to sit on (as their own "safe space" to lay in any part of the school building) or to wrap around themselves, soft toys for comfort, fidget toys for repetitive calming rhythm, a photograph that brings feelings of happiness or reassurance and any items/activities that help the child or young person regulate themselves; colouring or zen-doodling/zentangle/mindful art helps with regulation since it utilises the notion that any activity that uses repetitive strokes (colouring or doodling) provides rhythm, aids relaxation and gives the brain valuable "time out" (Pillay, 2016).

It can help to also have a card depicting a face or an emoji representing that emotion with a brief description of how they may feel and list of things next to it that may help them if they are feeling angry, sad, cross or worried (downloadable resources).

4. **Reduce sensory overload.** We can help *change their physiology* (chapter 4) and *support* them by using weighted blankets, weighted cushions, a cuddly toy or ear defenders, as these objects may particularly help pupils avoid sensory overload. Providing the child with age-appropriate coping mechanisms, such as physical activities or a quiet walk in the playground, can also help manage their anger. Removing the pupil from the source of the over-stimulation, the noise or the busy environment should be done in a positive rather than a reprimanding manner. Relaxation techniques or breathing exercises can change their physiology too, to reduce signs of anxiety "(see Table 8.2, chapter 8)."

5. **Modelling and mirroring.**

The adult models appropriate responses/behaviour for the pupil to mirror (copy). Similar to *co-regulation*, *remaining calm and composed* ourselves is needed, as children often **mirror** the behaviour of the adults around them (Greene, 2021). Very young children and toddlers may even mirror facial expressions and reactions. In *marked-mirroring*, we can copy (mirror) an exaggerated version of the child's distressed face and then gradually move our face into a calm state (Crittendon, 2005). We can also physically *show* them how to relax their body and make a calm choice or, *write down* where and how they should sit, for example. We can model good reactions by remaining calm and talking through ways of responding. These skills can be taught through direct instruction, modelled by the teacher and reinforced through regular practice.

Using shared gesture to *soothe* can be effective when the gesture is a type of pre-discussed code between the adult and child – the adult could indicate a "hug" sign as a signal that the child should reach for their safety blanket to prevent an outburst; kind, non-aggressive gestures work best as a supportive, shared language rather than causing further negativity (such as by wagging a finger).

Positive reinforcement can follow successful mirroring and pupil self-regulation, to encourage such actions in the future. A parent picking up on these cues can demonstrate a calm, thoughtful approach (modelling *emotional regulation*). Caring and responsive interactions (modelling) help a child maintain a secure parental-attachment (chapter 3); the secure situation allows them to internalise the *emotional regulation strategies* which they experienced (mirroring), thus equipping the child for future situations, including those outside the parent-child relationship (Brumariu, 2015). These internal resources provide a scaffold for a child's emotional experience and therefore it guides them towards increasingly sophisticated self-regulating strategies (Crugnola et al., 2013).

6. **Use distraction to limit obsessional thinking.**

Obsessional thinking may become common, so *distraction* is a good technique (see chapter 5). Children may visit certain websites and this *search history* can help identify what thoughts are pre-occupying them. Thoughts that begin with "I should…," "what if…" may trigger anxiety. Anger and anxiety are natural responses to change and uncertainty, therefore anxiety is reduced by *predictability* and by *structure*, namely within the classroom environment, but balanced by *flexibility* in approach.

7. **Creative opportunities to *express* their emotions**.

Providing children with opportunities to express their feelings through creative outlets, in a safe and supportive environment, can help manage their anger. *Journaling, art, or group discussions are* examples which allow the child to process their emotions in a safe and healthy way.

Another strategy, if symptoms persist, is to provide children with appropriate art, play or drama therapies, or talking therapies such as counselling and wellbeing *support*. This can include individual or group counselling, as well as referral to outside mental health professionals as needed.

> The capacity of art, music, and dance to circumvent the speechlessness that comes with terror may be one reason they are used as trauma treatments in cultures around the world.
>
> (Van der Kolk, 2015, p. 290)

When angry, they cannot communicate well (chapter 4), hence, allowing free expression through creative media can be a therapeutic tool.

8. **Identify trigger points: one-to-one pupil meets with named adult, at start of school day.**

   When the pupil arrives at the start of the school day, meeting a named adult gives the pupil an opportunity to talk through the plan for the day, identify any trigger points, pre-empt situations or address any busy corridor or location-based issues. Discussing known changes prevents the pupil being surprised by unexpected alterations to their schedule, teacher or timetable.

   If further additional, protective approaches are needed, reduce the pupil's transition stress points. Consider developing a nurture group or primary-style class base, where there is one teacher, or the teacher(s) move to the pupil(s) rather than pupils move around school to the teachers (Hughes and Schlösser, 2014; NurtureUK, 2023). Some lessons will be challenging in nature or in subject, recognising this can pre-empt and prevent a situation arising where the pupil is *triggered*.

   The *"pupil-adult-meet"* starts the day well and addresses any practical issues (missing uniform, lost pen, no breakfast, late for school, chaotic morning routine) before they settle in their group; this allows staff members an awareness of why the pupil had no pen that day, for example, and prevents a punishment or an avoidable emotional eruption. We do not know what children have experienced prior to entering the school or college building that day – it may be a major achievement that they have managed to get themselves there in the first place (and worthy of praise and recognition).

   The start (or end) of the day meet also offers an opportunity for the pupils and the teacher to greet (or say goodbye to) each other in a welcoming, creative and fun way. This builds relationship (Alexander, 2019) and, importantly, shows that relationship comes first for children who have undergone trauma or loss; being warmly greeted by name and made to feel valued or "noticed" is a priority to create a secure atmosphere. For further ideas, see "P.A.C.E." (**P**layfulness, **A**cceptance, **C**uriosity and **E**mpathy) in section F. 'Acceptance', see point '3. Build trust, relationship and connection: P.A.C.E.'

Three key interventions: We are all human and therefore are unable to perfectly apply all strategies, all of the time. It can help to have staff decide three key interventions which are carried out consistently by everyone and across the school.

Choosing just three could include:

- A named adult for the pupil and a start-of-day meet.
- An *SOS bag* or use of a *Regulation Station*.
- A safe space (which could be a fixed area, small "light" room or blanket to sit on, in their SOS bag).

> See *top five key characteristics* and *top five support suggestions* for *"anger and distress"* in end of chapter Summary Table.

C. GUILT and BARGAINING

During the grief stage of *bargaining* a child may experience feelings of guilt, self-blame and a desire to make deals, or bargains, to change the outcome of a traumatic event or loss (Kübler-Ross, 1969, 1997). This stage is a normal part of the grieving process; the child is not necessarily looking for solutions but rather a means to make sense of their loss. They are negotiating and doing compromise as a way to bring relief or bring closure. It suggests that they are trying to postpone the inevitable, with words such as, "If you let me... then I'll...," "I did do..., so please can I...?"

SUPPORTING "BARGAINING".

Bargaining is about control, or loss of control. Everything is in negotiation because the child or young person is reaching out to us and trying to be on top of things. We need to:

- be present and listen,
- ensure our negotiation is *non-judgemental and cheerful*,
- check any promise we make is *realistic and achievable.* A pupil may plead, "Can I? Yes, or no?" but we do not have to decide immediately; it is alright to say, "I need to think/talk to/ check," before committing to a promise we cannot carry through.

Bargaining is closely linked to *regaining control*, by trying to make sense of a "purpose" or "greater reason" behind it. The survivor therefore tries to do something good because of the "burden of guilt" (Lifton, 1967, in Horowitz, 2011, p. 53) at having survived, or to gain the sense that the loss was not in vain, but rather "something good came out of it," even if that "something" is *lessons learnt.*

Guilt can also arise because, when needed, the young person felt they "*did not do enough*" or "*were not there at the time*" or "*got off lightly, when others did not.*" They were not in control of the situation and now need to feel as if they are. Guilt can lead to action as an attempt to regain lost control.

Guilt can be strongly linked to shame, and children or young people may feel bad for how they reacted (or how they did not react) during a traumatic event, whether it was to placate someone or survive an atrocity (Van der Kolk, 2015). Feeling they should *act out, retaliate* or *cause harm* can lead to later guilt about their *hostile impulses*, even years after the event. Additionally, the recent trauma may trigger feelings from a previous trauma as the child intrinsically makes an association with past events.

Conversely *guilt*, from feeling ambivalent or simply accepting the trauma, can occur. Not blaming anyone but putting it down to "just an accident" can be a coping mechanism. Every situation is unique, everyone's feelings are personal to themselves and are shaped by their past experiences, personality and upbringing. There is no "right" or "wrong" reaction, although sometimes a surface-level calmness and lack of emotion may be due to supressing the honest and real feelings, as these can simply be too much to bear. Two extremes of this are being completely *emotionally overwhelmed* (such as in catatonic state of numbness), compared with the nonchalantly acting *as if nothing has happened (if closed off from the trauma they do not have to face their grief or loss).* The latter is part of a dissociative process, as if the grieving child is saying, "if I feel nothing, then nothing has taken place." It appears as *apathy* yet is acting as an invisible barrier between the traumatic event and the young person themselves (Horowitz, 2011). Often this barrier gives way (with time), to reveal a child who may feel despair, helplessness or depression mingled with guilt and shame; then they may blame themselves and think that they "should have done x to save him," or "I should have helped," or even, "I am responsible, because if I had/hadn't done x then this would not have happened." As with all extremes of emotion, it requires sensitive *support*.

C. Practical *support* for GUILT and *support* for BARGAINING.

1.	Negotiation should be non-judgemental and cheerful.
2.	Promises made should be realistic and achievable.
3.	Avoid dismissing or minimising their emotions. Reduce feelings of guilt and self-blame.
4.	Validate their feelings. Encourage them to talk.
5.	*Don't "guilt trip" or tell them that "they're lucky" or to "count their blessings."*
6.	Seek professional help – grief counselling.
7.	Keep in mind prior factors that may affect strategies – temperament, health, parent's own childhood.
8.	Therapeutic story telling or story telling Apps for children.

1. **Negotiation should be non-judgemental and cheerful.** Maintain calm, consistency; use P.A.C.E. (see F. below).
2. **Promises made should be realistic and achievable.**
   Pause before committing and respond "I need to think/check/talk to" before agreeing to anything.

3. **Avoid dismissing or minimising their emotions.**

   Do not dismiss the depth of guilt, as saying "it's not your fault" or "you'll be alright, don't worry" does not provide reassurance to a young person who is worried and fearful. However, verifying what they are feeling and talking through what will happen next allows the child to express their true emotions. They will feel "heard" and this provides reassurance that the trauma was not their fault; it can help reduce feelings of guilt and self-blame (National Child Traumatic Stress Network, 2023).

4. *Listening, validation and empathy.*

   Listening: Encouraging children to talk about their feelings and concerns

   - provides emotional *support*,
   - helps children process their emotions and
   - works through their feelings of guilt and shame; being ashamed can inhibit children, causing them to "bottle things up" and not talk about them.

   It is important for the adult, parent or teacher, to acknowledge their emotions and let them know that they are *valid* as this can reduce feelings of guilt and shame (study by Cohen et al., 2004).

   Supporting and calming a child during this stage is to provide them with an *empathetic* and non-judgmental listening ear. Encourage the child to talk about their feelings and experiences, but without trying to fix the situation.

5. *Don't "guilt trip" or tell them that "they're lucky".*

   Telling them to "*count their blessings*" or to "*be grateful*" *because they are xyz* offers no consolation and can lead to a pupil thinking that "it happened" because they "did not do X."

   Guilt, a deep-seated emotion that people return to and play through in their heads, is often linked to being ashamed that they survived, weren't there, had it too easy, did not heed the cues, were not vigilant enough or did the wrong thing. Even talking through and apologising to a deceased friend/family member can *support* a young person – the apology or words that need to remain unspoken could be approached by an act such as planting a tree or writing a letter.

6. **Seek professional help – grief counselling.**

   If the symptoms of guilt persist and interfere with daily life, mental health professionals or counsellors can help the children or young people process the trauma, understand their emotions and develop coping strategies. Seek *support* from an appropriate website, charity or agency (downloadable resources).

7. **Keep in mind prior factors that may affect the effectiveness of the strategies.**

   As we read in chapter 6, various prior factors may alter the strategy's effectiveness or present a barrier to be worked around. These include:

   - temperament,
   - environment,
   - physical and mental health,
   - parent's own childhood and
   - cultural beliefs and values.

8. **Therapeutic story telling** (also see chapter 8). Read a children's book together that helps explain trauma, grief or loss to children. Books are also available which show the connection between emotions and bodily sensations. Both these interventions connect emotional and cognitive development (Perrow, 2023; Soboti, 2022). Alternatively, use a story telling App for children (such as "RainbowTales.App").

> See *top five key characteristics and top five support suggestions for "guilt and bargaining"* in end of chapter Summary Table.

D. DEPRESSION

This encompasses feelings of sadness, fear, regret, guilt, shame, hopelessness and helplessness. During any traumatic collective event, as we watch the news or hear stories from close friends, we may feel isolated, insignificant or anxious. Our children and young people may be frozen in activity or have given up, they may have lost trust in others, mistrust their faith or may push others away.

Impacts of depression include either crying whilst talking about the loss and the "hole" that lies ahead (a reactive depression) or a depression with no speaking (but possibly just crying), where there is no energy to even say words out loud; voicing it may be too taxing, or simply too painful. These are "normal" expected reaction to a traumatic event (Horowitz, 2011).

Children who are experiencing depression as a result of grief, trauma or loss may require additional *support* in the classroom, as an individual or within a small group. *Support* for depression requires *validation* and *compassion* – and *acts of care, support and empathy* are needed.

It is hard not to medicalise depression during this stage, and while we should be vigilant in case the child is becoming unwell long-term, we should be mindful that *it is a natural part of grief* (chapter 2).

D. Practical *support* for DEPRESSION.

1.	*Challenge negative thoughts together.*
2.	Use alternative tools for two-way communication.
3.	*Create a safe and supportive environment. Comfy and relaxing.*
4.	Identify and name *who is in their team.* Give hope practically. Let them know that they are not alone.
5.	Encourage child to seek social *support* and *support* systems
6.	Healthy habits: food, *self-care* and connecting with nature.
7.	*Psychoeducation:* educate others about the child's situation, to provide *support* and understanding.
8.	*Make a choice (from pre-prepared personalised list) of an activity or task to lift your mood.*

We can ***verbally give hope:***

1. ***Challenge negative thoughts together.***
   Naming it and speaking words such as "This is the depression taking over your thoughts at the moment, can we *challenge that together*?" validates those feelings and it lets the child know you are alongside them. It challenges those negative thoughts and beliefs that relate to the traumatic event (Cohen et al., 2017).
   Naming it also gives pupils an opportunity to understand why they might be behaving as they are (Bowlby, 1980) and the *challenge* is a proactive response.
2. **Use alternative tools for two-way communication.**
   Children and young people may find expressing themselves easier through tools such as a social story, comic strip conversation, Lego, play, art, journaling, widgits (Widgit Online, 2023), through gesture or via remote communication (e.g., Teams, Google Meet, Zoom). The adult can use similar means to reply.
   Communication tools provide a platform to share thoughts and receive understanding whilst being less invasive than one-to-one interpersonal conversation. A communication tool allows *thinking time*, to express all they are going through. ***Creative media*** can also be shared with more than one adult, should the pupil choose to share.
   Other communication tools which allow the child to identify with circumstance or emotions within text are fiction or non-fiction stories (downloadable resources), figure play, YouTube videos (choose carefully) or podcasts. They can be utilised by school staff to give a child the chance to show their inner turmoil, or for adult supporters to encourage, guide and give hope. Open communication, **active listening** (see above) and providing opportunities help achieve this. Studies have shown that a WhatsApp local or community group can also be a tool for improved communication opportunities (Woodward, 2020).
   For someone with communication or language needs or choosing not to speak, a ***communication keyring*** (downloadable resource) can be created together. This consists of small, laminated cards of symbols or photographs which each depict an emotion, expression, or a short phrase – these can be attached together by means of a hole punch and a keyring clip; using these can help the child convey their emotions, or their needs. A communication mat, in the 'Your Voice, Your Choice' tool, is an alternative method (Bloom et al., 2020).
   If physically apart and using Zoom (or similar), two-way communication can be facilitated through:

   - reading a bedtime story,
   - doing "homework" or journaling together,
   - writing in the chat box,

- playing clapping games – to benefit from the security and *soothing* repetition of rocking and rhythm,
- shared gesture can act as an alternative to direct contact e.g., blowing a kiss, an "air" high-five, fist-bump or placing a hand on your heart and
- techniques to *soothe* and co-regulate – which encourage *self-soothing* and self-regulation can be found in the *soothing* and *self-soothing* table (chapter 6).

3. An important strategy is to **create a *safe and supportive environment***. When they are happy, children feel comfortable discussing their feelings, experiences and expressing their emotions (Rae, 2012). This can be achieved whether it is in person or at a distance. Making time, without distractions are key, whether together or apart.

   A physical safe space, such as a book corner, a time-out space, or a quiet room or corner of the classroom can be made into a relaxing and welcoming place to sit. As previously described with the *SOS bag*, a portable blanket can be laid down to create the child's own safe and personal space wherever they are. When a child is agitated, it can indicate aggression and therefore entering their personal space might escalate the situation. When the pupil is calmer, entering their personal space can be useful to move forward or refocus on a task when the situation allows.

We can ***give hope in a practical way***:

4. **We can identify and name *who is in their team*** and therefore who can provide emotional, social, practical and financial *support*.

   The young person may be able to suggest people and think of some far and wide. It is important they know that they cannot get well alone, *they need people*. Practically, draw a picture of "their team," all the people together who they can call on for *support*. Often it is asking for help that is the hardest, but if known people are named, and those adults are committed, this gives the child or young person the permission to approach them when they need it. Team members could include parents/carers, relatives, close friends, school-staff, a counsellor or mental health professional from CAMHS (Child and Adolescent Mental Health Service), any social worker or health visitor or a doctor (see "My Team" template, downloadable resources). Providing emotional *support* to the child lets them know that they are not alone (Cohen et al., 2017).

   Encourage the pupil to seek social *support* from friends and family, or to consider joining a *support* group (Cohen et al., 2017). Alternatively, focus on the child's strengths, hobbies and interests, to provide social activities they would enjoy. Opportunities to interact, develop and maintain positive relationships (Joshi, 2022) can be sociable and fun!

5. **Healthy habits: food, *self-care* and connecting with nature.**

   Encourage healthy habits and *support* the child to engage in exercise, healthy eating and a good sleep pattern. Likewise, address any physical needs too such as sleep disturbances or changes in appetite; the benefits of getting a good night's sleep cannot be underestimated. A sleep tracker book or phone App may help identify areas where changes in a routine could improve healthy habits.

   Depression affects the brain, memory and concentration, so low mood and low activity are expected during the depression phrase. We may need to **suggest *self-care*** such as "Are you going to do your nails? Have a bath?"

   To aid relaxation, to help a child manage their feelings, a walk or connecting with nature can offer much needed "time-out" to assimilate their emotions without having too many demands placed on them. Mindfulness activities (being present and using their five main senses to notice the world around) and connecting with nature can change their physiology positively towards an upward emotional spiral (Segal, et al., 2013) (template – downloadable resources, healthy sleep routine).

6. ***Offer psychoeducation.***

   Educating other teachers, staff and classmates about the child's situation and how they can provide *support* and understanding can be achieved through training, books, websites and resources (see downloadable resources). Similarly, providing psychoeducation to the child and their family about depression (and anxiety), as a normal reaction to trauma, can encourage compassionate responses. It is hard not to medicalise depression during this stage, and while we should be vigilant in case the child is becoming unwell, we should be mindful that it is a *natural part of the grief process*.

7. **Prepare a box or a list of favourite activities.**

   Engaging in a chosen, preferred activity can offer an emotional lift or provide a distraction to help with emotional regulation. Since the activities will be the child's or young person's choice, this encourages a sense of regaining control. Familiar favourite activities give a sense of order, security and normalcy too.

An activity list or activity "**happy box**" may include:

- a small ball or skipping rope,
- colouring, doodling or journaling,
- some new stationary or felt pens,
- board games,
- a favourite book or comic,
- small toys, cars, figures, Lego or cuddly toy, for example,
- music to listen to – this can be a great *soother* and designed by the child (it makes a great, purposeful activity), and
- small items for *self-care*: i.e., hairbrush, hair bobbles, ribbon or nail varnish.

See *top five key characteristics and top five support suggestions for* "depression" *in end of chapter Summary Table*.

E. ANXIETY

There are numerous strategies that can be used for anxiety, but these interventions below can make a big difference. In my experience of teaching pupils with Social, Emotional and Mental Health (SEMH) difficulties, those with a diagnosis for anxiety had some general similarities in that they:

- Frequently catastrophised ("this will go bad," "that noise means someone will hurt me," "anything could happen next") and engaged perpetually in "negative self-talk" which begins the route to a "panic attack." Re-framing is a key intervention (see below).
- Experienced panic attacks. Changing their physiology to trick the body (and brain) into thinking things are alright can be done using breathing and body relaxation techniques (Table 8.2).
- Could not cope well with unplanned changes, whether this is change of a routine, family eatery visit, timetable, teacher or other changes at home or in the school day. The child or young person uses all their energy to cope with their heightened awareness and vigilance in the threatening situation (to maintain homeostasis, described in chapter 4), therefore coping with additional, unplanned changes gives them something else to think and genuinely worry about.
- Cannot think clearly so are largely unable to reason, compute knowledge or learn (chapter 4) (Bloom et al., 2020). Their cognitive functioning is low; therefore, occupying their brain and body with an activity beneficially engages them; giving "time-out" from their cycle of negative thinking can help neutralise their extreme anxiety.
- Often feel completely exhausted from being nervous, anxious or stressed.

The premise for these understandable reactions is that after experiencing a stressful event, or preceding a known anxiety-inducing event, there are typically three reasons to *think, feel, communicate or act*. These reasons are:

1. to *understand stimuli and plan* responses ("What was that noise?" "Who is that?" "What should I do next?"),
2. to *restore personal* safety and to feel and share *positive social emotions* ("I didn't feel safe, I told the group, gained positive affirmation and felt safer, then we all had a good time together."),
3. to self-regulate to return to *feeling capable* with their *emotions* (e.g., fear, shame, joy, melt-down, detachment, spiralling), *cognitions* (e.g., remembering, planning, concentrating on a task), and *perceptions* (your intuitive sense of a situation) or *thoughts* (thinking about, daydreaming, opinions or views).

The most important aspect in the below triangle is the summit, that is *reviewing the stimuli* (the cause of the emotional state) and evaluating to plan and take action (Figure 7.1). This sequence (more fully described in the neuroscience chapter, chapter 4) involves the child or young person being aware of cues from the environment (exteroception) and cues from their bodily responses

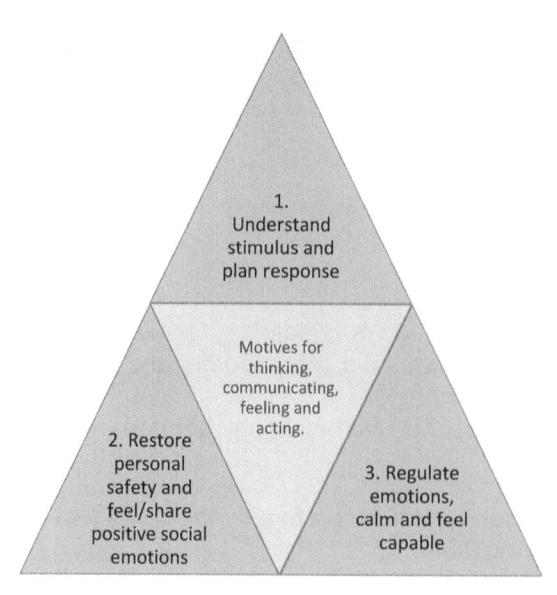

Figure 7.1 An illustration to depict the three reasons for the personal actions taken after a traumatic event (Taylor, 2023).

(interoception) in order to decide whether there is a threat and, if so, the best ways of coping; this evaluation leads to the emotion (such as fear, joy, anger, anxiety). This process may involve a slower, thoughtful, cognitive reflection or may rapidly engage the threat-detection system to give a *fight-flight-fawn-freeze-flop-flock response*, depending on the nature of any threat. The *emotion* is the result of what the brain perceived cognitively (Barrett, 2021) and the emotion, the anxiety, is the *incentive* to respond to any threat.

The anxiety causes heightened alertness; the child or young person feels the need for extra vigilance. Cues may be *accurate* or may be *misinterpreted*, but in school a pupil would have increased fear and, potentially, unjustified "startle" reactions and may be "jumpy." "**SOOTH-ING**" strategies, from the previous chapter, can be applied to the second part of the triangle to help achieve *positive social emotions*. However, a balance is needed by the adult when responding and *"soothing"* – if a child requires excessive reassurance or excessive security in "attachment," the young person may misinterpret this as being completely reassured and therefore complacent; this maladaptive form of coping can lead to other states caused by grief and loss, such as being in denial, numb or removing themselves from reality (Horowitz, 2011) due to a lack of awareness or understanding i.e., "being lulled into a false sense of security."

E. Practical *support* for ANXIETY: in addition to the strategies for depression above.

1.	*Breathing exercises. Teach relaxation techniques.*
2.	*Engage in physical (whole body movement) activity.*
3.	*Coping with unplanned daily change – adult start of day meet.*
4.	*Sleep routine: support family guidance.*
5.	*Construct and encourage use of a memory box.*
6.	*Adapt: adapt the day, routine or school timetable for a personalised approach.*
7.	*Grounding/mindfulness examples.*
8.	*Re-framing negative thinking – use stages.*

1. ***Teach relaxation*** techniques and breathing exercises.

    Relaxation techniques, such as deep breathing (the visual image of triangle breathing, or mountain breathing, works well), as does progressive muscle relaxation (tighten and squeeze every muscle in turn in the body and gradually loosen them one by one). This also helps physical symptoms and tension that exist due to anxiety (see Table 8.2, chapter 8 and resources template in the downloadable resources).

2. ***Engage in activity.***

    Encourage engagement in a simple ball-throwing game or other physical activity, as this has been shown to reduce symptoms of anxiety (Joshi, 2022). Alternatively, blowing bubbles, building with Lego, a board game, hands-on task (sorting pencil pots or washing up after art, for example) or craft activity can occupy the child's thoughts and help them enjoy momentary relief from a pattern of anxious thinking and its associated symptoms.

3. ***Adult one-to-one meet at start of day: coping with unplanned daily change.***

    A start of day check-in with a known, named trusted adult gives opportunity to be greeted by a valued familiar face, thus lessening any brewing anxiety. It is a key time to discuss any known changes to the day, to prevent the pupil being surprised by unexpected alterations to their expected schedule, teacher or timetable.

4. ***Sleep routine.***

    Anxious children often have trouble getting to sleep; sleep disturbance or nightmares may exacerbate their anxiety. *Support* to improve it may involve a physical change to their room or sleep pattern, or adult advice (friend, family, doctor or other professional). The family may need *support* to adjust their child's bedtime routine. A young person may benefit from guidance on bedtime healthy habits. A frequent suggestion is to avoid technology for at least 30–60 minutes before going to sleep. Some young people find the silence difficult and enjoy quiet background music, a radio on or other noise such as "white noise" or mindful sounds (whale song and seaside sounds, for example).

    The environment can be adjusted to give some light, depending on preferences. The "intrusive thoughts, dreams or nightmares" safety plan can sit by a bedside, along with objects that offer comfort. A cuddly toy or blanket to snuggle or pull tight can also help the physiology to encourage relaxation.

    A familiar and regular routine, such as bath-time and a story, offers reassurance and builds expectations of an approaching bedtime. However, flexibility on special occasions or holidays can acknowledge these treat times and the expectation that the school term will see a return to a predictable evening routine.

    For further advice, the group "Sleep Support" (2023) offers help.

5. ***A memory box* or a happy bag.**

    Fill a small box or bag with photographs, objects, images and items which bring a happy memory, representations of safety (i.e., security blanket or cuddly toy) or something that links with a joyous event in some way.

6. ***Adapt***.

    Adapt the day, routine or school timetable to offer a personalised approach to meeting needs and alleviating stress and worry. Structured routine gives the pupil the security of an expected framework, however, flexibility is also needed; it is not a case of *one size fits all* and just because something *has always been done like this* does not mean that it *always has to be done like this*.

    A shortened school day, a bespoke timetable or activities such as animal therapy or extra physical activities may help move the child(ren) through a difficult experience. One pupil's favourite lesson may be another pupil's worst fear. It helps to talk to and ask the child. Having a voice and being heard can make a difficult day more bearable.

7. ***Grounding/mindfulness.***

    Obsessional thinking may become common, so grounding or *distraction* is a good technique (see Table 8.2, chapter 8).

    Children may visit certain websites and this "search history" can help identify what thoughts are pre-occupying them. Thoughts that begin with "I should…," "What if…" may trigger anxiety. Anxiety is a natural response to change and uncertainty, therefore, anxiety is reduced by *predictability* and by *structure* – namely within the classroom environment but balanced by *flexibility* in approach.

8. ***Re-framing negative thinking.***

    Re-framing negative thinking involves shifting the child's perspective and finding alternative, more positive interpretations of situations or thoughts. It is a helpful technique for children or young people who *catastrophise* by imagining the worst-case scenario or for a pupil who has a low self-esteem or always thinks that something bad will happen. Whilst some aspects of their thinking may be realistic at times of a traumatic event, this *support* endeavours to prevent repeated negative cyclical thinking, or children emotionally plummeting in a downward spiral. It is possible to use this with a class, with the case of a collective or group trauma; research provides evidence that active-participation, discussion-based learning techniques (using case study examples) can be more effective for pupil-learning outcomes than seated, class-based taught sessions (Hughes and Schlösser, 2014).

Counselling or Cognitive Behaviour Therapies (CBT) are types of professional-led talking therapies which aim to adjust the child's thinking and challenge negative thoughts and beliefs that relate to the traumatic event (Cohen et al., 2017). CBT techniques can help the child or young person re frame their negative thinking and reduce avoidance behaviours whilst developing coping skills.

Strategies and techniques for *reframing* are:

a. Recognise negative thoughts: encourage the pupil to be aware of their thoughts that are not always facts (Segal et al., 2013). An awareness of their judgements, and observing their own negative thinking patterns, allows the individual to recognise the impact on their emotions and behaviour.

b. Challenge negative thoughts: once negative thinking is identified, its accuracy can be challenged; *support* the pupil in having the power to *choose* how to interpret and question the evidence or beliefs, and therefore they can *choose* how to respond to situations.

c. Be aware of cognitive distortions: these are irrational patterns of thinking such as "all-or-nothing" thinking, overgeneralisation ("it has happened once, it will happen everywhere") or personalisation ("it's my fault, if only I hadn't…" or "if only I had just…").

d. Find evidence that contradicts the negative response: consider possibilities, or past experiences where they overcame challenges (Seligman, 2002). Seek out any positives, no matter how small they may seem. Seek alternative explanations too for their situation as when they see that there are factors which are beyond their control, it can lead to more understanding and less self-blame.

e. Use *cognitive restructuring*: guide the pupil to replace negative thoughts with more positive realistic ones that are more balanced or more empowering (Carr, 2011). This cultivates optimism too. Re-framing with positive affirmations involves consciously choosing to think positively (find the one good thing in the situation) and repeating affirming statements such as "I am capable of handling this" or "I have found out that people are kind and are there for me." This is constructive and moves their thoughts into a more positive light.

f. Practice gratitude: encourage "*an attitude of gratitude*" which could be the basis of a class collage or art wall. A child or young person could keep a journal focusing on the things they appreciate and are grateful for, to combat the negatives and foster a more positive mindset.

g. Encourage positive self-talk: help the young person be aware of their internal dialogue and guide them to replace critical or negative thoughts with positive ones. This can be personalised and could include making a chart or diagram together. Teach them to speak to themselves with kindness and compassion (Neff, 2003; Sammons, 2019).

h. Practice and repetition make this cognitive re-framing a habit that becomes more automatic and ingrained. Children and young people need to monitor their thinking and look out for the negativity that may creep in (they need adult *support* to do so) in order to make adjustments when negative thinking resurfaces and maintain a positive approach (Seligman, 2002).

i. Make an "accurate thinking plan" bespoke for the individual child or young person (downloadable resources) that encourages "helpful thinking" which is realistic and notes possibilities and positive moments. A group or whole class lesson on types of negative thinking, reframing it and using "helpful thinking" can be used to introduce the concept.

j. Make positive interactions possible: a child surrounded by individuals who are a positive influence will experience positive social interactions and healthy relationships which can help counteract negative thinking patterns. The positive aspects of "epistemic trust" are described in the "**STRENGTHEN**" chapter (chapter 8).

k. Seek *support* or professional help: suggest that the person seeks *support* from friends, family or (if negative thinking persists and significantly impacts daily life) professionals such as therapists, counsellors or a mental health professional (NHS, 2023). Sometimes, a fresh perspective can help re frame negative thinking and provide additional tools for managing negative thoughts; a professional can provide specialised techniques tailored to the child's individual needs (more on this in the section below).

Reframing negative thinking is a process that takes time and practice. It is important to approach it with patience and understanding. These stages are not necessarily linear and may overlap or repeat. The process of reframing negative thinking is dynamic and ongoing. Encourage and *support* the young person to be consistent in applying these strategies and remind them that progress may be gradual but achievable with perseverance; self-compassion and positive reminders of progress are key.

> See *top five key characteristics and top five support suggestions* for "anxiety" in end of chapter Summary Table.

Professional help and *support*

The above practical strategies can be effective, yet easy to apply within a school or home-schooling environment. However, some children or young people may need specific professional *support*.

If the pupil's grief reactions persist or intensify over time, if they are significantly impacting their daily functioning or if you think the child or young person has prolonged mental health needs which impact their daily living, consider involving a **mental health professional** who specialises in **grief counselling or trauma and loss;** they can provide specialist *support* for complicated grief, such as ongoing depression, severe anxiety attacks, guilt, anger or suicidal thoughts. Whilst waiting for appointments, a referral to a school counsellor, educational psychologist, Speech, Language and Communication Specialist or other mental health service (or charity) as appropriate. Remember 999 and Emergency Departments (A&E) are there for mental health as well as physical health if an emergency occurs. In education, the document "HM Government (2022): Right Support, Right Place, Right Time" gives guidance. Providing children with appropriate ***counselling and mental health support*** can include individual or group counselling, as well as referral to outside mental health professionals as needed (NHS, 2023; Mind, 2023: Young Minds, 2023).

Trauma-focused therapy

Trauma-focused therapy is an evidence-based treatment that can help children who have experienced trauma; it focuses on helping children process their traumatic experiences. It effectively reduces symptoms of post-traumatic stress disorder, depression and anxiety (Cohen et al., 2004, 2017).

Professional help: for severe, multiple or long-term traumatic response

Although supporting children and young people through severe long-term traumatic responses is usually held within the realms of the specialist, it is being briefly mentioned here to acknowledge that it exists and is often presented by several long-term emotions occurring at once (a "co-morbid condition," or "co-morbidity" and means having a diagnosis for two or more conditions).

Children and young people emerging from a war, a large-scale natural disaster or a unique event (such as 9/11) may have witnessed atrocities and present as having extreme stress, anxiety and depression, coupled with intrusive thoughts, nightmares or sleep disturbances. They may act very sad, angry and despairing; other features may be tension, irritability and/or exhaustion. Some may have delayed reactions or denial.

The level and nature of this impact is dependent upon the child's or young person's personality attributes and whether trauma has been previously experienced. Young people who have encountered a previous trauma have an earlier and greater response than those who have had no previous traumatic experiences (Van der Kolk, 2015). Also, understandably, prolonged exposure to a traumatic experience can deepen the level of response and worsen those associated negative emotions.

The duration and intensity of prolonged, severe stress may bring a life-long change of personality traits, values and ethos. Thus, this impacts their growth and development into adulthood. Even the way they "parent," *support*, relate and discipline may stem from their own experiences. When working with the family of a child who has undergone traumatic stress, it is worth remembering that the parents and carers may have endured insurmountable distress too.

When reactions and responses have not surfaced during the actual traumatic event, it may be due to numbness or denial, or to a "psychic [psychological] closing off" (Lifton, 1967, in Horowitz, 2011) this *dissociative process* is a *defence mechanism*.

During the event, the child may try to carry on as normal, but prolonged exposure to the stressor eventually will lead to a point where the stress is manifested in some way. There can be a delay in symptoms manifesting. An example of a response changing over time could be:

- Denial at first.
- Stress mounts.
- Then later, intrusive symptoms – restlessness, disturbed sleep, feeling sick, a slight hand tremor or shaking, not feeling able to eat, hyper-startled responses ("jumps" easily).
- The need to talk over and over about what happened.
- Unexpected and sudden reminders can spark a hyper-vigilance or a startled response – it can also poke old (dormant) memories and cause.
- Sudden anxiety or a stomach-churning sensation.

This is just an example and not a definitive process.

What do Children and Young People (CYP) struggle with? Managing associated known symptoms

Research (Wray et al., 2023) with children and young people determined that the general reactive symptoms, that impact daily living, that they mostly speak about are:

- A lack of energy and feeling tired and some compared physical activity with being at home.
- Struggling with getting ready in the morning for school was common for many different reasons, including a lack of energy or disorganisation.
- Some school tasks were found to be particularly challenging, especially maths, and could cause great distress.
- Doing things under a time pressure could exacerbate their stress, whether that was related to something routine or more complex situations or issues, such as examinations, homework online with a time limit or making important decisions about their future.
- The challenges associated with feeling different from their classmates were a key theme, with one participant saying it made her feel nervous to do things she struggled with – and another saying she sometimes felt annoyed and upset at being the only pupil with a learning *support* assistant because she could do things on her own and lacked personal space.
- Not wanting to feel different to others, recounting the importance of meeting other children who were similar to themselves was valuable.
- Feeling different and being aware of their limitations appeared to exacerbate feelings of anxiety, with some explaining their concerns about asking for help in front of their peers.
- Moving schools or other big change.
- Teaching assistants were viewed as being largely helpful as they were available, present and there for them; however, children and young people had mixed views about teachers themselves, some were perceived as not interested in helping them, lacking time to help, being insensitive to their needs or as making things worse when trying to help.

These are areas to be aware of as vigilance can negate against these risk factors.

Importantly, **psychological isolation**, *the child or young person not being able to share their experience or feel anyone understands, is a key factor in symptoms continuing.* Remember, everyone's grieving process is unique, and it is essential to approach them with empathy, patience and flexibility. By offering reassurance and normalising their reactions, you can help the pupil navigate their grief and gradually move towards healing and acceptance.

A new reality – or a new version of the previous reality

Children and young people who have experienced a traumatic event not only may require and seek help but may also resent that help, even showing anger towards the source of that help. This is part of them reforming their known life into a new reality. Whether they have experienced grief, loss (in all its forms), change or injury, they will be coming to terms with the traumatic event to understand it; the emotions described in this *support* section are denial, guilt, shame, anger, depression and anxiety which will have decimated their trust in life as they knew it. They need to find meaning in what they have endured, they will want to connect with people, find significance in their life and come-to-terms with the trauma experienced (Horowitz, 2011). Additionally, enduring a trauma or psychological fear, angst or despair is a time of great stress, and stress can bring to the surface certain vulnerabilities or predispositions in personality traits, those close to the child or young person may notice that "they have changed."

A desire to take action

Emerging from the trauma the experience becomes absorbed by our "schema," our personality and our future approaches to the world's concepts. Every experience shapes our children and young people, and therefore new features emerge within their personality and belief systems. This may bring a **desire for action**, since action is about regaining control and can end the feeling of being "under threat." Anger can be channelled into something positive as they want to "do something about it," therefore rage is replaced by a sense of justice.

By considering the neuroscience (chapter 4), successfully "conquering," "overcoming" or "getting even" can reduce the heightened emotional response in the limbic system. Therefore, taking action becomes a new coping skill too; the child or young person has a new reality and may adopt a new identity at home, at school or both. This also helps move the child towards a state of acceptance.

F.   ACCEPTANCE

Trauma is an event or a series of events that overwhelm the child's or young person's ability to cope, and it may leave them feeling helpless, unsafe or powerless. Children can experience trauma in many forms such as physical, emotional and sexual abuse, natural disasters, neglect, accident and violence. Recent world events such as the COVID-19 pandemic, war, displacement or fleeing as a refugee, economic poverty or natural disasters can have long-lasting effects on children's social and cognitive development. The physical, emotional, psychological and social distress it causes impedes wellbeing and instigates emotional reactions. They may feel overwhelmed, anxious, depressed, guilt, shame – all those responses discussed in this chapter. As highlighted, emotional states are individual for each child and young person; there is not a set order to the emotions that they pass through. Strong emotions resulting from grief, loss, bereavement or trauma may be exhibited all at once, they may change throughout a day, an emotion may last for weeks or months or they may bounce between responses regularly (chapter 2).

Due to the nature of trauma, they may *feel*, or may *be*, disconnected from their peers, friends, family and community.

They may take time to reach the "acceptance" stage, and when they do, it may not be permanent. This phase is characterised by the realisation that fighting change is not going to make it go away and is a restoration of equilibrium (Horowitz, 2011) when the pupil accepts and moves on. However, it is a crucial phase in the recovery process where the child is coming to terms with the traumatic event and what has happened, they start to make meaning of it and begin to consider moving forward.

This "acceptance" stage is depicted by calmness; children start to acknowledge the reality of what has happened to them, through this realisation they can begin to process their emotions and thoughts – they realise, they accept and, consequently, calmness brings more possibilities.

Some young people may make the most of the situation and explore these new opportunities. For example, a child displaced and living within a different community or country will discover new experiences and openings, and during the pandemic, many families rapidly became familiar with online communication tools and platforms, and social media.

Acceptance does not mean that the child or young person is over the trauma or that they have forgotten about it, rather, it means that they are no longer in denial and are ready to face the challenges of healing. The child has begun to accept their situation and start to look towards the future (Kübler-Ross, 1969).

Supporting children during this stage involves helping them make ongoing progress towards recovery. These **SUPPORT** strategies are not disruptive and can be used by teachers, parents, carers or the professionals alongside them. Reaching the stage of acceptance potentially may have a massive knock-on-effect for the carer/teacher/parent – but especially the parent. An adult working with a child who has begun to show *acceptance* may experience a strong emotional reaction. Whether that manifests as overwhelming relief, sadness or joy, being emotionally prepared can help mitigate against any negative reactions in the supportive adult. Chapter 9 considers the care for those doing the caring.

SUPPORT during "ACCEPTANCE".

In addition to their range of emotions, children and young people may have questions about the trauma, such as asking why it happened, who was to blame, what will happen next or will it happen again? The children and young people need age/stage-appropriate *support* to help them make sense of their experience, cope with their feelings, understand why they have acted/reacted as they have and rebuild their sense of safety and trust.

There are many ways to help with this, many have been briefly covered in the *Support* sections above but will be included and developed here to bring cohesion.

F. Practical *support* at the "ACCEPTANCE" stage.

1.	Foster positive, supportive relationships and community connections.
2.	Offer ongoing emotional *support* and validation.
3.	Build trust, relationship and connection – by using "P.A.C.E." (Hughes, 2006).
4.	Create a sense of normality.
5.	Teach coping skills and ability to make self-judgements (resilience).
6.	*Support* and encourage new opportunities – hand holding until they can run.
7.	Provide appropriate material.
8.	Cognitive and emotional development – e.g., therapeutic story writing.

1. **Foster positive, supportive relationships and community connections.**

    A strong *support* system, that includes positive role models, is crucial for children who have experienced trauma for them to gain *support*, guidance and better, long-term, mental health outcomes (Levine and Kline, 2006). Children feeling heard and validated by the adults in their lives helps children feel *safe and secure and* more comfortable exploring their feelings and thoughts about the traumatic event (National Child Traumatic Stress Network, 2023). Research shows these positive relationships build resilience and coping skills (Bretherton and Oppenheim, 2003; Tang et al., 2018). In-school connections are usually among the strongest relationships outside a child's own family; these, plus an accepting environment developed on nurture principles (NurtureUk, 2023; Rae, 2012) contribute to a powerful school community which can influence for the good.

    If children have lost *community* or find connections difficult to make, explore *children and family community resources*, such as *support* groups or counselling services, to help children develop coping skills, or see D.4 above. Providing a sense of belonging and security help rebuild a sense of safety and trust (National Child Traumatic Stress Network, 2023). This *rebuilding* is more likely to be successful if geared towards the child's strengths (such as a musical talent), interests (such as a football or dance club) or needs (for example, young people moving to the UK from war-torn Ukraine were offered opportunities to meet other Ukraine nationals who were in the same position); these offer opportunities for the child to participate in social activities and positive interactions with like-minded peers (Joshi, 2022).

2. **Offer ongoing emotional *support* and validation** as the child moves through the *acceptance stage* and beyond.

    Help the child develop skills for effective **communication** and problem solving to improve their relationships and sense of competence in navigating life's challenges. Educating other teachers, staff and classmates about the child's situation improves their understanding to make tailored emotional *support* possible (Parkes, 2001). It may be appropriate to use resources suggested in (8) below.

    Children in an "acceptance phase," now in a place where they can engage cognitively and discuss their circumstance, need their feelings listened to and **validated**. Validation involves acknowledging and accepting a person's thoughts, feelings and behaviours as understandable and justifiable, given their unique experiences and circumstances (Perry and Szalavitz, 2017). Even if these feelings are difficult or uncomfortable, it is essential the adult does not display "shock," "disapproval" or "criticism," as casting judgement could break the relationship or induce shame or self-blame. Adults should reassure children that it is normal to have mixed emotions after a traumatic event and that they are not alone. An empathetic, non-judgemental listening ear encourages the child to express themselves; feeling heard and understood builds open communication and trust; it creates an emotionally safe environment. Trust is strengthened by the adult continuing to be aware of the **child's specific needs and triggers** and providing them with accommodations as necessary.

3. **Build trust, relationship and connection: P.A.C.E.**

   Children are not born with the ability to regulate their emotions; through their relationships and interactions, they are nurtured and learn how to respond (Geddes, 2006). For adults to model positive relationship attitudes/actions, they need to:

   - show unconditional care and acceptance,
   - show genuine interest in pupils' lives and interests/passions and
   - "notice," "hold-in-mind" and remember things the pupils have told them or done well at; recall and chat about these at a later date.

   Healthy relationships help children explore, understand, recover, grow and heal from trauma. A central idea to these relationships is "**P.A.C.E.**" (Hughes, 2006): **P**layfulness, **A**cceptance, **C**uriosity and **E**mpathy.

   P.A.C.E. nurtures *attunement*, *regulation* and a *secure attachment*; its aim is to help staff engage with children and young people who have suffered trauma, grief or loss, to build trust.

P – PLAYFULNESS.

Laughing and having fun together help us feel more connected and facilitate learning. Create a positive, shared, fun experience and a feeling of lightness by original or innovative lesson approaches, and by having time for relationship and joy within that connection. Ending a lesson or a school day happily can bring this shared feeling too. Look for opportunities to make an activity (game, quiz, task, lesson, topic, school visit) enjoyable. A playful approach can build relationship without personal space being invaded; it allows closeness but without feeling too intense. A child in trauma may find affection uncomfortable, yet a "playful" approach can help children feel more open as it feels safe and relaxed but does not include making a judgment nor being criticised.

When children experience these positive emotions, they can become dysregulated and then miss out on the opportunities for a happier time; regulating positive emotions is just as hard for them as regulating shame, anxiety or guilt, for example; they all can feel uncomfortable (Alexander, 2019). It may take a while to develop these relationships, but when children smile, laugh or giggle, they become less withdrawn and more responsive. Humour can diffuse a difficult situation; Ideas are:

- *Engage in activities and games together – physical games (ball throwing), jigsaws or board games.*
- *Play games which build to an exciting finish.*
- *Warm and personalised greetings.*
- *Show that you are interested in and delighted by what the child is doing.*
- *Find moments for silliness.*
- *Incorporate rhythmic actions into teaching.*
- *Defuse stressful demands.*

A – ACCEPTANCE.

Actively communicate to the pupil that their views and behaviours are accepted, as are their wishes, feelings, urges, motives and perceptions that are behind their outward behaviour. This behaviour is an attempt to communicate their depth and strength of emotion.

It is about accepting, without judgment or evaluation, their inner life, thoughts and compulsions. There is no *right* or *wrong* to these.

Differentiate between behaviour and the child themselves. Always check your verbal, paralinguistic and non-verbal behaviour to ensure you convey acceptance.

Example: Situation: We could have a child lashing out at a friend. You're aware that they had a falling out recently.

- Before we talk about how inappropriate the behaviour was, we can say, "*I know you were angry about what he said last time, but lashing out can hurt people. Let's try talking to him about it.*" Accepting the emotion behind the action reduces the potential for shame and helps the child to be more able and willing to change their behaviour.

ACCEPTANCE WITH LIMITS is crucial in a school setting. Example phrases are (Alexander, 2019, p. 204):

- *"Not helpful, kiddo, and I still care about you."*
- *"I'm here for you, and we need to work out what just happened."*
- *"That's not how we treat one another here; let's figure this out together."*
- *"I can like you a lot and not like something you did."*
- *"We all make mistakes; this one doesn't make you a bad kid."*

BUMPING INTO BOUNDARIES IN RELATIONSHIPS helps children feel safe. Our teenagers need to feel and know parameters (chapter 4) as bouncing against these rules or boundaries helps develop their coping skills and navigate life. Hence, any negative, natural or logical consequences help them learn information for future decision-making. Making choices that we do not want them to make is an important learning opportunity. Allowing them chance to make decisions for themselves builds their coping-mechanisms and life-skills; they will learn from the outcomes. It is important not to get angry when they break the rules or push boundaries – this is all part of "learning." Importantly, the most important thing they can learn is that they are safe and *accepted* in their relationship with us.

C – CURIOSITY.

Curiosity, without judgment, is about us wondering *why* a pupil acted as they did, *what* they feel, *what* is the meaning behind their behaviour. It is our curiosity about "what makes them tick," asking and chatting about why they acted/reacted as they did and working through it together. It is *how* we help children and young people understand themselves, become aware of their inner life, reflect upon the reasons for their behaviour, and (if needed) communicate it to them and, subsequently, help them to communicate it to others (i.e., parents, counsellor or psychiatrist). Curiosity lets the child know that the adults understand.

Children often know their behaviour was inappropriate but do not know why they did it or are reluctant to tell adults why. With curiosity, the adults are conveying their intention to simply *understand why* (not lecture) and to help the child with understanding, to help them heal and change after trauma or loss.

Examples:

- *"What do you think was going on? What do you think that was about?"* or
- *"I wonder what…?"* (Said out loud, without anticipating an answer or response from a child). This is different from asking the child, *"Why did you do that?"* with the expectation of a reply. It is not interpretation or fact gathering. It's just about getting to know the child and letting them know that.
- It could involve making a guess out loud about what a child may be thinking and feeling, as if having a non-threatening conversation with yourself, with the child in the room.
- "Help me understand what happened; can you start at the beginning?"
- "I'm listening; tell me more."
- "What were you feeling then/now?"

Curiosity prevents an adult being frustrated or assuming a young person had bad intentions. It allows an openness in conversation that may help the pupil reflect further to discover the thought, feeling, perception or motive that was stressful, frightening or confusing that caused their behavioural reaction.

Even when we have no idea why a child is behaving in a particular way, curiosity gives the child an invitation to talk about it and validates the thoughts and feelings underlying their behaviour.

E – EMPATHY.

After the pupil has voiced their inner life, we can show empathy by imagining what it felt like to be them. Empathy demonstrates compassion, helps them feel understood, which again promotes regulation and connection; the adult proves they will not "shy away" when emotions run high, or the relationship has hit a tricky point.

The adult is demonstrating that they know how difficult the experience was for the child and that they will not have to deal with the distress alone. Knowing that they have *support* and have someone who is "there for them" communicates strength of relationship, love, commitment and can give confidence that they will not be abandoned at a time when they most need *support*. It can be hard to accept *support* if we feel that our distress is too much for the other person; hence, going through this together can *strengthen* the relationship, it can give a deeper emotional connection. The teacher is showing that they also connect to the emotions behind the behaviour.

Examples

We need to communicate empathy with our eyes, our facial expression and our tone of voice. When the child is visibly upset or angry, we can emphasise certain parts of our statement and match the emotional expression.

- *"Wow this is really hard for you right now."*
- *"I noticed your expression; did I worry you when...."*
- *"This is really bothering you SO much."*
- *"You are SO upset about this! This is REALLY tough."*
- *"You seem really worried about this."*
- *"I can see that you're angry at the moment."*
- *"I think that trying this is a bit scary for you."*
- We can follow up with more elaborate statements which wonder about the connections between the feeling and a specific situation. This mixes in the C of PACE – Curiosity.
- *"It hurt so much when she didn't ask you to play. You were probably thinking 'Why did she do that?' It was a real shock for you."*
- *"You wanted to have another turn so badly. You were so excited about it and it's so unfair that we ran out of time."*
- *"It seems to you like he hates you. That must be really hard. I know you like him a lot, so this is pretty confusing."*

Using P.A.C.E.

It should be noted that a *playful* approach is likely to be the last part of the P.A.C.E. acronym that we apply when we are first building a relationship with the child who has experienced trauma as they will need our *Acceptance*, *Curiosity* and *Empathy* far more in the early days. However, *playfulness* is crucial for showing that there is room for fun and relaxing interactions, despite the difficult moments.

P.A.C.E. focuses on the whole child, not simply the behaviour, to help pupils feel secure with the adults and reflect upon themselves, their thoughts, feelings and behaviour, building the skills that are needed for maintaining a satisfying life, developing self-belief and resilience.

For adults, using P.A.C.E. can help reduce the level of conflict, defensiveness and withdrawal that tends to be ever present in the lives of troubled children. Using PACE enables the adult to see the strengths and positive features that lie underneath more negative and/or challenging behaviour.

Generally, practically what we can do:

- Being louder about celebrating small successes – in class, vocally or with a reward system. Or, as a teacher, phone home to give praise; this builds a positive home-school relationship too!
- Using a journal/planner to record successes, personal beliefs or new skills.
- Reviewing school-based strategies or routines for the child – is this still working/does this still need to be there? Do their personalised interventions or *"support* plan" need to change?
- Record and celebrate. Use: pictures, displays, school newsletter, letter or phone call home (for the good things only).

4. **Create a sense of normality.**

    After experiencing trauma, children may struggle to return to their normal routines and activities. Promoting a sense of normalcy can help children feel more comfortable and secure, regain confidence and restore their sense of control. Encourage children to engage in activities they enjoyed before the traumatic event, such as sports, hobbies or spending time with friends; opportunities for social interaction and peer *support* help children feel less isolated and increase their sense of belonging (National Child Traumatic Stress Network, 2023).

Part of providing a sense of normalcy is routine and emphasising the importance of *self-care* (see *SELF-CARE*, chapter 9).

5. **Teach coping skills and ability to make self-judgements.**

    Coping skills and resilience can be gained by increasing children's independence. *Support* children and adolescents in their choices - but allowing them to make their own decisions (and cope with the consequences) teaches a child to make judgements. School-based informal "resilience" groups can follow a programme to actively develop this skill too.

To *support* a healthy wellbeing and help children and young people feel empowered:

- *Support* them to judge when to use, for example: time-out, relaxation, breathing exercises, mindfulness and grounding, to help manage any residual symptoms of trauma (see Table 8.2).
- Encourage children to set and work towards **achievable goals**, to build a sense of agency and accomplishment.
- Provide opportunities for the child to feel empowered and in control of their own life, such as allowing them to make decisions about their own treatment or therapy. This can help restore their self-esteem.
- Help the child build a sense of hope and optimism for the future, by focusing on their goals and aspirations, and encouraging them to develop plans for achieving them.
- Focusing on any **personal growth or newfound strength** can help the child develop coping skills.

6. **New opportunities: hand holding until they can walk and run, small steps.**
   Acceptance brings more peace and with it comes the ability to undergo challenge; hence, new opportunities may be explored. With the case of the COVID-19 pandemic, "new" activities such an online lessons or dance classes, home-schooling, the use of the TikTok app or teaching older relatives to "Zoom" call have all encouraged *participation and challenge*.
   Viewing a video (that we have specifically made to explain changes or times of transition) can also *aid adaptation* – for example, for a return to a school, but not as we know it!

7. **Appropriate material**
   Children will have questions about the trauma and need age-appropriate information to help them understand what has happened. Adults can provide clear and concise explanations that are tailored to the child(ren)'s developmental level and language skills. Too much information or graphic details can overwhelm or frighten the child or young person; it is important, however, for it be factually accurate to counteract any scaremongering that has existed through social media or among their peers. Age-appropriate books, videos, websites or other resources can help explain the trauma in a way that is accessible and engaging for the child (see downloadable resources).
   Providing education and information about the traumatic event can help children understand what happened to "get their head around it" and reduce their anxiety and fear. Education and information can explain the cause and effects of the traumatic event, discuss coping strategies and provide resources for mental health *support*. This assists young people make sense of what happened, feel more in control and reduces their risk of developing long-term mental health difficulties (Furr et al., 2010).

8. **Cognitive and emotional development: therapeutic story writing.**
   This intervention improves both academic achievement and wellbeing. It is an intervention that can improve the pupils' chances of success by addressing their emotional needs whilst developing their cognitive needs.
   A small group (four to six children) meet weekly for an hour, for ten weeks to write stories inspired by an "opener" supplied by the Therapeutic Story writing Group.

Each session begins with a mindfulness moment and a feelings check-in for children and adults. Then one pupil's story from the previous session is read and a new story opener is given – typically a phrase or a sentence. Then the children and the teacher/practitioner write a story, share their stories and draw pictures. The session ends with a mime game.

(Holmes, 2022)

Teachers and educators gain insight into the relationship between characters in the story and prevalent emotions; the story may be used as a metaphor for what the pupils are experiencing. This helps children process their emotions, expand their emotional vocabulary, and this, in turn, helps them communicate their feelings, be better understood and feel less frustrated. The pupils can project their concerns and fears onto the characters and work through their feelings, within a relatively (physically and emotionally) safe environment. The research highlights evidence of the benefits, with the children describing their experiences positively and enthusiastically (Centre for Therapeutic Storywriting, 2023).

Individual circumstances and responses

The strategies described in this "Acceptance" section can help children feel safe and secure, process their traumatic experiences and improve their mental health outcomes. Pupils who find it impossible to engage in such activities may not be at this "acceptance" stage of the grief cycle; likewise, pupils may flit between the emotions described in sections A–F. Differences in life-situations and traumatic experiences may help explain the wide variety of reactions and responses to the little things that happen in everyday life.

> See *top five key characteristics and top five SUPPORT suggestions for "acceptance"* in end of chapter Summary Table.

Conclusion

This chapter has described responses in children that are triggered by traumatic events. Trauma can be a difficult experience for children and young people to process, particularly when it involves grief, loss and other significant changes. However, with the right *support*, children can begin to come to terms with their trauma, accept it and move forward with their lives, with their new adapted belief systems in place.

Serious life events have shattered their world, as they knew it. *Support* enables the child to acclimatise to a new way of living and integrate the experience into their schema (their knowledge of how the world is made up). Essential to any *support* is a relationship that is safe, secure and supportive. The processes and interventions that aid the recovery process and help the new information be internalised and processed realistically are discussed in the next chapter, *"STRENGTHEN" (chapter 8).*

Summary

	• *Top tips for "SUPPORT" technique (chapter 7)*
1.	The key approach – that underpins all *SUPPORT* strategies. • Maintain your own adult self-regulation (see chapter 5) to present a controlled, approachable self. • Be tuned into trauma – even on the good days! Be vigilant in spotting early cues of distress and remember what worked well previously. • Create a positive and supportive home and/or classroom environment, with bespoke interventions, where children feel safe and valued.
2.	Other key means of practical *support*: • Use a search engine to discover age-appropriate resources that fit with the current situation. • Contact families who have experienced a trauma, to acknowledge their loss and to express *support*. • Intervene as appropriate and help them practice, to develop their resilience. This also helps children learn to cope when the teacher, parent or carer are not present. • Utilise other community *support* (or national *support*) mechanisms as appropriate. • Set up channels for communication – to share news, gain updated information and feel a sense of belonging. • Prepare children and young people for any practice or real government national text message. • Gather the "survivors" views of their needs. This may change throughout time.
3.	*Support for shock and denial (also called "numbing" or "avoidance").* Top five key characteristics and top five *support* suggestions for "shock and denial."

Common characteristics	Key support suggestions
Acts "numb," as if emotionless – acting as if *nothing has happened.*	Offer reassurance that emotions are expected ones, and they are now safe/out of danger.
Has intrusive thoughts, dreams or "flashbacks."	*Develop a safety plan for intrusive thoughts, etc.*
Use of defence mechanisms; talk of "the good old days."	Name emotions (use visual resources) and describe what is happening to them. Educate.
Personality changes that are "out of character."	*Be present and listen empathetically.*
Talking about the event often (to process it).	*Support* an urgent need to complete a task.

4.	*Support* for anger, and distress – which can include separation anxiety. Top five key characteristics and top five *support* suggestions for "anger and distress."

Common characteristics	Key support suggestions
Anger, tantrums or "it's not fair."	Pick up on early warning signs and know triggers. Check "search history" – identify pre-occupying thoughts. Distraction limits obsessional thinking and engages in an activity to bring a natural break.
Being angry with themselves or others.	Visually explain anger and use regulation activities. Creative ways to express emotions.
Persistently seeking information (off news, internet, friends or messaging) – as a means of regaining control.	Reduce sensory overload: weighted blankets, safe space, relaxation techniques. Change their physiology: breathing and *soothing* techniques.
Guilt. Blaming everyone, blaming themselves.	Model calm behaviour and a calm choice, and mirror what to do. Co-regulate to self-regulate.
Obsessional thinking (I should, what if). Joins group action or peaceful protest.	Meet a named adult at start of day to identify any likely trigger points in the day.

5.	*Support* for bargaining: guilt and shame. Top five key characteristics and top five support suggestions for "guilt and bargaining."

Common characteristics	*Key support suggestions*
Trying to be in control. "Can I, yes, or no?"	Be present and listen. Maintain calm consistency.
Negotiating: "If you let me…, then I'll…." "I did do…., so please can I…?"	Negotiation should be non-judgemental and cheerful.
Guilt from not doing enough or acting/reacting as they did at the time. Shame can be closely linked to this.	Promises made should be realistic and achievable. Pause before committing, "I need to think/check/talk to."
Closing themselves off from the trauma shows as "apathy."	Avoid dismissing their emotions. Validate and be empathetic. Do not guilt trip them.
Association with past events.	Use therapeutic story telling or grief counselling as *support* systems.

6.	*Support* for depression – top five key characteristics and top five *support* suggestions for "depression."

Common characteristics	*Key support suggestions*
Sadness, hopelessness, helplessness, low activity or frozen in activity.	Encourage healthy habits (food, walking). Suggest *self-care* such as "Are you going to do your nails? Have a bath?"
Given up. Feels hopeless and helpless.	"This is the depression taking over your thoughts, can we…challenge that together?"
Guilt or shame. Fear, regret.	Verbally and practically give hope. We can identify and name who is in their team and therefore who can provide emotional, social, practical and financial *support.* Name "who is in their team." They need people.
Isolated, alone, lonely, lost faith in others. Feels insignificant, anxious	Create a "happy box" together of favoured activities.
Crying and talking or crying/distraught silently.	Encourage social *support* opportunities. Use two-way communication tools creatively if physically apart.

7	*Support* for anxiety – top five key characteristics and top five *support* suggestions for "anxiety."	
	Common characteristics	*Key support suggestions*
	Frequently catastrophises – "this will go badly."	Breathing exercises to regulate physiology.
	Does not cope well with unplanned change – gets anxious and hyper-vigilant.	Adult start-of-day meet to cope with unplanned change.
	Body tension, breathing, face changes to fear.	Create a memory box or a "happy bag."
	They cannot think clearly, reason or learn.	Use grounding, mindfulness or relaxation.
	Often feel completely exhausted from anxiety.	Reframing negative thinking.
8	*Support* during acceptance – top five key characteristics and top five *support* suggestions for "acceptance."	
	Common characteristics	*Key support suggestions*
	More peace, and calmer in nature.	Build trust, relationship and community connections.
	Acknowledges the reality of the situation.	Create a sense of normalcy and develop child's ability to make self-judgements and decisions.
	Makes ongoing progress towards recovery.	Encourage take up of new opportunities.
	Ready to face the challenge of healing.	Set up a therapeutic story writing group.
	Open to new possibilities and ready to take new opportunities.	Appropriately use the P.A.C.E.and all its component parts (Hughes, 2006): **P**layfulness, **A**cceptance, **C**uriosity and **E**mpathy.

8 *STRENGTHEN*

Reconstructing emotions and hopes for the future

Chapter overview

- The previous chapter described **SUPPORT** strategies relevant to all emotions and showed when at an acceptance/peaceful stage of their non-linear "grief process," children and young people may be able to talk through some of those "big feelings" that felt overwhelming at the time and look to a brighter future.
- This chapter describes how human connection builds stronger relationships which can forge epistemic trust.
- This is a good foundation for interventions which build optimism; positive psychology focuses on identifying and enhancing the positive aspects of our daily lives, it builds personal strengths and qualities through targeted experiences.

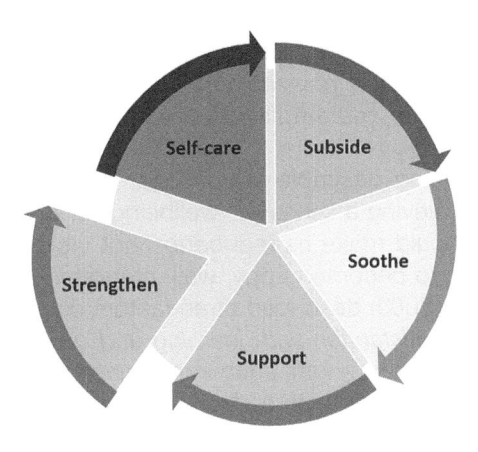

Links with neuroscience

The previous chapter focused on a range of emotions, many of which were linked to distress in some shape or form.

Distressing emotions are an obstacle to happiness and thriving (Carr, 2011) since they involve making negative comparisons ("it's not fair" or "I was happy before x happened") and highlighting how, prior to the trauma or loss, we may have taken "good times/things/people" for granted (Seligman, 2002). When the child or young person is in a place of relative peace and acceptance, it offers an opportunity to give hope for the future, stir their optimism and to appreciate the positive aspects of the people and opportunities around them. A positive outcome would be for their overwhelming reactions to "loss" to gradually be replaced by an intrinsic motivation and a determination to be a "good human" living a positive existence. A young person may receive positive feedback that is either intrinsic (they like how it makes them feel) or extrinsic (they receive verbal praise or tangible reward). This positive feedback for their mood or actions helps the brain re-evaluate what it thinks it knows and then adjust accordingly.

The brain works via a system of checks and balances and chooses its next cognitive move based on the feedback it received from what it just did (Barrett, 2021), as we read in chapter 4. Positive feedback also helps us cope with stress. Our adrenal system goes into overdrive when we are stressed, but hearing the words "that's right," "good job" or "nice work" keeps us relaxed. Essentially, for pupils, this information about their "performance" helps their brains know what neurons to grow or which ones to prune (brain *plasticity*, chapter 4). Positive feedback releases

DOI: 10.4324/9781003275268-11

Table 8.1 Happiness levels (Bentham, 1817) illustrated by Taylor (2023).

Level one	**Momentary feelings** Joy e.g., eating, warmth. Pleasure.	*More immediate, sensual and emotional.* *More absolute and reliably measurable.*	*More cognitive and relative.* *More moral and political.* *Involving more cultural norms and values.*
Level two	**Judgements about feelings** Wellbeing. Satisfaction.		
Level three	**Quality of life** Esteem. Position in society., Fulfilling one's potential.		

serotonin into the brain, reinforcing feelings of calm and happiness. Feedback, in the classroom and in life, is one of the most important ways to help teenagers learn efficiently (Feinstein, 2009).

Since the brain possesses this ability for "neuroplasticity" and can constantly lose those connections which are no longer used, sustained practice of a new behaviour or thought process is needed to stimulate growth and forge new neural pathways. An example of where this is beneficial is when practicing "reframing negative thinking" (described in chapter 7). There are **practical ways to incorporate new, beneficial habits** into a child or young person's daily routine to foster positivity and encourage happiness; this has many benefits.

Happy people are deemed to be more sociable, energetic, caring and cooperative with stable, supportive relationships and wide social networks. Showing creativity and flexibility, they are believed to be productive and better leaders/negotiators with stronger immune systems and are healthier, both mentally and physically (Ra, 2011). Seligman et al. (2005) provided evidence that promoting healthier, more fulfilled lives helps ward off unhappiness and builds personal resilience.

Additional attributes describing desirable educational goals include being "well-adjusted," having "high self-esteem," achieving a sense of "wellbeing" or developing a "positive outlook." All assume that education should make us feel *better*, not worse; indeed teachers, responsibly, want to prepare students to become happy, well-integrated, citizens contributing to wider life (Liver, 2014). Diener (2006, 2009) described three factors contributing to "happiness": *close social relationships*, *personal satisfaction with learning and growth* and *meaningful goals* that derive from their values and fit their strength, enabling progress to be possible. A rich, supportive school environment, grounded in care, with a strong educational relationship, provides opportunities for pupils to develop these socially valued aspects-of-self; embedded values can work towards the *three factors* said to improve pupils' "happiness."

Bentham (1817) described three happiness levels, with each level, also including all the qualities of the level below (see Table 8.1 above).

This model *supports* Seligman's (2002) four decades of research which concludes that there are three pillars for happiness: *Pleasure* (level one), *Absorption* in a task (level two) and *Meaning*: life with a purpose (level three). The term "subjective wellbeing" (coined by Diener, 2009) considers that happiness is composed of both **cognitive** and **emotional** aspects. Positive feelings include emotions such as joyful, proud, excited, cheerful and interested (Suldo, 2016), which are the antithesis of the many negative feelings described in chapters 2 and 7 (i.e., ashamed, angry, scared, sad and guilty). Seligman (2002) introduced a ground-breaking and renewed emphasis on happiness and related concepts. He put forward the **three pillars of positive psychology** which included:

- Positive emotions and experiences (e.g., happiness).
- Positive individual traits (e.g., character strengths).
- Positive institutions (e.g., healthy schools and families).

Positive psychology aims to improve the quality of life through studying these three aspects. It is the scientific study of what makes life most worth living, focusing on both individual and societal wellbeing.

Positive psychology is a relatively new field of study, but it has grown rapidly in recent years. This is due, in part, to the increasing recognition that happiness and wellbeing are not just the absence of negative emotions but also the presence of positive emotions, strengths and virtues (Diener and Seligman, 2002).

Positive Psychology Interventions (PPIs)

The main goal of many positive psychology interventions is to increase *happiness (subjective wellbeing)* in children and young people. While it cannot be directly "taught," it can be fostered through deliberate evidence-based approaches and resources which have been examined in research and determined to fuel a positive life-trajectory (Suldo, 2016). Research evidence has established some *risk factors* that have a negative impact on mental health and some *protective factors* that *support* good wellbeing; notably our *life circumstance* has an impact, whereupon pupils of *higher socioeconomic status*, overall, have better mental health than students of lower socioeconomic status; the implication is that for some children and young people, the **SUPPORT** strategies are a lifeline.

Better *academic achievement* and *higher self-esteem* also predict stability in mental health; this therefore suggests a bi-lateral relationship where a component of good mental health and wellbeing is intrinsic motivation to achieve, and conversely, achievements and feelings of success lead to good subjective wellbeing. Here, **SUPPORT** strategies, interventions and group projects at an individual, family, peer-group, school and community level can have a dramatic and positive impact on life circumstance and also on a community's wellbeing.

Interestingly, and somewhat surprisingly, research determined that stressful life events did not predict instability in mental health, "suggesting that the presence or absence of adverse life circumstances did not cast a lasting shadow among teenagers" (Suldo, 2016, p. 46). This gives hope that *support* and interventions can help the child or young person overcome the challenges surrounding a traumatic event.

When we can assist young people move forward

When our children and young people are challenged through experiencing a traumatic event, we can *support* their emotions and behaviours using ideas from chapters 5–7. Following these experiences come opportunities for change (Carr, 2011), which may present themselves.

- During a "rite of passage" or stage of life e.g., as a pupil moves from primary to secondary school.
- Making (or breaking) long-term habits such as a healthy lifestyle, better mood management.
- Within normal day-to-day tasks, such as coping with a morning routine, "life laundry" or homework deadlines.
- After a traumatic event, such as pandemic, bereavement, moving house (or country) or family financial poverty.

While we have seen how these traumatic events (independent or combined) can challenge the coping resources of our pupils, they also offer opportunities for the growth, change and development of strengths.

Two concepts which assist with this opportunity are "positive psychology" and "epistemic trust."

Epistemic trust

Research into **epistemic trust** (epistemology being the "science of learning") has determined that a pupil is more likely to respond positively to any (positive psychology) suggestion made by the supporting adult, when the adult has forged trust with them (AMBIT, 2017). The depth of the trust depends on how well the child or young person connects with their teacher. It is this trust and connection that increases their ability to learn. It is dependent on the adult relating to them by:

- Making eye contact.
- Looking at what they are looking at.
- Listening to them.
- "Noticing" something about them or remembering something the pupil has told them and asking about it at a later event (e.g., "I'm going to visit my Nan on Saturday," and on Monday the teacher remembers to ask how the trip went).
- Trying to "get inside their head."
- Demonstrating this by verbalising i.e., the teacher shares their own (uncertain) understanding of what that pupil is conveying then corrects their own misunderstandings to convey to the child that the teacher now has a better idea of what they are thinking/feeling/stuck on.

There may be a moment when the pupil lights up or indicates that the adult "gets it." This "mentalising" the grappling (to be on the same wavelength and understand the nuances of the pupil's feelings) brings a connection that develops into epistemic trust.

This is the strong base for a child to hopefully be ready to take up your next suggestion; they feel validated, understood and heard, and so may trust in the advice or idea being suggested, as they now know that they can rely on you. This connection builds epistemic trust. It also illustrates the effort needed by the adult to connect, listen, verbalise, ask, listen, re-iterate what they heard – it is a meeting of minds, of morals and values.

In a sense, **it prepares a clearing in which learning can occur**; this includes social-emotional learning as well as through the education curriculum. It is this social-emotional learning theme that applies more closely with this book's contents. The whole of the supportive relationship stems from this ability to develop this two-way process of epistemic trust.

Therefore, a key point is to have a named adult, one with whom this pupil most strongly connects, to offer the "*support*" suggested in this chapter. This idea underpins the "***SUPPORT*** " and the "***STRENGTHEN***" chapters, as these chapters give example of strategies which benefit from these interpersonal "connections" being made and forged.

How positive psychology can help

Positive psychology is concerned with improving happiness and wellbeing as it focuses on identifying and enhancing the positive aspects of human experience, rather than solely treating mental illness (Seligman, 2002). The field of positive psychology incorporates scientific research, theories and evidence-based practices to understand *what* contributes to a fulfilling and meaningful life and *how* to achieve this (Suldo, 2016). Its practical tools and interventions have been shown to benefit children and young people by promoting their subjective wellbeing; this *support* aims to:

- Proactively build personal *strengths* such as gratitude, optimism, happiness, wisdom, creativity, hope and resilience.
- Increase resilience and the ability to cope with challenge: by developing strengths such as optimism and resilience, individuals can better cope with stress and adversity, to "bounce back" from setbacks more easily.
- Cultivate "good" emotions – promoting positive emotions such as joy, love and awe.
- Cultivate positive mental health (improving mental and physical health). Interventions have been shown to reduce symptoms of anxiety and depression, and to improve physical health such as lowering blood pressure and improve the immune system (Lyubomirsky, 2008).
- Enhance life by increasing wellbeing and life-satisfaction; interventions can help individuals cultivate positive emotions and experiences; this can lead to greater overall wellbeing and life satisfaction (Seligman et al., 2005) and help towards finding *meaning* and *purpose*.
- Foster positive enhanced relationships: interventions can improve communication skills and help individuals build stronger, more supportive connections with others easily (Seligman et al., 2005), to allow them to flourish in communities (Seligman, 2002).
- Promote positive child development and positive parenting.
- Enhance creativity and productivity.
- Improve academic performance and engagement.

PPIs have also been tested in school-aged children and adolescents through education services.
The targets and activities that have been examined most often in research studies with pupils (Suldo, 2016) include:

- Gratitude: with activities such as *counting-your-blessings*, recording positive events in a journal or performing a gratitude visit (writing and delivering a thankyou letter).
- Kindness: enhanced through performing three to five acts of kindness in a designated day.
- Personal identification of strengths, often through a "you at your best" writing about a time the student excelled, followed by reflection on personal strengths shown at that time.
- Use of character strengths: from a list of positive traits valued across cultures.
- Hope and goal-directed thinking: involving activities such as visualising their desired future (goals) and creating pathways (steps to pursue) towards that vision.
- Optimistic thinking style: explaining life events from the past to extrapolate the positives (helpful thinking or positive re-framing is similar) which will help when considering events in the future.

- Serenity: often fostered through meditation mediation to train awareness of the present moment.

Positive psychology interventions

Using some of the above PPIs was shown to increase positive emotions (Suldo, 2016). As a result, the following four personal resources were enhanced:

1. *Mental resources*: improved mindfulness where they are "present" i.e., aware of their surroundings and able to enjoy the pleasant aspects of any occasion, increased creativity resulting in developing multiple pathways to reach certain goals. These are all better "habits of mind."
2. *Psychological resources*: developed character strengths such as having purpose in life and optimism combined with self-acceptance and improved self-esteem.
3. *Social resources*: developing the ability to have greater connection in relationships in which trust is built; this more satisfying is a more attractive quality to others and gives the perception of greater *support* from closer friends.
4. *Physical resources*: reduced stress-related hormones/neurochemicals and an increase in ones which improve bonding and wellbeing leads to better health; an enhanced immune system and better sleep are other positive physical outcomes.

These PPIs are evidence-based techniques that can help children and young people increase their positive emotions, *strengthen* their relationships and promote their sense of meaning and purpose.

Aims and potential impact of PPIs

The overall aim, and potential impact, of these interventions is to:

1. Alter *personal inner concepts*: such as emotions, values and interests; this includes altering mood and finding ways to achieve calm and serenity at times when it is needed (using breathing techniques, mindfulness/meditation and grounding).
2. Develop *character strengths*: a character strength is defined as (a) thoughts, feelings and actions which are present in a range of the individual's behaviours and are generalisable across different situations and times, (b) they must contribute to fulfilling a good life (for self and others) and (c) they must be morally valued in their own right, irrespective of the outcome (Peterson and Seligman, cited in Hefferon and Boniwell, 2011).
3. Engage *problem solving strategies* and forward-planning; this encompasses promoting positive self-talk and cognitive re-framing, recognising obstacles and moving forward into purposeful activities.
4. *Build relationship* (includes epistemic trust) and create a positive school climate and culture. The stimulus to achieve this is controlled and purposeful.

These four aims all **strengthen**; they offer hope and encourage optimism. Suggestions of practical **SUPPORT** strategies to use with school-age children are suggested in the table below using these four headings, representing each of the aims:

1. **Strategies to promote PERSONAL INNER CONCEPTS: emotions, mood and values.**

These strategies help practise emotions ahead of a situation. They help teach the brain in advance, the most helpful way to respond in any given situation. Just as we can create and alter our thinking patterns (as in "re-framing negative thinking"), we can create our emotions. It can be helpful to practise positive thoughts and positive emotions – as repeated practise alters the brain pathways (see brain plasticity in chapter 4) and therefore it gets easier to experience positive feelings (rather than feelings that accompany a worrying thought being repeated over and over).

Promoting positive emotions and experiences (such as gratitude, joy and hope) helps improve resilience and boosts optimism. These positive emotions can help to counterbalance negative emotions and increase pupils' sense of wellbeing and good mental health (Lyubomirsky, 2008).

Table 8.2 A table to illustrate positive psychology approaches which support PERSONAL INNER CONCEPTS: emotions, values and interests.

Emotions and Mood				
Emotional regulation supporting a child to be aware of emotions and self-regulate (also see chapters 5 and 6)	Make a card (age-appropriate) depicting a colour next to an image and emotion. Use it to help the child or young person identify, communicate and choose an activity appropriate to how they feel. If "sad" or "angry," use some of the *personalised* interventions listed (completed in an adult-pupil time together). If calm or happy, complete an activity.			
	Images chosen by child for "calm"	Images chosen for "sad or worried"	Images chosen for "joy and happiness"	Images chosen to represent "anger"
	Calm	**Sad or worried**	**Happy and joyful**	**Angry**
	Fill a box with calm images or activities that work for the child (decide together) – it encourages the pupil to make a positive activity choice and perpetuate their calm brain.	Gratitude exercise and use the happy memory box. A worry box to write worries down and post in or a worry doll to talk to. Re-framing.	Write or draw what made you happy and add it to your memory box. The pupil can also use the memory box when they are sad.	Breathing exercises. Use SOS bag. Go to safe space or sit on their blanket. Wrap weighted blanket around.
	Emotion coaching – promoting positive emotions can lead to improved academic performance and greater emotional regulation (Gilbert et al., 2021).			
	Emotions come in many shades. Let's come up with five words to describe how you feel today.			
Countering negative beliefs	To counter negative beliefs with positive ones, keep a diary of mood or urge change episodes containing the following three columns: • The activity that led to the change in mood or urge. • The beliefs that led to the change in mood or urge. • The consequent mood or urge rating after the activity on a 10-point scale (Carr, 2011).			
Gratitude Gratitude activities increase positive emotions and social connections, which can enhance trust and cooperation (Hefferon and Boniwell, 2011).	Use a gratitude journal to increase positive and decrease negative emotions among pupils through activities such as gratitude journaling; wellbeing is enhanced where pupils are encouraged to reflect on things that they are thankful for each day (Seligman et al., 2005).			
	Activity: list three things that they are grateful for since yesterday.			
	Gratitude exercises: write a letter of appreciation to one person to whom you are grateful or appreciative (or art, poem, card) – or for something kind that someone had done for them, but they had never thanked.			
	Classroom teaching about *grateful thinking* to understand why they may "feel good" or "feel happy" at sending the letter and understanding how people feel at receiving random acts of kindness, and why.			
	Draw a picture of what you are grateful for.			
Kindness	Encourage the child or young person to perform one, two or three acts of kindness that day, or in a week (depending on developmental stage). This can be as simple as thanking their parent/carer for food.			
Serenity and Calm				
Breathing exercises help steady the physiology of the body, bring calm and lower the heart rate.	**Breathing exercises:** **Mountain breathing:** ▲▲ trace up and down your first finger, as you move up the finger breath in, at the fingernail hold your breath, trace down the other side of your finger as you breath slowly out. Repeat with your middle-finger and so on. **Triangle breathing:** ▲ visualise an equilateral triangle, each side represents a different phase on the breathing cycle. As you picture the first side, inhale slowly. Visualise the second side as you hold your breath and finally exhale while you imagine the third side of the triangle. Repeat.			

(Continued)

Table 8.2 (Continued)

	Box breathing: ☐ inhale slowly and deeply through your nose for a count of 4, hold for 4 and exhale slowly through your mouth for a count of 4, hold your breath for a count of 4 (repeat cycle). **4–6–8 breathing:** inhale slowly through your nose for a count of 4, hold for 6 and exhale slowly through your mouth for a count of 8. Repeat the cycle several times trying to lengthen the time.
Mindfulness and meditation Daily meditation can help children become attuned to their own emotions and body awareness which increases their perception of the emotions in others – it reduces symptoms of anxiety and depression and improves wellbeing.	**Body scan meditation** Sit, stand or lie down. You may close your eyes. Be aware of your body moving from your head downwards and tense each area as you go. After ending at the feet scan back upwards, consciously relaxing each muscle in turn. **Walking meditation** Find a quiet or peaceful place to walk. As you move, be aware of the physical sensations of each step. Notice the contact with the ground and your shift of weight. Observe the sights, sounds and sensations around you. **Loving kindness meditation** Sit comfortably, close your eyes if you can, take a few deep breaths. Generate feelings of loving kindness towards yourself; tell yourself something that is nice about you or that you did well at today/this week. Repeat a simple phrase in your head such as "may I be happy, safe and live with ease." Extend these feelings of love and wellbeing to others who are close to you and then expand to include "neutral" people. Notice nice qualities in them. Practice this.
Grounding This controls any symptoms of trauma by turning attention away from the trauma, anxiety, flashbacks or other uncomfortable feelings by concentrating on something else.	**5-4-3-2-1:** **5** 👀 what are 5 things you see? Notice the pattern, texture, light or fine details. **4** ✋ – what are 4 things that you can feel? Notice the feeling of your clothing, the sun's warmth or the chair you are sitting on. **3** 👂 – what are 3 things that you can hear? Notice close sounds and distant sounds. **2** 🔺 – what are 2 things that you can smell? Notice cut grass or fragrance, for example. **1** 👅 – what is 1 thing that you can taste Carry a mint, a sweet or a snack to use for this. **Categories:** choose three categories from the boxed list below and try to name as many items as possible for that category. For a variation, try naming the items alphabetically, or adding one more thing to a list each time and repeating the list (as in the game "I went to market and bought a…"). Movies. Animals. Fruit and vegetables. Colours. Countries. Books. Cars. Football teams. Cereals. Famous people. Cities. Sports. Animals. Famous people. Clothing items. Games. **Mental exercises** • Name all the objects you see. • Describe the steps in preparing your favourite meal or baking a cake. • Count backwards from 100 in 6s. • Pick up an object and describe it in detail. Describe its: colour, texture, feel, scent, size and any other qualities you notice. spell your full name and the names of three other people backwards. • Read something backwards letter by letter, or • spell something backwards and pronounce the new word. • Think of an object and draw it in your mind or in the air with your finger. Draw something familiar like your home, a vehicle or a pet. • Name everyone in your favourite football or basketball team.
Music	Listening to music (on a phone, iPod or pc) is relaxing and absorbing. Have headphones handy or ask the pupils to bring in their own earplugs. Encourage the pupil to prepare their own playlist. Music has a positive influence, it can relax, or compel people to clap, tap a table, or dance, anything that acts as an outlet for the rhythm and tune that they are experiencing as a whole-body feeling. This regulates breathing, releases "good" hormones/neurochemicals. It calms, energises them and reflects and creates their moods. Neuroscientists found that music impacts both the academic and emotional wellbeing of teenagers; factually, brain-wise, music enters the inner ear to begin igniting numerous areas of the brain. First the brain stem, then the thalamus, and finally to the temporal lobes; "the various patterns of the beat engage neurons associated with emotions, experiences, and knowledge, allowing us to feel tranquil, invigorated, or

(*Continued*)

Table 8.2 (Continued)

	just plain happy" (Kluball, 2000, in Feinstein 2009, p. 79) – hence, listening to music has a positive emotional and intellectual impact, but research regarding participating in making music points to improvements in memory, visual-spatial relations (maths and science), and self-esteem.
Use resources	We are not necessarily trained therapists but there are excellent resources and one of them is by Paul Stallard (2019) *"Think Good, Feel Good: A Cognitive Behavioural Therapy Workbook for Children and Young People."* Search other programmes or projects available or suitable for school use.

2. **Strategies to promote CHARACTER STRENGTHS and PERSONAL QUALITIES, including physical health and immune system (see Table 8.3).**

The use of *character strengths' interventions*, such as identifying and using one's strengths in new ways, has been shown to improve happiness, engagement and academic performance among pupils (Seligman, 2002).

Table 8.3 A table to illustrate positive psychology approaches which develop CHARACTER STRENGTHS and PERSONAL QUALITIES, including physical health and the immune system.

Strength's teaching	• Classroom teaching to understand positive qualities and what their peers regard as their "strengths" – to build their own strengths and recognise it in others. • Look at characters in a story to identify their strengths (in the situation in the book). • Parent psychoeducation or parent evenings which describes the positive strengths in their child. • Class-teacher–facilitated sessions of "strength-spotting" in others. • Through circle-time (Mosley, 1998)
Conflict resolution and restorative practice	**Develop social and emotional learning** skills, both socially and within the curriculum. Games can develop qualities such as empathy, active listening and conflict resolution skills which can help pupils to better understand and communicate with others, leading to more positive relationships and improved communication.
	Practice active listening to help pupils better understand others' perspectives and feelings, leading to improved communication and more positive relationships (chapter 7). Paired conversation, question-answer sessions or circle-time are effective platforms for this.
Remove obstacles	Recognise and address any obstacles or challenges that may impede pupils' happiness and flourishing. This may involve providing *support* and resources for pupils who are struggling with mental health issues or facing difficult life circumstances, as well as addressing any systemic or structural barriers that may exist within the school or wider community (Suldo, 2016).
Resilience and optimism	*Invite interesting local figures into school* to talk about their experiences; this can cultivate a sense of awe and be inspiring. A talk by someone who had a negative experience which they overcame can act as a good role model. *Praise personal qualities* such as resilience, optimism, kindness, as this encourages a positive culture and highlights these positive qualities. NB see *list of strengths as personal qualities and traits* (below).
Wellbeing and mental health	**Promote a healthy lifestyle** habit such as regular exercise, healthy eating and adequate sleep. Classroom education in Personal, Social and Health Education (PSHE) lessons can equip the pupils with knowledge. Practically, goal setting and self-monitoring have been shown to be effective in encouraging healthy lifestyle behaviours and improving physical outcomes. **Encourage sports, hobbies or interests.** Provide a list of local clubs or craft groups. Look out for free family events in the local area, often libraries or community centres are a good source for these. **Invite representatives from local activity groups into the school.** Often, meeting people while on the safe territory of a familiar setting is an easier first step to joining a club, or pet care class or theatre group.

(*Continued*)

Table 8.3 (Continued)

Using character strengths Explore strengths as personal qualities.	**Create a sense of purpose and meaning:** by encouraging pupils to identify and pursue their strengths, interests and values, they can develop a sense of purpose and meaning in their lives, which can contribute to their overall wellbeing. **List of strengths to encourage and have as a focus of lessons** (Hefferon and Boniwell, 2011)**:** **Wisdom and knowledge** • Curiosity and interest. • Love of learning. • Judgement, critical thinking and open-mindedness. • Practical intelligence, creativity, originality and ingenuity. • Perspective. **Courage** • Valour. • Industry and perseverance. • Integrity, honesty and authenticity. • Zest and enthusiasm. **Love** • Intimacy and reciprocal attachment. • Kindness, generosity and nurturance. • Social intelligence, personal intelligence and emotional intelligence. **Justice** • Citizenship, duty, loyalty and teamwork. • Equity and fairness. • Leadership.
	Temperance • Forgiveness and mercy. • Modesty and humility. • Prudence and caution. • Self-control and self-regulation. **Transcendence** • Awe, wonder, appreciation of beauty and excellence. • Gratitude. • Hope, optimism and future-mindedness. • Playfulness and humour • Spirituality, sense of purpose, faith and religiousness.
Choose or develop a hobby or interest	Choose to engage in an existing hobby or interest – or start a new one (see the online resources). Search "List of hobbies" on an internet search engine. See https://simple.wikipedia.org/wiki/List_of_hobbies to help with making a choice.

3. **Strategies to promote PROBLEM SOLVING STRATEGIES and FORWARD-PLANNING, including interests (see Table 8.4).**

Problem solving strategies and forward-planning are part of our *executive functioning*; carrying out these deductive and reasoning tasks within a positive framework gives a greater chance for feelings of success. Approaches which *support* this are in Table 8.4.

Table 8.4 A table to illustrate positive psychology approaches which support PROBLEM SOLVING STRATEGIES and FORWARD-PLANNING.

Problem solving	Teaching pupils effective problem solving strategies and coping skills, such as mindfulness, grounding, breathing and relaxation techniques; this helps them to independently and pro-actively navigate life's challenges. Over time it builds skills, confidence and resilience (see Table 8.2).
	Set problem solving: • Set exercises to use key strengths (see table above). • Decide and pursue goals (using a young person's identified key strengths).
	If stress, anxiety or other mental health problems impede pupil's wellbeing, **provide support and resources** such as counselling service, peer *support* programmes or specialist help; overcoming obstacles or challenges enables future planning.
Careers, work placement to match interests	**Purposeful engagement in activities** that align with their values and interests is the first step in planning for a future. • Match any work placements or school educational visits to pupil's interests. • Careers education or guidance with college application can also benefit by ensuring a strong match to a pupil's strengths.

(*Continued*)

Table 8.4 (Continued)

Growth mindset	**Foster a growth mindset**, which is the belief that abilities can be developed through hard work and dedication (Dweck, 2007). • Praise qualities such as effort and perseverance rather than innate ability. • This can improve relationships and communications by securing a more positive and open attitude towards feedback, mistakes and challenges. • Encourage pupils to view mistakes and challenges as opportunities for growth and learning, rather than as sources of failure or shame. • Develop resilience: this mindset can enhance pupils' resilience by increasing their ability to bounce back from adversity and maintain a positive outlook in the face of challenges.
Positive self-talk and cognitive re-framing (reduce catastro-phising)	**Promote positive self-talk and** cognitive re-framing (see chapter 7, E.8.), to re-frame negative thoughts and beliefs into more positive and adaptive ones – this reduces the impact of negative self-talk and increases pupils' ability to cope with stress and adversity, by boosting their optimism and resilience (Seligman et al., 2005). • Identify negative thoughts and beliefs and replace them with more positive and adaptive ones. For example, a pupil who experiences negative thoughts about their academic abilities might be encouraged to reframe these thoughts by focusing on their strengths and past successes, and by reminding themselves that it is normal to experience occasional setbacks or difficulties. • Include gratitude exercises, positive visualisation and positive affirmations. Circle-time or golden time is often a good place for these (Lyubomirsky et al., 2005). • Use positive news items or non-fiction story to offer positive examples.
Learning	Principles learnt can also be applied to the learning environment; this scaffolding will *support* learning (Rosenshine, 2012) whether it is education-based learning or learning a new skill or hobby. The sub-text of supporting pupils is that by using interventions to improve wellbeing, learning will (in turn) be improved (Aubrey and Riley, 2022).
Problem solving LEGO THERAPY	*"Building Friendships"* is one example of a Lego-based group activity with playful learning. It is designed to *support* the development of social connections, communication and emotional wellbeing through collaborative building with LEGO® bricks. It uses roles of builder/engineer/supplier to encourage interaction and cooperation between three children with a facilitator. The aim is for this increased interaction to continue beyond the activity. The Lego website has case study examples of their work with neurodiverse pupils (LEGO®, 2023).

4. **Strategies to promote a POSITIVE CULTURE and RELATIONSHIP BUILDING, including physical needs, action and interaction. (see Table 8.5).**

Building relationships is more successful with a layer of epistemic trust forming a solid base for healthy inter-personal connection. A positive culture begins with individuals each combining to create a positive school climate and culture together. Table 8.5 suggests stimuli to help achieve this.

Table 8.5 A table to illustrate positive psychology approaches which support POSITIVE CULTURE and RELATIONSHIP BUILDING, including physical needs, action and interaction.

Safety and bonding	*A safe space which is inviting, comfortable and attractive: colourful cushions, blankets or throws, soft string lighting or moving bubble lamps can make this feel a special place to be. A blanket can be made to feel a special "safe space." It is portable so can be carried wherever the pupil moves to as their very own place to sit (when needed).*
	Activities together encourage bonding. Board games (Mercier and Lubart, 2021), physical activities, collaborative working, designing a poster together and "play" are examples.
Epistemic trust and culture	Epistemic trust refers to the trust individuals have in the accuracy and reliability of information and knowledge they receive from others. This is an important component of social trust and is needed for effective communication and cooperation in social interactions (AMBIT, 2017). Use positive communication and interaction styles, such as active listening, empathy and positive feedback to increase trust and enhance relationship (chapter 7).
	Promote positive group norms and values, such as honesty, fairness and respect. These can enhance trust and cooperation within groups and increase the likelihood of accurate and reliable knowledge transmission. Approach topics such as *stereotyping* or *isolating minority groups* to increase these values.

Table 8.5 (Continued)

Active listening	Engage in active listening and encouraging listening. See chapters 5 and 6 for more information.
Circle of Security Think about the experiences of our children and young people through their eyes – and gain insight that the child's thoughts/ feelings may be very different to our own.	**The Circle of Security** is built on the theory that our own experience of being parented directly affects the way we parent. We may not be aware of how we parent, or what triggers us when the child is having an outburst or meltdown. The Circle of Security encourages parents and caregivers to become aware of their own unconscious attachment behaviours, personal views, strengths and what their challenges are. The aim is to help them know a more secure attachment (*The Circle of Security Network, 2023*). **A *support* mechanism** to achieve this is through work with the families or "parenting classes" put on at the school. Three main exploratory questions are asked: 1. What do you think this felt like for ****? 2. When **** had those experiences what sorts of thoughts and feelings did this trigger in you? 3. What do you imagine I am thinking and feeling when I think about your reactions to **** feelings? (Asen and Fonagy, 2021).
Unconditional positive regard	*Urie Bronfenbrenner emphasised the importance of adults being involved in a reciprocal, yet irrationally strong, **emotional attachment relationship** that is enduring (Brendtro, 2006, citing Bronfenbrenner, 1991, p. 2; Bronfenbrenner, 2005).* Unconditional positive regard (Rogers, 1959) is a concept that means there are no conditions of acceptance, no feeling of "I like you only if you are … or if you behave impeccably… or if you are quiet in class" and so on. It means caring for the child or young person, having empathy and accepting their values, feeling, beliefs, actions and past experiences, through a non-judgemental and respectful attitude. The child or young person is viewed as a separate person, with permission to have their own feelings and emotions. It can build relationships for pupils who have faced trauma or loss. It gives the pupils a chance to succeed, since there is someone who believes in them and has a connection. Pupils *liking* their teacher builds relationship, connection, esteem and learning (Pierson, 2013). Some practical strategies that can *support* this in school include: • Process praise which is specific and targeted. Find a process to praise i.e., what the child or young person is doing and how they are acting (use the "values" list above) rather than the *end-product* of their schoolwork. • School staff demonstrating unconditional positive regard towards each other and to all pupils. • Letting all pupils know that they each have their own ***SUPPORT*** strategies personal for them, so that: a. they know interventions are highly personalised and so feel valued, and b. it prevents cries of "it's not fair" when one student is allowed something (e.g., "time out" or staying indoors at lunchtime, or leaving the lesson early to avoid busy corridors) that another pupil does not have. • Concepts already discussed earlier, such as active listening, praise and encouragement, a safe and inclusive environment, constructive feedback, mindfulness practices, strategies to raise self-awareness of emotions, the adult apologising, respect, non-judgemental conflict resolution practices.
Physical health and boost immune system Strategies other than improved healthy habits	Positive emotions have been shown to have a beneficial effect on the immune system as they increase the activity of natural killer cells and other immune system components (Cohen et al., 2004). Hence, create positive emotional experiences, involving joy, gratitude and love/caring. Table 8.2 gives examples.
	Mindfulness, relaxation, grounding and breathing techniques have been shown to improve the immune system function and physical health outcomes. These activities (described above) and other physical activities such as yoga help reduce stress and, in turn, lower the risk of chronic disease.
	Strong social *support* and positive relationships improve our physical and mental health. *Support* from friends and family, or joining a new social group, related to hobbies or interests, can be of benefit (also see chapter 7).

(Continued)

Table 8.5 (Continued)

Stimulus control	Stimulus control involves changing our environment so that it contains fewer triggers for effects of trauma or problem behaviour, and more cues for productive alternatives. For example, noise, heat and overstimulation can invoke sensory issues. In the long term, a useful goal is to become capable of tolerating situations that trigger problem reactions or behaviours. Tolerance for these trigger situations may be developed in the following way: • List all cues and triggers for problem reactions, difficult emotions, unwanted intrusions or problem behaviour and assign each a number between 1 and 100 to indicate the strength with which it elicits a reaction. List strategies to avoid, contain or cope with the highest scoring triggers (for example) (Carr, 2011).
Fear and autonomic responses	• Try to encourage a child or young person to notice their own feelings as they deconstruct the ingredients of their emotions, especially their body sensations e.g., a fast-beating heart does not necessarily mean their brain has detected a threat or there is something to fear. Their heart may be beating faster because they are excited or are getting ready to exercise. • If someone fears, say, a spider, ask them to describe the spider using as many emotion words as possible, e.g., "The spider in front of me makes me feel disgusting, nerve-wracking and jittery but it is kind of intriguing." Learn about the spider, its habits, home and likes and dislikes. Knowing about something can reduce its fear and the uncertainty. This requires knowledge of the child or young person.
Positive relationship and social *support*: improve communication (Ford and Parker, 2016)	**Activities that involve talking.** These can also enhance good communication and joint problem solving skills which is a precursor to adolescent autonomy. • Use the features of "Circle of Security" described above. • Restorative practice. • Actively developing *epistemic trust* enhances relationship. • Participate in a shared activity, to improve communication, or chat generally, whilst doing so e.g., rule-based board/table-top or physical game, baking, complete a jigsaw, learn a new skill together. • Ask the child or young person to teach you (the adult) a new skill; there may be something they are good at, such as playing an instrument, doing nails, a dance routine, words to a song, a (healthy) "TikTok" craze or a playground/clapping game. In addition to positive psychology interventions, a positive psychology approach can also improve mental health and wellbeing by promoting positive relationships, which give social *support*. This acts as a protective factor against developing mental health difficulties.
Planning for the future	**Looking forward with optimism** • List things to look forward to. • Make plans. • Research organisations, such as for the next stage in life at college, university, workplace, training, voluntary work or apprenticeships. • Gain counselling or other professional *support*. Even if this was received at the time, with age and maturity levels come other questions. • Take up or develop a hobby to boost wellbeing. • Arrange a trip, a visit or to see a friend. • Record good times to encourage moving forward; it acts as a reminder that they "could do it."
Comfort corner: a safe space to talk	**Develop and make use of a comfort corner.** Sit there together just to "be" or use it as a safe place to talk (The Family Place, 2023). • Use a corner of a room, a cupboard, a tent, a "den" or a blanket to sit on. • Place activities in the space that encourage calm (decide together), items may include: cushions, playdough, cuddly toy, fidget toys, construction toys, quiet games, music through headphones, bubble lights or books. • Adults use the corner together with the child to *strengthen* connection and regulate emotional energy. • Once in the corner, ask the child how their energy is. Then choose one of the activities to bring calm. • Talk to build trust. After the activity, ask the child how they feel, or how their energy is. Explain why they feel calmer. Create **guidelines** for use of the comfort corner to include it should be used by one child at a time, and only with an adult present. Using the identified place should open-up conversation; it is a place to be still and sit one-to-one.

Conclusion

Neuroscientific research from recent years has shown that our brains are not "hard-wired" by a certain age, but rather, they remain malleable and flexible. This ability to change physically and psychologically, as we read in chapter 4, is known as plasticity. It is this aspect that gives us optimism and hope as we work with our young people.

This chapter has built on the "attachment theory" described in chapter 3, to present ways in which greater connections, stronger relationships and epistemic trust can grow – and develop into a catalyst for working effectively with the child or young person. When they feel valued and *supported*, the **SUPPORT** strategies (from the last chapter) and the suggestions to "*strengthen*" them (from this chapter) are likely to be more effective. If they trust us then they will be more inclined to *trust our suggestions too* and work *with* us, not *against* us.

During and after times of heightened stress, where pupils may have experienced trauma or loss, the need for the adult to remain sensitive and calm is at its greatest. Showing care and understanding within our interactions and communications builds a secure attachment which aids children and young people in regulating their emotions. When there is trust and compassion, good conversations can happen, children should feel more able to speak with honesty and openness, to express themselves and their worries. It is through having a "good relationship" that "change" can happen.

A positive psychology approach can *support* children and young people beyond their emotional upheaval (relating to the traumatic event) and take them forward into a future with a brighter outlook. PPIs are evidence-based techniques that improve wellbeing and mental health; they promote positive emotions, *strengthen* relationships and enhance a sense of meaning and purpose (Seligman et al., 2005; Suldo, 2016).

This enables the children and young people to bring their strengths and sound values to any situation that they are faced with, whether the situation brings challenges or opportunities, or both! Our pupils will possess *historical strengths*, *personal strengths* and *contextual strengths* (Carr, 2011).

- *Historical strengths*: early experiences that later equip us to cope with demanding situations. Historical strengths include: early secure attachment, the childhood experience of parenting, positive school experiences and past experiences of coping successfully with adversity.
- *Personal strengths*: attributes which help us solve complex problems. Personal strengths include: our character, intelligence, creativity, wisdom, emotional intelligence, easy temperament, positive personality traits, positive motives, self-esteem, positive coping strategies, physical health and a strong immune system.
- *Contextual strengths*: positive features of our current social network and lifestyle. They include positive relationships within our earliest family set up, our current family and our social *support* network/friendships. Contextual strengths also include fulfilment through participating in leisure activities, or other hobbies and roles that are part of our lifestyle.

Our children and young people coping with trauma or loss is one of life's biggest challenges and so is supporting them. Sometimes, they will not be ready to engage or deal with their emotions or trials. At other times, they may have moved beyond the "acceptance" phase, be ready to face new opportunities head on (Carr, 2011) and accept adult facilitated *support*. Interventions described in this chapter are ones to guide, and to make the most of brain plasticity by forging new connections to achieve more positive life outcomes.

Above all other strategies, students who feel *high levels of a sense of belonging* are likely to thrive the most. In a study of 12,000 high school students, those who felt valued, liked and appreciated at school, loved at home and felt fairly treated had the ingredients which facilitated a strong sense of connection. Those students endured less stressful feelings than students who felt disconnected, they also later exhibited far fewer at-risk behaviours such as depression, alcohol abuse or violence (Harris and Udry, 2022). *Belonging* makes us feel happy, it adds to our social and emotional wellbeing (Feinstein, 2009) and in turn this helps us survive and thrive. The chart (Figure 1.2, chapter 1) depicting stages we go through in the event of a collective trauma makes more sense in the light of this; human nature, on the whole, brings its positive strengths and qualities to the fore and aims to create group belonging, even in the face of adversity.

Garnering connections and trust were shown to be the most effective way to build relationship and belonging. Supportive adults, teachers and/or their parent-figure need to attune to the child or young person, listen and take note of their communications. Communications can be verbal, or non-verbal through gesture, body language, facial expression and behaviour. Adults do not need to have all the answers, indeed trying to "fix" the situation can impede a relationship as it is forming a judgement, and when young people feel judged or criticised, they are likely to resent the adult input or "being told what to do." They may even experience feelings of shame and humiliation, which will prevent them reflecting on the experience and learning new emotional-resilience skills. Teenagers need adults to lend them their thinking brains (chapter 4 described the many changes happening in puberty that limit this capacity) to *support* them developing reflection, insight and curiosity; these qualities *enable* them to achieve goals in the future, take responsibility and move forward with more optimism. The strategies discussed in this **STRENGTHEN** chapter aim to do just that. Generally, **building independence through choice and personal responsibility**, planning events, projects, visits or assignments together is an effective way to tap into individual interests. To engage the child or young person, allow them to make choices; letting them choose helps them to be in the driving seat – taking control at a time when a trauma or loss has prevented any sense of control.

Summary

	Top tips for "STRENGTHEN" techniques (chapter 8)
1.	When the child or young person is in a place of relative peace and **acceptance**, it offers an opportunity to give hope for the future, stir their optimism and to appreciate the positive aspects of the people and opportunities around them. A positive outcome would be for their overwhelming reactions to "loss" to gradually be replaced by an intrinsic motivation and a determination to be a "good human" living a positive existence. A young person may receive positive feedback that is either intrinsic (they like how it makes them feel) or extrinsic (they receive verbal praise, tangible reward or other positive feedback) – positive feedback for their mood or actions (for example) helps the brain re-evaluate what it thinks it knows – and then adjust accordingly.
2.	**Positive psychology** is concerned with improving happiness and wellbeing as it focuses on identifying and enhancing the positive aspects of human experience, rather than solely treating mental illness (Seligman, 2002). Positive psychology interventions can be used to increase *happiness* (often referred to as *subjective wellbeing*), in children and young people. While it cannot be directly "taught," it can be fostered through deliberate evidence-based approaches and resources which have been examined in research and determined to fuel a positive life-trajectory (Suldo, 2016). The benefits are improved: 1. *Mental resources* – enhanced mindfulness where they are "present." 2. *Psychological resources* – character strengths such as having optimistic purpose in life. 3. *Social resources* – the ability to have greater connection in trusting relationships. 4. *Physical resources* – reduced stress-related hormones and an increase in ones which improve bonding and wellbeing lead to better health; an enhanced immune system and better sleep are other positive physical outcomes.
3.	**Epistemic trust:** a pupil is more likely to respond positively to any (positive psychology) suggestion made by the supporting adult when the adult has forged trust with them. The depth of the trust depends on how well the child or young person connects with their teacher. It is this trust and connection that increases their ability to learn – it is dependent on the adult relating to them.
4.	**An aim of these interventions is to: (1)** alter *personal inner concepts* such as emotions, values and interests; this includes altering mood and finding ways to achieve calm and serenity at times when it is needed (using breathing techniques, mindfulness/meditation and grounding). **See Table 8.2 above.**
5.	**An aim of these interventions is to: (2)** develop *character strengths*: a character strength is defined as (a) thoughts, feelings and actions which are present in a range of the individual's behaviours and are generalisable across different situations and times, (b) they must contribute to fulfilling a good life (for self and others) and (c) they must be morally valued in their own right, irrespective of the outcome. **See Table 8.3 above.**
6.	**An aim of these interventions is to: (3)** Engage *problem solving strategies* and forward-planning; this encompasses promoting positive self-talk and cognitive re-framing, recognising obstacles and moving forward into purposeful activities. **See Table 8.4 above.**
7.	**An aim of these interventions is to: (4)** *Build relationship* (includes epistemic trust) and create a positive school climate and culture. **See Table 8.5 above.**
8.	Having connection and building relationship were the most effective means to give a sense of belonging and help pupils thrive (using the strategies described). Attachment theory showed that stronger relationships helped *epistemic trust* grow and develop into a catalyst for working effectively with the child or young person. Brain plasticity is the aspect that gives us optimism and hope as we work with our young people. Positive psychology approaches can *support* children and young people beyond their emotional upheaval relating to the traumatic event and take them forward into a future with a brighter outlook. Generally, **building independence through choice and personal responsibility**, planning events, projects, visits or assignments together is an effective way to tap into individual interests. Let them choose to engage them and help them be in the driving seat – taking control at a time when a trauma or loss has prevented any sense of control.

9 *SELF-CARE*
Caring for the carers

Chapter overview

Caring for the carers. Self-care for those who are doing the caring is considered in three ways:
- How the school ethos, and how we as colleagues, can reduce and not add to stress and improve wellbeing.
- Acts of *self-care* for the carers.
- How shared story can help the healing process as we learn from each other's experiences.

Trauma triggers an attempt to make sense of the world; it can be a challenge to maintain one's "professional identity" whilst facing one's own vulnerabilities when confronted with a threatening scenario.

- *Teacher stress is closely linked to the extent to which a teacher (or other educational professional) feels they can cope (both physically and emotionally) with the demands they aim to meet.*
- *Developing talents, self-expression and rising to a challenge are aspects of teaching which are enjoyable, whilst surpassing a challenge brings satisfaction. It is not the challenges inherent within education that give the issue, but the unending and relentless nature of so many that can lower staff wellbeing.*
- *This chapter gives evidence for the need of effective wellbeing support within education, along with evidence and a description of the huge positive impact that good wellbeing and good mental health have on the workforce.*
- *Risk factors and protective factors are described, to raise awareness for those working within an education system in which self-reflection and appraisal occur in abundance.*
- *A range of implementations, practical strategies, interventions and self-care for all staff are described; emphasis is placed on the important influence of senior leaders in promoting a positive ethos and healthy environment.*

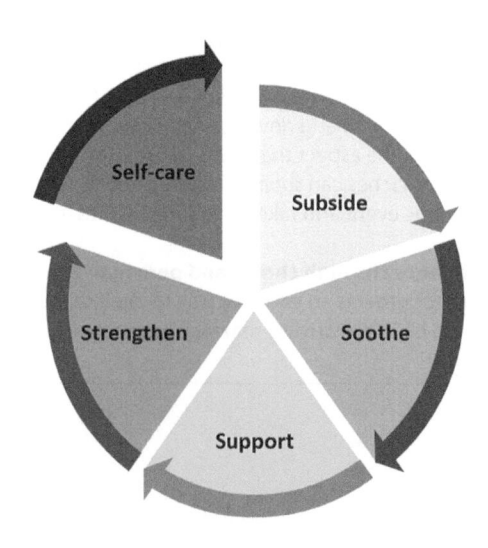

DOI: 10.4324/9781003275268-12

Introduction

Implementing the strategies, described in chapters 5–8, is not easy to maintain. Supporting children and young people who have undergone traumatic, stressful experiences can be exhausting, particularly when this coincides with the many changes happening in the adolescent brain and body (as we read in chapter 4). Children and young people require tolerant, non-judgemental, compassionate adults who are alongside them for the long-haul; this can be a rewarding and creative opportunity. However, maintaining exterior calm, being empathetic, validating emotions, active listening and implementing strategies to *support* and *strengthen* can also take its toll. I have known many staff reach a stage of "compassion fatigue" where they are exhausted from continually "giving out" (Figley, 2002). It is not that they do not care anymore but staff themselves need their batteries topped up; the same for parenting – it is an endless role, one that is usually cherished but can be tiring. Carrying the emotional load of your child or a pupil can be heavy, and it is natural to feel overwhelmed, helpless or unsettled from time to time. Add to the scenario the fact that adults, parents, teachers or other professionals may be on the receiving end of hurtful behaviours, blame, anger or judgement and, potentially, have undergone the same collective traumatic experience as the pupil, it is clear that they require a solid supportive foundation to underpin their efforts and hold them up. Adults need to be kind to themselves, and kind to other adults they work or live alongside, particularly as together they will be trying to navigate a shifting landscape. This chapter *"SELF-CARE: Caring for the carers"* aims to highlight issues relating to being in a caring role and suggestions to *support* those doing so.

Challenges within education: school ethos and the teacher's role

Teachers not only face multiple interactions from pupils/students, parents, colleagues, administrators and other professionals, they also have numerous tasks in addition to that of educating, referred to in the past as "the hidden curriculum." In their role, teachers often act to raise self-esteem in their pupils, consider the children's wellbeing, write school reports (worded in a positive manner to encourage), have meetings about how to bring out the best in pupils, act with compassion and empathy, *support* poor mental health, improve wellbeing and resolve conflict effectively. However, it is very difficult to be effective if the teacher is feeling "stressed" or if the school environment they are in does not adhere to supportive values and practices (Rogers, 2011). Teacher stress is linked to emotions such as anger, frustration, anxiety and depression that results from the challenge of meeting the educational, physical, social-emotional and wellbeing needs of the pupils. Beyond the classroom, whole-school factors may increase teacher stress, such as lack of resources (that is, lack of time, money, equipment or human resources (HR)), interactions with colleagues and unceasing evaluations and quality assurance checks (in all their variety: lesson observations, learning walks, appraisal and, of course, Ofsted).

Stress is closely linked to the extent to which a teacher (or other educational professional) feels they can cope (both physically and emotionally) with the demands they aim to meet. Successful coping acts as a buffer against stresses, whereas poor coping increases stress. Over time continual patterns of low-coping and high-stress lead to teacher burnout (Herman et al., 2020a) due to chronic emotional exhaustion, feeling "not with it," and reduced feelings of accomplishment – both physical and mental health issues result. This is the main reason teachers leave the profession, and their low levels of self-efficacy (a belief that they can succeed at a specific challenge) (Herman and Reinke, 2015) result in ill-health, high staff-turnover and diminishing sense of community (not to mention, expense for the school's budget).

The term *"**Quality of Life**"* is often used to express an implied standard in a work-life balance; however, the "quality of *work*-life" goes beyond merely financial wellbeing. The ideal *quality of life* relates to our subjective wellbeing or happiness. Aspects of working life that are enjoyable and worthwhile include developing talents, self-expression and rising to a challenge (Glicken and Robinson, 2013). Surpassing a challenge brings satisfaction. It is not the challenges inherent within education that give the issue, but the unending and relentless nature of so many that can lower staff wellbeing.

Evidence of the need for good wellbeing *support*

Good mental health and wellbeing *support* within education has become a necessity rather than an optional extra. The Harvard Business Review (2021), saw this *support* move into the "essential" category from the "desirable" category within education. This is understandable when considering UK teaching staff and education professionals report some of the highest rates of work-related illness, of which stress, depression and anxiety are the major reason (Health and Safety Executive, 2022; Ofsted, 2019). Teachers rated their wellbeing as "low-to-moderate," driven down by issues such as a lack of resources, high workload, lack of work-life balance and a lack of *support* from leaders. However, positive aspects that enhanced wellbeing were good relationships with colleagues and a strong school culture. This knowledge can be used to enhance teacher wellbeing and retain staff.

An annual survey, of more than 3,082 education staff, found that in 2022 record numbers of UK teachers and education staff had considered leaving the sector during the previous academic year due to pressures on their mental health and wellbeing (Education Support, 2023). In the past academic year, results showed:

- 76% of educators experience symptoms of poor mental health due to their work (87% for senior leaders).
- 72% of educators are stressed (rising to 84% for senior leaders).
- 59% of staff have considered leaving education due to pressures on their mental health and wellbeing.
- 55% have actively sought to change or leave their current job.
- 68% of staff cited volume of workload as the main reason for thinking about leaving their jobs (83% for senior leaders).
- 45% of educators always go into work when unwell (rising to 61% for senior leaders).
- 42% of educators think that their organisation's culture has a negative impact on their wellbeing.
- 59% of educators have considered leaving the sector in the past two years due to pressures on their mental health.

Two other recent studies found that more than 90% of teachers reported high levels of stress (Herman et al., 2018, 2020a). These are concerning statistics that need our attention.

Evidence of the positive impact of good wellbeing

This evidences the challenges inherent to educational institutions and determines that action needs to be taken pro-actively and consistently. Where this has occurred, boosting employee wellbeing and supporting staff mental health have seen some very positive responses. Evidence suggests that employee wellbeing boosts *productivity and performance*, that when feeling well, employees display *healthier behaviours and greater decision-making skills* (Mentally Healthy Schools, 2023). *Higher employee morale* also results in employees *feeling more competent* and *employees feel valued* when their needs are met physically, mentally and financially (Workable, 2023).

Further evidence of the huge positive impact that good wellbeing and good mental health have on the workforce:

Staff who have a *high-stress, but low-coping* profile have higher burnout with lower effectiveness, higher self-reported depression, more negative staff-pupil interactions and lower pupil learning outcomes, whereas a *low stress/high coping* profile has lower burnout, greater parent involvement and higher prosocial skills in comparison (Herman et al., 2020a, 2020b).

However, teachers who report **high engagement in intentional coping strategies** (e.g., *self-care* activities, social and leisure activity) experience *lower* levels of burnout than teachers who indicate lower levels of coping engagement (Herman et al., 2018, 2020a, 2020b). Yet, teacher training courses do not generally include stress management (Ansley et al., 2021) to reduce burnout and promote teacher efficacy, despite the many benefits it offers.

Good staff wellbeing has many benefits

Staff who feel valued and supported are able to manage moments of heightened stress, maintain a positive relationship with pupils, thereby impacting their educational outcomes positively and in turn reap improved job satisfaction. Improved job satisfaction leads to less staff absence, with greater staff retention (Anna Freud, 2022), hence the benefits are:

- Positive impact on themselves and on pupils, including improved educational outcomes, as both staff and children and young people are more engaged and benefit from a positive learning environment*.
- Boosts *productivity and performance*.
- Greater social cohesion and sense of community, as staff stay longer, and relationships deepen.
- Happier working atmosphere for children and adults, and a happier atmosphere increases wellbeing.
- Positive role model of staff getting along; this also promotes social-emotional learning (SEL) and positive behaviour.
- Increased productivity of staff members.
- *Higher employee morale* also results in employees *feeling more competent*.
- Reduced absences from work in relation to sickness (both short term and long term).
- Staff being able to manage stress better and develop healthier coping strategies.
- Employees display *healthier behaviours and greater decision-making skills*.
- *Employees feel valued* when their needs are met physically, mentally and financially.
- Improved job satisfaction, which can *support* retention.
- Greater parent involvement and higher prosocial skills in comparison (Herman et al., 2020a).
- Staff feeling valued, therefore know they are supported and invested in.
- Less staff ill-health and lower rates of staff turnover (which helps the school budget) (Barnes, 2007).
- Higher rates of positive interactions with pupils and fewer harsh reprimands (Herman and Reinke, 2015).

… and ultimately, the school or college, and its pupils, benefit! A sentiment expressed in, *"Well teachers, Well students!"* (McCallum and Price, 2010, p. 1).

School ethos

The above list demonstrates the very real need for the **school ethos** to be one which effectively *supports* its staff to maintain, and even improve, their wellbeing.

The ethos of how a school, or other professional institution, operates often lies in the hands of its senior leaders, and in turn they have a relationship with those above them. Whatever the basis of these bi-directional relationships, those with seemingly less control are the staff team who have less delegated authority (i.e., *lower down in the pecking order*), yet they are the ones who daily work face-to-face with the children and their families. If they are working in a conducive environment, these staff can have a tremendous positive impact on our pupils and, consequently, on our society. When we want pupils to flourish, we encourage them, we tailor the learning to meet their needs, we attempt to keep their self-esteem raised, we help them feel good about themselves, and when there are personal, academic or social struggles, we find bespoke and innovative ways to *support* them whilst showing unconditional positive regard. Thus, it stands to reason that to help the *staff* thrive or feel supported they should be treated the same way! It is easier to be a more effective teacher if we feel we are treated in the way that we are treating the pupils. Similarly, senior leaders are often the last to get thanked and appreciated; *caring* works both ways, as does positive (or constructive) feedback. Open, honest and robust working relationships require an atmosphere of trust and respect for communication to be effective; so much more can be achieved when reflection and evaluation occur *and* have a positive impact on practice. This leads to good staff wellbeing, and the numerous benefits are listed above.

Positive and safe relationship amid traumatic circumstances

When working in difficult circumstances, or with challenging pupils, often staff will still *go the extra mile* when they are happy, and when there is a positive and safe relationship between staff and leaders. A safe relationship is one where the staff do not have any fear or anxiety about what may happen; they feel able to ask when they need help, they do not sense a negative judgement being placed on them for requiring *support*, they feel free to ask for advice and allow other staff members or leaders to witness their experimental lessons (not "safe" tried and tested ones, but untried experiences planned to make the learning exciting). This all takes courage or requires very safe and secure relationships; being *open* means being *vulnerable* when we do not *feel safe*, and that can be too great a risk in hostile or toxic working environments.

Ironically, then the very place things that need to be improved is the very place where improvement is too scary. Fear, anxiety and stress can prevent things improving, and poor staff wellbeing is detrimental. Importantly, what we say and what we do (or *don't* do) can play on the minds of another professional; we can (unknowingly, or otherwise) instigate a downward spiral in a colleague's mood as they *reflect*. Alternatively, we can take on the personal responsibility of ensuring all our encounters instigate an upward spiral. Aiming to leave a conversation with the other person feeling a little happier than when the chat started could be an aim. Wellbeing and our mental health have a bi-directional impact, generally when one is "up," so is the other, and this affects our reflections about the job and ourselves.

Reflection

As professional practitioners, whether we are an educator, health or social care professional, reflection is integral. Reflecting informally (through a friendly chat), formally (through quality assurance systems) or self-reflection such as "mulling things over," all contribute towards an awareness of our own skills, knowledge and lived experience.

A sense of social and professional competence is integral to our sense of self, capability and academic attainment. However, one mistuned comment can cause this sense to ebb away, and feelings of being unappreciated and devalued can take over. A system purely focused on attainment can erode self-esteem; thankfully, most institutions now have an awareness of mental health, and a "staff wellbeing policy" usually exists.

When to be aware that we are under stress

Reflecting realistically is *intrinsic* to the teaching profession. However, when excessive demand is placed upon us as a professional, then we are subject to "overload" and rather than *reflect objectively*, or realistically, we "feel stressed"; this can lead to types of *thinking* that lead us on a downward spiral, to "catastrophising," imagining the worst-case scenario or "dramatising," when an issue "feels bigger" than it really is.

These natural responses are often caused by **risk-factors** such as too many tasks to complete, unrealistic demands (which may include coping, unsupported, with a personal or health issue), enforced workplace change, too short a timeframe to complete tasks or a heightened stressful situation, to name but a few. Sooner or later, we will be unable to keep all our plates spinning and this shows as **physiological changes** (chapter 4). Once we lack emotional energy, or are subject to "burn out," it is inevitable that we may experience one or more of the following:

- bursts of anger,
- worry,
- not sleeping well,
- ill health,
- anxiety,
- lack of resilience,
- depression,
- a desire to step away from the situation/leave/long-term absence.

We are all human, so no one is immune from these feelings, not leaders nor mental health professionals.

There are **risk factors** and **protective factors** that come into play; *risk factors* increase the likelihood of poor wellbeing; however, *protective factors* improve wellbeing. Having briefly introduced examples of *risk factors*, the theme will be developed.

Low staff wellbeing: risk factors

There is no doubt that the teaching profession is highly stressful (Eddy et al., 2022; Herman et al., 2018, 2020a, 2020b; Howard and Johnson, 2004; Ofsted, 2019). High stress can lead to burnout, which can be characterised by emotional exhaustion, feelings of failure (lower feelings of personal accomplishment) or feelings of detachment (depersonalisation). In turn, this depersonalisation can lead to a distant, or even callous, attitude towards others (Glicken and Robinson, 2013).

This can harm the working atmosphere between colleagues and can also harm pupils. Since adults, including teachers, influence child development, their own state of wellbeing can impact the classroom. Not only does it become personally difficult for the staff member to feel effective, additionally, anxiety and stress can hinder the ability to remain calm, to manage social-emotional competence, and therefore teach as effectively (Arens and Morin, 2016; Herman et al., 2020a, 2020b). Hence, stress and these negative emotional factors can hinder a teacher's ability to deliver education (Arens and Morin, 2016). A stressed teacher is more likely to react unpredictably or act harsher than usual (Herman et al., 2018). This erodes a good teacher-pupil relationship and brings a negative atmosphere, not conducive to a positive experience for all. Additionally, the highest rates of staff-turnover are found in schools with greater pupil needs and in schools where pupils from marginalised socio-economic backgrounds form a majority (Simon and Johnson, 2015). This leads to "a vicious cycle of the rapid changing of unprepared teachers teaching students with the highest academic needs" (Barnes et al., 2007, in Eddy et al., 2022, p. 103543). This also proves a direct link between teacher wellbeing and pupil experience; pupils need teachers to benefit from a positive work experience to give them the greatest chance of sticking around and building a positive, established school community. Teachers "can't give it away, if they haven't got it" (Long, 2023). In turn, good teacher wellbeing should positively impact the pupils' education and learning.

Wellbeing after a major event

Wellbeing is linked to a holistic health encompassing physical and emotional wellness. SEL is the process of acquiring and applying knowledge and skills to develop this "wellness"; through SEL, we develop healthy identities, manage emotions, achieve personal/collective goals and make responsible/caring decisions. Hence, developing social-emotional competence is defined as prosocial characteristics which include self-awareness, social awareness, responsible decision-making, self-management and relationship management (Collaborative for Academic, Social, and Emotional Learning (CASEL), 2023) – these are the CASEL 5 competencies.

Good wellbeing therefore involves a feeling that life is well-balanced on a social and a personal level (Mental Health Foundation, 2023), sometimes referred to as the "work-life balance." If staff wellbeing is so impactful on social-emotional and educational learning, then it should be high on a school agenda; however, it should hold an importance all the time and not just because of a traumatic event such as the COVID-19 pandemic, natural disaster or other turmoil. To use an analogy, when farmers plant crops, they prep the ground first and ensure that the field is in a healthy condition, they don't wait until the country has run out of wheat before planting the next crops – so it should be with staff wellbeing. Ensuring that the best possible *support* is in place, all the time should equip staff for those turbulent times.

After a traumatic incident, natural disaster or other taxing situation, such as a pandemic or displacement as a refugee, recovery from the major event is needed in addition to the usual working practices within schools. Admittedly, during a national or a collective trauma, government practices may alter daily (chapter 1) offering an additional challenge. However, during the covid pandemic, for example, school leaders were encouraged to reduce staff workload, place "quality assurance processes" on "pause" and concentrate on pupil and staff wellbeing; the extent to which an individual establishment achieved this varied, nevertheless valuable lessons have been learnt from this experience and from case study example.

Applying this to organisations recovering from major stressful events (Malinen et al., 2018) determined that:

1. Focusing on wellbeing can help staff to maintain performance and cope better with other stresses caused by the situation.
2. Senior management teams need to take time to understand the school's/community's/ region's recovery status and not impose their own timelines for return to "business as usual."
3. Greater visibility and communications from senior leaders are needed, not only during the immediate aftermath but over the longer term of recovery; these communications should acknowledge the challenges faced.
4. Flexibility and a greater degree of autonomy aid local sites to adapt, as necessary, to their changed environment.

Using this knowledge, practical strategies can be gleaned which act as "protective" (supportive) factors for staff.

Supporting wellbeing: practical protective factors

One main way to reduce the stress (not add to) and improve the wellbeing in others is to create an environment in which non-judgemental and supportive conversation can happen, without fear of recrimination. An open-door policy, an honesty in sharing amongst the Senior Leadership Team (SLT) and a proactive leadership, which operates within the "Ethical Leadership Framework" (Ethical Leadership Commission, 2019), all can work towards achieving this.

Engagement in **healthy coping strategies** (e.g., exercise, mindfulness, relaxation techniques) is a protective factor against educator stress and burnout (Herman et al., 2020a, 2020b). Even with the best working situations, teachers have intense, stressful job demands (Ansley et al., 2021). Unmanaged and unsupported stress is detrimental to themselves, to the school and to the pupils; therefore, it is essential to develop a skill set for effective coping strategies to build social-emotional competencies and improve the learning environment, teacher interactions and, therefore, pupil outcomes (Ansley et al., 2021). Training, online programs or courses are ways to help develop a skill set.

Thus, to possibly increase access and buy-in among participants, these programs may be provided through internet-based platforms. Asynchronous online interventions – that allow flexible scheduling, individual pacing and the option to participate from any location – could increase the feasibility of participation.

Characteristics of positive learning environments* include healthy relationships with students and other school staff, promotion of SEL and positive behaviour *supports* and implementation of evidence-based instructional strategies (Ansley et al., 2021).

The list below shows practical steps that can be taken at the various levels:
Three levels of *support* and their associated strategies can be constructed as a whole-staff group exercise. Below is a starter example outline:

- "*Universal support*" refers to the fact that this is continuously, consistently and widely available, irrespective of circumstance (Anna Freud, 2022).
- "*Directed support*" refers to next-level group **SUPPORT** strategies for the specific purpose of addressing responses to a traumatic event or circumstance.
- "*Specialist support*" is used for a perceived specific mental health or wellbeing difficulty with an individual – as shown in chapter 2, various expected emotional reactions or phases of grief, trauma or loss can exist, which may be brief or long-lasting.

Universal support

- Staff-wellbeing policy.
- A comfortable physical environment.

- Dedicated staff rooms (a staff "safe place" that looks inviting and comfortable).
- Good, timely and effective "change management."
- Regular SLT weekly drop-in sessions for any concern.
- Staff "buddy system" or mentoring groups for day-to-day work.
- Clear communication of information regarding school matters.
- Communicated information about external and internal lines of wellbeing *support* – for personal or work issues.
- Staff wellbeing team established and supported to offer regular events.
- Culture of no-blame and no stigma for mental health needs of school community.
- Feedback boxes for staff to anonymously share ideas for improvement (whether it is with working practices or school ethos).
- Daily work-related interventions. Treating each other thoughtfully and respectfully, within a no-blame culture.

Directed support

- Supervision (see below).
- Wellbeing events for staff.
- Solution circle sessions between staff (O'Brien et al., 1996).
- Training and continuous professional development, and training around mental health.
- Regular mandatory wellbeing check-in meetings for all staff using a personal or peer *support* mode.
- Teacher stress-management programme (see below).
- Bibliotherapy and webinar-based interventions (see below).
- Over-a-cup-of-coffee or strolling conversation (see below).

Specialist support

- Crisis *support*.
- Helpful, positive and proactive *support* from HR staff.
- Education *support* partnership.
- Referrals to occupational health.
- Employee assistance programmes.
- Cognitive-behavioural approaches to stress management (see below).
- The Coping-Competence-Context (3C) theory (Herman et al., 2020b) (see below).
- Creating a document that lists these layers of strategies can be made specific for your school or college setting. A few of these are further explained below.

Strategies to *support* staff wellbeing

SUPPORT: over-a-cup-of-coffee chat, or strolling

Myers (1994) and DeWolfe (2000) have extensive experience of best practice after a collective traumatic event. They suggested that one of the most effective styles of wellbeing and mental health staff interventions is through casually "roaming" through the workplace, circulating among employees and chatting with staff members.

Whether this is a senior leader or a mental health professional who engages in this strolling "stress-management" technique, it has the intentional purpose of chatting, asking questions and giving advice, noting any environmental stressors or making plans to meet more formally in a break-time. The benefits were that someone goes to the teachers, rather than the teachers needing to seek out someone for their own *support*. The "over-a-cup-of-coffee" style strategy has been shown to be the approach that staff respond best to in a situation where they have been the ones managing the emotional fall-out from a traumatic event. This method is also the best way to informally take note that an employee's stress is interfering with their ability to carry out their teaching duties, for example, and therefore an on-the-spot supportive solution can be to suggest they have a 30-minute break (at least), take time out away from the classroom environment, rest, eat, drink or have a walk. It may be that accompanying the teacher will help further, or just the act of noticing and taking this small supportive action, lets the teacher know they are supported. The teacher feeling this *support* can make all the difference; however, follow up is needed.

Whilst walking and talking, skills that may help are (DeWolfe, 2000):

1. *Active listening:* using non-verbal cues, giving minimal encouragements (nods and "uh-huhs"), conveying empathy, paraphrasing, reflecting feelings, summarising, differentiating content and feelings.
2. *Asking questions interviewing techniques*: asking open and closed questions, focusing with questions, but avoiding using questions to give advice or make judgments.
3. *Providing support and encouragement*: establishing rapport, empowering the survivor, giving positive feedback about coping strengths, offering suggestions, but avoiding communication blocks, and unhelpful phrases.

SUPPORT: daily work-related interventions (Anna Freud, 2022, 2023)

Other practical hands-on practices senior leaders can engage in are:

a. **Model good working practices, and *self-care*, to encourage a work/life balance for self and all staff.** This can include encouraging and taking regular breaks, finishing work on time, regular meetings with line managers/appraisees to check working hours/*support* healthy practice, not taking work home and asking for help and *support* when needed. The SLT should not just talk about doing these things, but they should model them too.
b. **Communicate clearly with staff, particularly around any changes that might be taking place at school.** Good and effective change management that does not cause an increase in stress/working time is a skill. Similarly, excessive change causes stress, whether it be changes to exam boards used (and therefore unfamiliar curriculum content), room use, timetable or the numerous data bases schools use. Chapter 2, Figure 2.1, can be used to illustrate the emotions experienced during enforced workforce change; if possible, consult with staff beforehand about changes to make choices together, then offer reasoning, reassurance with an implementation schedule, plus adequate training. All too often it is the staff that are directly affected by the change who have the least say when senior leaders implement something new. Also remember to feedback on the positives and things that are going well, as an encouragement, and senior leaders should evaluate the effectiveness of the change using a forum that permits honesty and/or anonymity. If things aren't working well, reverting back should always be an option.
c. **Encourage a sense of community.** As per (b) deciding together, and staff "being heard" and valued, brings community. A sense of community can be achieved by allowing opportunities for all staff to get together (reinforcing that all staff are important) and having non-work-related activities and clubs for staff.
d. **Keep staff wellbeing and development on the agenda.** Offer open meetings or resilience-based workshops for all staff, to help normalise the process of speaking about wellbeing. This can be done via lunch time seminars or inset days rather than adding to the working day. It can include topics such as managing stress, work-life balance or be an opportunity to problem-solve current issues. It can also be useful to provide opportunities for colleagues to regularly share and debrief with each other.
e. **Provide school staff with regular opportunities to feedback on any thoughts or concerns regarding staff wellbeing and how to improve it.** This overlaps with (b) and (d). Importantly though (e) is, in a sense, a positive psychology intervention, allowing moving forward practically and with optimism. This can help to develop a more inclusive and compassionate school culture (Riley, 2022).

SUPPORT: teacher stress-management programmes

Many programmes have been developed to *support* teachers, but although success varies from programme to programme, many show a small impact and have a strong effectiveness evidence-base, developed to reduce teacher stress. Mindfulness programmes are increasing in popularity and appear to have a similar level of impact (von der Embse et al., 2019).

SUPPORT: cognitive-behavioural approaches to stress management

These are usually short-term and focused on solving a problem (Beck, 2020). Techniques include many of those found within the "re-framing," mindfulness and relaxation techniques (chapter 8 tables), such as:

a. Behavioural activation: participation in rewarding and stimulating activities increases enjoyment.
b. Cognitive restructuring: "re-framing" by noticing, evaluating and changing thinking patterns.
c. Relaxation techniques: breathing exercises, and body relaxation.
d. Systematic desensitisation: gradually increasing exposure to feared environments or stimuli to reduce anxiety.

Recent research (Ansley et al., 2021) found an online stress intervention which included a, b and c plus social *support* improved coping and personal accomplishment and reduced teacher burnout.

SUPPORT: bibliotherapy and webinar-based interventions

Rather than attend live in-person sessions or group training, book-based and online formats are convenient asynchronous formats, there to pick up at any time. They are self-directed interventions, practised independently to improve wellbeing. Studies have determined this to be as effective whether they are in-person or phone therapy sessions (Blanton et al., 2020; Eddy et al., 2022). Alternatively, reading a book as an in-school "book group" and processing it together was also helpful.

SUPPORT: the 3C theory (Herman et al., 2020b)

Prior theory and research have suggested that *improving teacher coping* and *reducing stress* is directly associated with improved classroom management and teacher-student relations (Herman et al., 2018, 2020b) and, in turn, improved wellbeing for all.

*   This 3C *support* takes a different approach, as wellbeing is the *end result*, rather than the initial aim and purpose of this theoretical approach. It includes:
*   The Competence pathway: the aim is to improve teacher skill, particularly in classroom management, as a major determinant of teacher stress and burnout.
*   The Context pathway: considers aspects of the school environment (e.g., leadership, expectations, resources, relationships) and societal factors (e.g., education laws, policies, media) that contribute to teacher stress.
*   The Coping pathway: individual competence, accompanied with positive, effective *support* e.g., peer-mentoring or team-teaching.

This 3C theory suggests that improving teacher performance, including increasing positive interactions with students and, ultimately, improving student outcomes, requires a combination of effective coping, competence and contextual *supports*. Thus, the suggestion for any workplace is that a combination of looking inward at the school factors and ethos, looking outward at the wider political spectrum of teaching and supporting teachers (and others employed in education) requires a stronger three-way *support* framework. That said, the willingness of the school and its leadership to be open to change, and the ability to have safe and supportive relationships which can challenge existing processes, will affect its effectiveness. While there are a whole range of self-help books, this book "Stress Management for Teachers: A Proactive Guide" by Herman and Reinke (2015) (available from book outlets) focuses on:

*   Changing perceptions of stress and coping *supports* to reduce stress and anxiety.
*   Adaptive thinking strategies, including re-framing and coping thoughts.
*   Personal behaviour strategies, along with behaviour management in the classroom, to increase positive interactions with pupils.
*   Effective communication strategies with school leaders and making an assertive request for contextual school change.
*   Wellness planning and building motivation.

Whilst these suggestions each contains an element of classroom behaviour management, it is for the benefit of describing the available resources and supporting trauma and loss. Pupil behaviour is their outward communication tool; with so much happening in their minds and lives, various behaviours manifest; as we read earlier, how we respond is vital. Beneficially, gaining this knowledge and understanding (that behaviour equals communication) allows our compassionate *support* to follow.

SUPPORT: supervision – what it can look like in school

Supervision is a practice, taken from the health service sector, which my most recent place of employment offered to all school staff (Anna Freud, 2022, 2023). Supervision is a supportive one-to-one time where a teacher who is finding something particularly challenging, or is supporting children going through a traumatic experience, can take time for themselves. It offers an opportunity to take time, to think about the troubling issue(s); however, it works best if it is a scheduled regular planned meeting with a staff member, rather than just happening *after* a situation has arisen (using the *prevention is better than cure* approach). In supervision, the staff member is the focus, with the aim being to *support* them with work tasks and challenges. Supervision recognises and acknowledges that staff stress may impact on their capacity to manage their work well; staff stress is not viewed as a negative trait but rather as *expected* as part of the job. It acknowledges that the professional is in a role that induces stress and therefore requires appropriate *protective factors* to *support* them. It provides an open forum where the problem can be discussed and it prevents the teacher from being alone in managing it; this is particularly important for education staff who are dealing with children and young people who have undergone traumatic events, grief or any type of loss. Planned supervision ensures that staff always have the most appropriate *support* – if the sessions are planned, and happen regularly and reliably, then access is easier. Every staff member will have an individual experience of their job, so the content of a supervision session will be personalised for every individual. The practise of supervision is slowly becoming more widely known in schools. It is usually delivered by a healthcare professional, a pastoral care team or specialist mental health staff. There are various models of supervision, most emphasise its supportive nature rather than purely having a directive function; it prevents isolation and negative feelings spiralling and ensures that staff have the correct *support* made available to them.

DAILY SUPPORT: looking after our own wellbeing: acts of self-care

It is easy to say "*take time out for yourself and have a walk*" yet when we have numerous tasks to complete or are feeling exhausted, emotionally or physically, it may be the last thing we wish to do. However, many of the **SUPPORT** strategies suggested in chapters 5–8 can be adapted to be age appropriate for adults too. The related aspects of neuroscience also apply (chapter 4), such as brain plasticity in learning a new skill set or way of thinking, or in using breathing and mindfulness/grounding techniques to change the body's physiology, thereby *telling it* that we are relaxed (as heart rate is lowered and breathing is steadied to make us feel better). Exercise or a walk can also have this positive (*self-soothing*) physical impact. This is a list of simply, easy-to-apply ways to manage our own wellbeing:

A. Give yourself breaks, time-out, enjoyable outings or time for hobbies or socialising. Even if feeling inundated, we need a work-life balance, but importantly, when we are anxious, our minds and bodies need time away from anxious emotions or having challenging thoughts racing round and round our heads.
B. Consider taking up a new hobby or activity, as this change becomes our positive focus and widens a social circle.
C. Local *support* groups of professionals can also be helpful.
D. Identify people we have in our lives who are supportive. This can be simply a mental exercise where we hold people in our mind or one where we talk to people and ask them to act as a *support*.
E. Talking to people is important; if something has affected us at work or we are concerned for a pupil's traumatic state, it is important to speak to someone before leaving work in order to (i) process how we are feeling, (ii) ask for *support* and (iii) not carry the issue home with you. This can reassure and also improve the quality of our evening time.

F. Self-compassion is needed to be kind to ourselves. We are human, we are not infallible, we all make mistakes, and it can help to be realistic about this. Perhaps try looking at the issue from another adult's perspective, as imagining it from another viewpoint can help us realise that we did not mess up as much as we are telling ourselves we did.

G. Take time out for *self-care*, whether that is a cup of tea, a TV programme, a walk in the country, a bath, time with the family, a hair/nail appointment or time spent on a hobby. These things can physically and emotionally recharge our batteries.

H. Know your own personal limits and have the ability to say "no" when needed. There are many ways to say "no" as sometimes it can be very difficult to not agree to help when specifically asked. Keep phrases in your mind to use, such as:
    - *Sorry, I can't today, but let's arrange a time next week/month.*
    - *I'm really not very good at that but I can suggest… [another person/website, or other helpful route].*
    - *I'll have to say sorry I just can't manage the time at the moment.*
    - *Thank you for asking me, but I feel very ill-quipped and don't have those skills, so I can't be any help.*

I. Be flexible regarding change. Good "change management" may be necessary in the school, however, repeated or poorly managed *change* is a stressor. Additionally, everything in life does not always go to plan and sometimes things need to alter. Our ability to adapt and accept change, make new plans and hone good life-skills, will help prevent *change* being a catalyst for stress.

J. Re-frame issues by reflecting on your thoughts and asking if they are positive or negative, supportive or critical. Introduce more positive thoughts and ways of thinking to turn down the critical voice. Re-framing thinking (chapter 8) is a good skill to practice, and in turn it enables us to feel more equipped to *support* this technique in children and young people.

K. Engage in *kind* self-talk/being kind to ourselves. Be realistic rather than expect too much of ourselves.

CREATIVE SUPPORT: shared story

Using *shared story* or journaling can help the recovery and healing process (Holmes, 2022; SEP-SIS, 2023; Togetherall, 2023). Whilst this creative approach has been among the suggestions for pupils, it has also been found to benefit and *support* adults (Soboti, 2022). As we *support* our children and young people, sharing our story has many benefits for us:

- It is our voice about the situation. Rather than process the events internally, it is an opportunity to share our experiences with others.
- This might be a way of us reaching out, or a way for others to understand our feelings.
- It also involves putting ourselves "out there," so as others read, they may be able to relate to our words and maybe feel less alone – or help us feel less alone.
- It prevents us getting interrupted or losing our thread as we verbally tell it; written down it is our own story from beginning to end.
- We can reflect before we write, sharing as little or as much of ourselves as we wish; it is easier to choose our words carefully and have a final version that we are happy for others to read.
- The actual process of writing our story is therapeutic and empowering; we have taken charge and are in control of the pen and paper (or keypad).
- The written version can be used to read out to share in a one-to-one or a group setting – it helps prevent us stumbling over our words. Of course, we can go off-script or elaborate as needed – but having our story scripted is a helpful prop. It also means that we do not have to repeat ourselves (which can be exhausting) – we can allow any family, friend, colleague, mentor or counsellor (for example) to read it. This can help them understand our experiences and perspective.
- It helps us make sense of things. At the time we may *feel* the big emotions, but this can be too much (or too exhausting) to put into words. We are breaking the silence on our experiences and accepting them as valid and real. This may reduce the intensity or aloneness we feel and may also help others who have undergone a similar experience.
- Supporting pupils who have individually, or collectively, experienced trauma or loss, whilst simultaneously feeling the effects of the situation too, can take its toll and long-term issues may go under the radar – a written account is there to stay and is a form of evidence-gathering that can be recognised and acted upon.

- As the story is written, the associated intense feelings must be faced, hence success can be found by overcoming that hurdle. If emotions feel too real as you write, you can step away from it and return later. The story-writing can be paused. Fear of facing or reliving the traumatic experiences can prevent the story being told – it can signal that additional professional help, or counselling, is needed.
- The stage where we begin to feel at peace, accepting of events or optimistic for the future can be a good time to write. Our sense of overcoming challenge and hope for our ventures ahead will shine through, to encourage others.

To write: to reduce interruptions, find a quiet time and place to write.

- If you're not sure where to start, try a little "brainstorming." Write down your thoughts as they come up. They don't need to be full sentences; they don't even have to be sentences. Just get the words on the paper or computer screen. If it is stressful, take a break.
- Don't rush it, unless you feel you need to get it done all in one shot or you might not finish it.
- Do it for yourself. While you will be *sharing* your story, it still must be for you.
- Watch your expectations. You will not know how you will feel when you see your story online. Nor can you know how others will respond. It is best to let go of any expectations that you have.

Finally sharing your story, whether that is online, in person, verbally or in a letter, can be powerful. You have helped yourself and others who will read it (especially if online). They can learn about the situation, the associated emotions, moreover, you have taken charge of that aspect of your life, you have control and are in the driving seat of what you share. The story can be written in a journal and kept for private use only, or for when you choose to let someone else have a glimmer of your experiences and emotions. It is information that has value, that someone, somewhere could relate to and feel a little less alone. The stories can form a community of stories – community can be built through story. The story will only be shared if, and when, you choose; if you are not ready to share something so personal, if you do not feel safe or ready to do so or if you still feel too exhausted or vulnerable, it does not have to be shared. It is still valid and can be re-read at a later date.

CREATIVE SUPPORT: whole-school creative projects which have supported wellbeing

One-off whole-school projects can beneficially offer a creative experience, community outlet and bring together a wealth of views. This can be used to respond (emotionally) to a collective traumatic event or current news topic that brought disquiet, and thereby the project can also be utilised to *support* inclusion and/or address any systemic or cultural barriers that may prevent all staff (and pupils) feeling equally safe and valued.

For example, in response to the shock surrounding the news items about George Floyd's death, all staff and pupils at my school created a book, professionally printed. The large, hardback edition was a collection of our individual responses to the unfolding news events. Senior leaders encouraged staff and pupils to respond in any written or 2D format they chose, but with complete honesty and openness; they led by example. Our inner-city school community recognised that without these qualities, of honesty and openness, any attempts to have frank discussions or move forward as a community would be futile. For such a project, participants needed to feel safe to share. The resulting publication revealed poetry, prose, diary entries, artwork and sincere reflections that stirred the reader because of their authenticity. This creation was interwoven with appropriate and practical whole-school "training" sessions and conversation about *unconscious bias*.

Further whole-school responses to current issues or traumatic events have included activities such as:

- Responding to survivors' stories through filmed movement, music and mime; this formed powerful viewing and a conversation piece. Survivors felt heard and responded to; their peers gained insight and a level of healing happened.
- A creation of a large-scale art installation whereby text was used among sculptural pieces to reflect inner turmoil.
- A bespoke musical drama production addressing loneliness, age, wellbeing and mental health whereby a whole community contributed in whichever way was right for them – be it

behind-the-scenes, prop-making, making and recording music or on stage. Staff and pupil participated to create a platform for community cohesion and a place to shout out about their social, emotional and mental health successes. Those attending the performance gave remarkable feedback; the pupils' friends and family gained insight which brought community cohesion and increased collaboration between home and school.

- Doing something as a whole-school community to welcome and integrate all children; this is effective to create a sense of belonging, but even more so for pupils post extended absence (due to a pandemic, extended absence or displacement).
- A family coffee morning, perhaps displaying children's handmade craft items; this also helps keep families in our perspective as many may be troubled by traumatic stressors or mental health difficulties too.

Other vehicles to bring change and develop community (an important quality in overcoming trauma and loss, as we read in chapters 1 and 2) are aspects of the everyday curriculum and lessons which can lead to nationally recognised awards. Unicef's "Rights Respecting Schools" Award (Unicef, 2023) and the Equalities Award (EqualiTeach, 2023) are two examples of this; it also showcases the exceptional everyday schoolwork and topics that are vital but can often remain hidden. Working together brings a sense of achievement and helps overcome negative impacts of trauma/loss; it *supports* all adults, children and young people as they work through serious issues together using whichever project or creative outlet – this can act as a platform to question and improve school culture, ethos, policy and practice. Tackling serious issues sensitively, but creatively, should be a positive experience, reducing any barriers to *change*, giving a *voice* and bringing much needed *support*.

Summary

Stress is closely linked to the extent to which a teacher (or other educational professional) feels they can cope (both physically and emotionally) with the demands they aim to meet. Successful coping acts as a buffer against stressors, whereas poor coping increases stress. Over time continual patterns of low-coping and high-stress lead to teacher burnout, and a poorer "quality of life" stems from our lower subjective wellbeing or happiness.

The many challenges within education, and the evidence of the negative impact from teacher stress and burnout, highlight the need for good wellbeing *support*. Good staff wellbeing (with lowered stress and high-coping capability) has many listed benefits for the individual, for the school and for the pupils.

The school ethos and staff relationships need to be conducive to maintaining and improving staff mental health; this is particularly important after a traumatic event. Ensuring that the best possible *support* is in place all the time should equip staff for those turbulent times, such as times of individual or collective trauma; at those times, it can be a challenge to maintain one's "professional identity" whilst facing one's own vulnerabilities, when confronted with a threatening scenario.

Risk factors increase the likelihood of poor wellbeing, and *protective factors* improve wellbeing. Risk factors were described to raise awareness of circumstances which are not beneficial. Whereas positive, protective factors supported staff; the important role of senior leaders was emphasised, both in encouraging/modelling protective behaviours and underpinning an appropriate school ethos. Layers of universal, directed and specialist interventions were described to show practical easy-to-apply approaches that benefit staff and school culture. Among these, a few were expanded, and these are briefly described in the "Top tips" summary table below.

	Top tips for SELF-CARE: Caring for the carers (chapter 9)
1.	• **UNIVERSAL SUPPORT** – *support* for everyone, everywhere.

• Staff-wellbeing policy.	• Dedicated staff rooms (a staff "safe place" that looks inviting and comfortable).
• A comfortable physical environment.	• Communicated information about external and internal lines of wellbeing *support* – for personal or work issues.
• Good, timely and effective "change management."	• Staff wellbeing team established and supported to offer regular events.
• Regular Senior Leadership Team (SLT) weekly drop-in sessions, where staff can raise any concern.	• Culture of no-blame and no stigma for mental health needs of school community.
• Staff "buddy system" or mentoring groups for day-to-day work.	• Feedback boxes for staff to anonymously share ideas for improvement (whether it is with working practices or school ethos).
• Clear communication of information regarding school matters.	• Daily work-related interventions. Treating each other thoughtfully and respectfully, within a no-blame culture.

2.	• **DIRECTED SUPPORT:**
	SUPPORT: supervision. Regular, scheduled, one-to-one sessions – an opportunity to take time, to think about the work tasks and challenging/troubling issue(s); the staff member's *support* is the focus.
	SUPPORT: over-a-cup-of-coffee or strolling. Circulating and intentional chatting – noting any environmental stressors or making plans to meet more formally in a break-time.
	SUPPORT: bibliotherapy and webinar-based interventions. Asynchronous study and *support* programmes; often utilises book study, a "book club" or webinars.
	SUPPORT: teacher stress-management programmes. Real-time, often in-person sessions – developed for this purpose, includes *mindfulness* programmes.

3.	• **SPECIALIST SUPPORT: daily work-related interventions (Anna Freud, 2022, 2023)** Other practical hands-on practices senior leaders can engage in are: • Model good working practices, and *self-care*, to encourage a work/life balance for self and all staff. • Communicate clearly with staff, particularly around any changes that will be taking place. • Encourage a sense of community. • Keep *staff wellbeing and development* on the agenda. • Provide school staff with regular feedback opportunities regarding issues to improve staff wellbeing.
4.	• **SPECIALIST SUPPORT: cognitive-behavioural approaches to stress management** These are usually short-term and focused on solving a problem (real-time, in-person or online). Techniques include: a. Behavioural activation: participation in rewarding and increased activity is stimulating. b. Cognitive restructuring: "re-framing" by noticing, evaluating and changing thinking patterns. c. Relaxation techniques: breathing exercises, grounding, mindfulness and whole-body relaxation. d. Systematic desensitisation – gradually increasing exposure to feared environments or stimuli to reduce anxiety. NB adding social *support* improved coping and personal accomplishment, and reduced teacher burnout.
5.	• **SPECIALIST SUPPORT: the Coping-Competence-Context (3C) theory (Herman et al., 2020b).** This 3C theory suggests that improving teacher performance, including increasing positive interactions with students and, ultimately, improving student outcomes, require a combination of effective coping, competence, and contextual *supports*. • The Competence pathway: to improve teacher skill, particular in classroom management. • The Context pathway: considers aspects of the school environment (e.g., leadership, expectations, resources, relationships) and societal factors (e.g., education laws, policies, media) that contribute to teacher stress. • The Coping pathway: individual competence, accompanied with positive, effective *support* e.g., peer-mentoring or team-teaching.
6.	• **DAILY SUPPORT: looking after our own wellbeing: acts of self-care.** • Give yourself breaks, time-out, enjoyable outings or time for hobbies or socialising. • Consider taking up a new hobby or activity as a positive focus and this also widens our social circle. • Local *support* groups of professionals can also be helpful. • Identify people we have in our lives who are supportive. • Speak to someone before leaving work to: (i) process how we are feeling, (ii) ask for *support*, and (iii) not carry the issue home with you. This reassures and improves the quality of our evening time. • Self-compassion is needed to be kind to ourselves. try looking at the issue from another perspective. • Take time-out for *self-care* e.g., a cup of tea, TV programme, walk, bath, family-time or a hobby. • Know your own personal limits and say "no" when needed. • Be flexible regarding change. Our ability to adapt and accept change, make new plans and hone good life-skills, will help prevent *change* being a catalyst for stress. • Re-frame issues by reflecting and introduce more positive thoughts and ways of thinking, to turn down the critical voice. • Engage in *kind* self-talk. Be realistic and do not expect too much of ourselves.
7.	**CREATIVE *SUPPORT*: shared story.** Using *shared story* or journaling can help the recovery and healing process. It gives us a voice and chance to express ourselves at our own pace.
8.	**CREATIVE *SUPPORT*: whole-school creative projects which *support* wellbeing.** One-off whole-school projects can beneficially offer a creative experience, community outlet and bring together a wealth of views. It can be a forum for honest reflection and conversation.

References

Abramson, C. I. (2023) Why the study of comparative psychology is important to neuroscientists. *Frontiers in Behavioral Neuroscience*, 16, 1095033. https://doi.org/10.3389/fnbeh.2022.1095033

AbuHasan, Q., Reddy. V. and Siddiqui, W. (2022) *Neuroanatomy, Amygdala*. StatPearls Publishing. Available from: https://www.ncbi.nlm.nih.gov/books/NBK537102/

Adams, E. L., Master, L., Buxton, O. M. and Savage, J. S. (2022) Sleep parenting practices are associated with infant self-soothing behaviors when measured using actigraphy. *Sleep Medicine*, 95, 29–36. https://doi.org/10.1016/j.sleep.2022.04.018

Ainsworth, M. D. S. and Bell, S. M. (1970) Attachment, exploration, and separation: Illustrated by the behavior of one-year-olds in a strange situation. *Child Development*, 41(1), 49–67. https://doi.org/10.2307/1127388. JSTOR 1127388. PMID 5490680 https://www.jstor.org/stable/1127388?origin=crossref&seq=1

Ainsworth, M. D. S., Bell, S. M. and Stayton, D. J. (1991) Infant-mother attachment and social development: 'Socialisation' as a product of reciprocal responsiveness to signals. In Woodhead, M., Carr, R. and Light, P. (Eds.). *Child development in social context* 1: *Becoming a person* (pp. 30–55). London: Routledge in association with the Open University.

Ainsworth, M. D. S., Blehar, M. C., Waters, E. and Wall, S. (1979) *Patterns of attachment: A psychological study of the strange situation*. London and New York: Routledge, Taylor-Francis. https://doi.org/10.4324/9781315802428

Alexander, J. (2019) *Building Trauma-Sensitive Schools: Your Guide to Creating Safe, Supportive Learning Environments for All Students*, Brookes Publishing, 2019: ProQuest Ebook Central.

AMBIT (2017) Epistemic Trust for AMBIT (Adaptive Mentalization-Based Integrative Treatment). Anna Freud: National Center for Children and Families. AMBIT.tv, https://youtu.be/HrEgDdsohNo

Anatomography (2015) Anatomography from Wikipedia: The Free Encyclopedia. Database Centre for Life Science. https://en.wikipedia.org/wiki/Anatomography

Anna Freud. (2022) https://www.annafreud.org/media/7653/3rdanna-freud-booklet-staff-wellbeing-web-pdf-21-june.pdf [Accessed 02.11.2022].

Anna Freud. (2023) Anna Freud: Building the mental wellbeing of the next generation https://www.annafreud.org/ and https://www.annafreud.org/research/key-research-findings/ [Accessed 31.07.2023].

Andrews, S. (2023) Personal Communication from an Early Years Area Senco. Text and images emailed to Juliet Taylor. 19 June.

Anon. (2023) Anonymous personal communications. UK.

Ansley, B. M., Houchins, D. E., Varjas, K., Roach, A., Patterson, D. and Hendrick, R. (2021) The impact of an online stress intervention on burnout and teacher efficacy. *Teaching and Teacher Education*, 98, 103251. https://doi.org/10.1016/j.tate.2020.103251

Araujo, H. F., Kaplan, J., Damasio, H. and Damasio, A. (2015) Neural correlates of different self domains. *Brain and Behavior*, 5(12), e00409. https://doi.org/10.1002/brb3.409

Arens, A. K. and Morin, A. J. S. (2016) Relations between teachers' emotional exhaustion and students' educational outcomes. *Journal of Educational Psychology*, 108(6), 800–813 DOI: 10.1037/edu0000105

Asen, E. and Fonagy, P. (2021) *Mentalization based treatment with families*. New York, NY: The Guildford press.

Aubrey, K. and Riley, A. (2022) *Understanding and using educational theories*. 3rd Edition. Thousand Oaks: SAGE Publications.

Backman, I. (2022) *Revealing communications between brain and body*. Yale School of Medicine. https://m.yale.edu/xmb7

Banaroya, M. (2023) *Confronting Kid Conflict with Emotion Coaching: Help your kids resolve their conflict and handle big emotions*. The Gottman Institute. https://www.gottman.com/blog/confronting-kid-conflict-with-emotion-coaching/

Barnes, G., Crowe, E. and Schaefer, B. (2007) The cost of teacher turnover in five school districts: A pilot study. https://edsource.org/wp-content/uploads/old/NCTAF-Cost-of-Teacher-Turnover-2007-full-report.pdf

Barrett, L. F. (2018) *How emotions are made: The secret life of the brain*. London: Pan McMillan.

Barrett, L. F. (2020) https://blog.dropbox.com/topics/work-culture/the-mind-at-work--lisa-feldman-barrett-on-the-metabolism-of-emot

Barrett, L. F. (2021) *Seven and a half lessons about the brain*. London and Dublin, Ireland: Picador, Pan Macmillan.

Bauer, R. H., Gilpin, A. T. and Thibodeau-Nielsen, R. B. (2021) Executive functions and imaginative play: Exploring relations with prosocial behaviors using structural equation modeling. *Trends in Neuroscience and Education*, 25, 100165–100165. https://doi.org/10.1016/j.tine.2021.100165.

Beck, J. S. (2020) *Cognitive therapy: Basics and beyond* (3rd edition). New York: Guilford press.

Bentham, J. (1817) *A Table of the Springs of Human Action,* in Goldworth, A. *Deontology together with the Springs of Action,* Oxford: Clarendon

Bethlehem, R. A. I., Seidlitz, J., White, S. R. et al. (2022) Brain charts for the human lifespan. *Nature*, 604, 525–533. https://doi.org/10.1038/s41586-022-04554-y

Bion, W. R. (2019) *Four discussions with W. R. Bion*. London: The Harris Meltzer Trust.

Blakemore, S. -J. (2012) TEDGlobal https://www.ted.com/talks/sarah_jayne_blakemore_the_mysterious_workings_of_the_adolescent_brain?utm_campaign=tedspread&utm_medium=referral&utm_source=tedcomshare

Blakemore, S. -J. (2019) *Inventing ourselves: The secret life of the teenage brain*. London: Penguin Random House UK.

Blanton, B. S., Broemmel, A. D. and Rigell, A. (2020) Speaking volumes: Professional development through book studies. *American Educational Research Journal*, 57(3), 1014–1044. https://doi-org.oxfordbrookes.idm.oclc.org/10.3102%2F0002831219867327

Bloom, A., Critten, S., Johnson, H. and Wood, C. (2020) Evaluating a method for eliciting children's voice about educational support with children with speech, language and communication needs https://nasenjournals.onlinelibrary.wiley.com/doi/10.1111/1467-8578.12308

Bomber, L. M. (2011) *What about me? Inclusive strategies to support pupils with attachment difficulties make it through the school day*. London: Worth Publishing Ltd.

Bowlby, J. (1961) Processes of mourning. *International Journal of Psychoanalysis*, 42, 317–339.

Bowlby, J. (1971) [1969] *Attachment and loss* (Vol. 1: Attachment, 1st ed.). London: Pimlico.

Bowlby, J. (1973) *Attachment and loss: Anxiety and anger*. London: Hogarth Press (International psycho-analytical library, no. 95).

Bowlby, J. (1979) The Bowlby-Ainsworth attachment theory. *Behavioral and Brain Sciences*, 2(4), 637–638. https://doi.org/10.1017/S0140525X00064955

Bowlby, J. (1980) *Loss: Sadness & depression. Attachment and loss* (Vol. 3). London: Hogarth Press. (International psycho-analytical library no. 109). ISBN 0-465-04238-4. OCLC 59246032.

Bowlby, J. (1981) *Attachment and loss* (Vol. 3, 1st ed.). New York: Basic Books.

Bowlby, J. (1988) *A secure base: Parent-child attachment and healthy human development*. Routledge.

Brammer, C. (2023) Personal Communication. Conversation with Juliet Taylor. 25 March.

Brendtro, L. K. (2006) The vision of Urie Bronfenbrenner: Adults who are crazy about kids. *Reclaiming Children and Youth*, 15(3), 162–166. https://www.researchgate.net/publication/234721190_The_Vision_of_Urie_Bronfenbrenner_Adults_Who_Are_Crazy_about_Kids; https://www.researchgate.net/profile/Larry-Brendtro/publication/234721190_The_Vision_of_Urie_Bronfenbrenner_Adults_Who_Are_Crazy_about_Kids/links/5e20b793299bf1e1fab7f40e/The-Vision-of-Urie-Bronfenbrenner-Adults-Who-Are-Crazy-about-Kids.pdf; https://cyc-net.org/cyc-online/cyconline-nov2010-brendtro.html

Bretherton, I. and Oppenheim, D. (2003) Chapter 3: The MacArthur story stem battery: Development, administration, reliability, validity, and reflections about meaning. In Emde, R. N. and Wolf, D. (2003) *Revealing the inner worlds of young children: the macarthur story stem battery and parent-child narratives*. Cary: Oxford University Press: ProQuest Ebook Central.

Brierley, C. (2022) *Brain charts: Mapping the rapid growth and slow decline of the human brain over our lifetime*. University of Cambridge. https://www.cam.ac.uk/stories/BrainCharts

Bronfenbrenner, U. (1991). What do families do? *Institute for American Values*, Winter / Spring, p. 2.

Bronfenbrenner, U. (2005). Ecological models of human development. In *Readings on the development of children* (pp. 3–8). New York, NY: Worth Publishers.

Brumariu, L. E. (2015) Parent-child attachment and emotion regulation. *New Directions for Child and Adolescent Development*, 2015(148), 31–45. https://doi.org/10.1002/cad.20098. PMID: 26086126.

Burgess, M. (2013) *Factcheck: Schoolchildren "left behind" by shorter school days? | Help Me Investigate… Education*. [online] Available at: http://helpmeinvestigate.com/education/2013/04/longer-school-days-may-not-lead-to-better-education/

Cannon, W. B. (1915) *Bodily changes in pain, hunger, fear, and rage*. New York: Appleton-Century-Crofts.

Carpenter, B., Egerton, J., Cockbill, B., Bloom, T., Fotheringham, J. and Rawson, H. (2015) *Engaging Learners with Complex Learning Difficulties and Disabilities*. Abingdon: Routledge.

Carr, A. (2011) *Positive psychology: The science of happiness and human strengths* (2nd ed.). London: Routledge.

Carter, R., Aldridge, S., Page, M. and Parker, S. (2014) *The human brain book* (2nd ed.). New York: DK Publishing.

Centre for Early Childhood. (2022) *Big change starts small [2021]*. https://centreforearlychildhood.org/research/ and https://centreforearlychildhood.org/report/

Center for Substance Abuse Treatment (US). (2014) *Trauma-informed care in behavioral health services*. Rockville, MD: Substance Abuse and Mental Health Services Administration (SAMHSA) (US); (Treatment Improvement Protocol (TIP) Series, No. 57.) Chapter 3, Understanding the impact of trauma. Rockville, MD. Available from: https://www.ncbi.nlm.nih.gov/books/NBK207191/

Center on the Developing Child at Harvard University. (2011) *Building the brain's "air traffic control" system: How early experiences shape the development of executive function*. Working Paper No. 11. http://www. developing child.harvard.edu and https://harvardcenter.wpenginepowered.com/wp-content/uploads/2011/05/How-Early-Experiences-Shape-the-Development-of-Executive-Function.pdf

Centre for Therapeutic Storytelling (2023) Stories to support pupils' emotional literacy and academic skills. https://therapeuticstorywriting.co.uk/

Cerna, L. (2019) "Refugee education: Integration models and practices in OECD countries", *OECD Education Working Papers*, No. 203, OECD Publishing, Paris, https://doi.org/10.1787/a3251a00-en.

Chang, K. (2017) Living with vulnerability and resiliency: The psychological experience of collective trauma. *Acta Psychopathology*, 3, 53. https://doi.org/10.4172/2469-6676.100125.

Clark, A. (2019) *Surfing uncertainty: Prediction, action, and the embodied mind*. New York: Oxford University Press.

Clarke, J. I. and Dawson, C. (2009) *Growing up again: Parenting ourselves, parenting our children*. Minnesota, United States: Hazelden publishers.

Cohen, J. A., Manarino, A. P. and Deblinger, E. (2017) *Trauma-focused CBT for children and adolescents: Treatment options*. New York, NT: The Guildford Press. https://www.google.co.uk/books/edition/Trauma_Focused_CBT_for_Children_and_Adol/YlbQeyPkliQC?hl=en&gbpv=1&dq=Cohen,+J.+A.,+%26+Mannarino,+A.+P.+(2020).+Trauma-focused+CBT+for+children+and+adolescents:+Treatment+applications.&pg=PP1&printsec=frontcover

Cohen, J. A., Manarino, A. P. and Knudsen, K. (2004) Treating childhood traumatic grief: A pilot study. *Journal of the American Academy of Child & Adolescent Psychiatry*, 43(10), 1225–1233. https://doi.org/10.1097/01.chi.0000135620.15522.38.

Collaborative for Academic, Social, and Emotional Learning (CASEL) (2023) What is the CASEL Framework? https://casel.org/fundamentals-of-sel/what-is-the-casel-framework/

Colley, D. and Cooper, P. (ed.). (2017) *Attachment and emotional development in the classroom: Theory and practice.* London and Philadelphia: Jessica Kingsley Publishers.

Crittendon, P.M. (2005) *Keynote Address at the German Association of Infant Mental Health (GAIMH)*. Hamburg, Germany.

Crugnola C. R., Gazzotti, S., Spinelli, M., Ierardi, E., Caprin, C. and Albizzati, A. (2013) Maternal attachment influences mother–infant styles of regulation and play with objects at nine months. *Attachment & Human Development*, 15(2), 107–131, DOI: 10.1080/14616734.2013.745712

DeWolfe, D. J. (2000) *Training manual for human service workers in major disasters* (2nd ed.) Washington, DC: Center for Mental Health Services. Department of Health and Human Services Substance Abuse and Mental Health Services Administration (SAMHSA). https://www.hsdl.org/?view&did=4017 or https://eric.ed.gov/?id=ED459383

Diener, E. (2006) *BBC Test for Life Satisfaction.* University of Illinois. http://news.bbc.co.uk/1/hi/programmes/happiness_formula/4785402.stm

Diener, E. (2009) *The Science of Well-being: The Collected Works of Ed Diener: Social Indicators Research Series: 37.* Netherlands: Springer.

Diener, E. and Seligman, M. E. P. (2002) Very happy people. *Psychological Science*, 13(1), 81–84. https://doi.org/10.1111/1467-9280.00415

Dingman, M. (2017) *Know your brain: Telencephalon. Neuroscientifically challenged*. http://neuroscientifically challenged.com/blog/know-your-brain-telencephalon [Accessed 13.06.2023].

Dingman, M. (2019) *YourBrain, explained*. Boston, MA. Nicholas Brealey Publishing. Creator of 2-minute neuroscience videos and cited in https://neuroscientificallychallenged.com/posts/know-your-brain-amygdala [Accessed 19.07.2023].

Dorricott, S. (2023) Original artwork with permission from the illustrator to reproduce. Personal communication. Email to Juliet Taylor, 28 July.

Dreisoerner, A., Junker, N. M. and van Dick, R. (2020) The relationship among the components of self-compassion: A pilot study using a compassionate writing intervention to enhance self-kindness, common humanity, and mindfulness. *Journal of Happiness Studies*, 22, 21–47. https://doi.org/10.1007/s10902-019-00217-4

Dreisoerner, A., Junker, N. M., Schlotz, W., Heimrich, J., Bloemeke, S., Ditzen, B. and van Dick, R. (2021) Self-soothing touch and being hugged reduce cortisol responses to stress: A randomized controlled trial on stress, physical touch, and social identity. *Comprehensive Psychoneuroendocrinology*, 8, 100091. https://doi.org/10.1016/j.cpnec.2021.100091; https://www.sciencedirect.com/science/article/pii/S2666497621000655

Durston, S. and Casey, B. J. (2006) What have we learned about cognitive development from neuroimaging?. *Neuropsychologia*, *44*(11), 2149–2157. https://doi.org/10.1016/j.neuropsychologia.2005.10.010

Dweck, C. S. (2007) *Mindset: The new psychology of success*. New York, NY: Penguin Random House.

Eckstein, M., Almeida de Minas, A. C., Scheele, D., Kreuder, A. K., Hurlemann, R., Grinevich, V. and Ditzen, B. (2019) Oxytocin for learning calm and safety. *International Journal of Psychophysiology*, 136, 5–14. https://doi.org/10.1016/j.ijpsycho.2018.06.004

Education Support. (2023) Teacher wellbeing index 2022. https://www.educationsupport.org.uk/resources/for-organisations/research/teacher-wellbeing-index/. [Accessed 30.07.2023].

Eddy, C. L., Herman, K. C., Huang, F. and Reinke, W. M. (2022) Evaluation of a bibliotherapy-based stress intervention for teachers. *Teaching and Teacher Education*, 109, 103543. https://doi.org/10.1016/j.tate.2021.103543

Education Support. (2023) *1970s working conditions in the 2020s: Modernising the professional lives of teachers for the 21st century*. Full report: https://www.educationsupport.org.uk/media/bn2bk5a3/1970s-working-conditions-in-the-2020s.pdf on Website: https://www.educationsupport.org.uk/resources/for-organisations/research/1970s-working-conditions-in-the-2020s-modernising-the-professional-lives-of-teachers-for-the-21st-century/ (Accessed 06.06.2023).

Eisenberg, N., Fabes, R. A. and Murphy, B. C. (1996) Parents' reactions to children's negative emotions: Relations to children's social competence and comforting behavior. *Child Development*. 2227. https://doi.org/10.2307/1131620

EqualiTeach (2023) Equalities Award: Showcasing Your School's Commitment to Equality. https://www.equalitiesaward.co.uk/

Erikson, K. T. (1976a) Loss of community at buffalo creek. *The American Journal of Psychiatry*, 133(3), 302–305.

Erikson, K. T. (1976b) *Everything in its path: Destruction of community in the buffalo creek flood*. New York: Simon and Schuster Paperbacks.

Ethical Leadership Commission (2019) Navigating the Educational Moral Maze: The Final Report of the Ethical Leadership Commission. https://www.ascl.org.uk/ASCL/media/ASCL/Our%20view/Campaigns/Navigating-the-educational-moral-maze.pdf and https://www.nga.org.uk/media/k5pdvv4u/framework-for-ethical-leadership-in-education.pdf found within https://www.nga.org.uk/news-views/directory/ethical-leadership-in-education-campaign/

European Commission (2023) Support for People affected by Russia's Invasion of Ukraine. https://education.ec.europa.eu/support-for-people-affected-by-russias-invasion-of-ukraine

Fairchild, G., Toschi, N., Sully, K., Sonuga-Barke, E. J. S., Hagan, C. C., Diciotti, S., Goodyer, I. M., Calder, A. J. and Passamonti, L. (2016) Mapping the structural organization of the brain in conduct disorder: replication of findings in two independent samples. *Journal of Child Psychology and Psychiatry*. DOI: 10.1111/jcpp.12581

Farley, R. (2023) *Loss and identity*. Personal Communications. Email to Juliet Taylor, 30 July.

Feinstein, L., Duckworth, K. and Sabates, R. (2008) *Education and the family : passing success across the generations*. London: Routledge (Foundations and futures of education).

Feinstein, S. G. (ed.) (2009) *Secrets of the teenage brain: Research-based strategies for reaching and teaching today's adolescents*. Thousand Oaks: Corwin Press: ProQuest Ebook Central. [8 June 2023]. https://ebookcentral.proquest.com/lib/brookes/detail.action?docID=1993924.

Feldman, R. (2003) Infant-mother and infant-father synchrony: The coregulation of positive arousal. *Infant Mental Health Journal*, 1–23. https://doi.org/10.1002/imhj.10041

Felitti, V. (2016) *Dr. Vincent Felitti: Reflections on the adverse childhood experiences (ACE) study*. National Congress of American Indians. https://youtu.be/-ns8ko9-ljU

Field, T. M (1998) Massage therapy effects. *American Psychologist*, 53, 1270–1281. https://doi.org/10.1037/0003-066X.53.12.1270

Field, T. (2013) *Touch: The foundation of experience*. Zero to Three Press.

Figley, C. R. (2002) Compassion fatigue: Psychotherapists' chronic lack of self-care. *Journal of Clinical Psychology*, 58 (11), 1433–1441. Wiley periodicals. DOI: 10.1002/jclp.10090

Ford, T. and Parker, C. (2016) Emotional and behavioural difficulties and mental (ill)health, *Emotional and Behavioural Difficulties*, 21(1), 1–7, DOI: 10.1080/13632752.2016.1139300.

Freud, S. (1917) Essay "Mourning and Melancholia," in Freud, S., Strachey, J. and Richards, A. (1984). *On metapsychology: The theory of psychoanalysis*. Harmondsworth: Penguin (Pelican Freud library, vol. 11).

Freud, S., Strachey, J. and Richards, A. (1991) *On metapsychology: The theory of psychoanalysis:Beyond the pleasure principle, the ego and the Id and other works*. Harmondsworth: Penguin (Pelican Freud library, vol. 11).

Friston, K. and Picard, F. (2014) Predictions, perception, and a sense of self. *Neurology*, 83(12), 1112–1118. https://doi.org/10.1212/WNL.0000000000000798. Epub 2014 Aug 15. PMID: 25128179; PMCID: PMC4166359. https://www.ncbi.nlm.nih.gov/pmc/articles/PMC4166359/ [Accessed 29.03.2023].

Furr, J., Comer, J., Edmunds, J. and Kendall, P. (2010) Disasters and youth: A meta-analytic examination of posttraumatic stress, *Journal of Consulting and Clinical Psychology*, 78. DOI:10.1037/a0021482

Gazzaniga, M. S., Ivry, R. B. and Mangun, G. R. (2019) *Cognitive neuroscience: The biology of the mind* (5th ed.). New York: W. W. Norton and Company Publishers.

Geddes, H. (2006) *Attachment in the classroom: The links between children's early experience, emotional well being and performance in school*. London: Worth Publishing Ltd.

Giedd J. N. (2008). The teen brain: insights from neuroimaging. *The Journal of Adolescent Health: Official Publication of the Society for Adolescent Medicine*, *42*(4), 335–343. https://doi.org/10.1016/j.jadohealth.2008.01.007

Giedd, J. N., Blumenthal, J., Jeffries, N. O., Castellanos, F. X., Liu, H., Zijdenbos, A., Paus, T., Evans, A. C. and Rapoport, J. L. (1999) Brain development during childhood and adolescence: a longitudinal MRI study. *Nature Neuroscience*, *2*(10), 861–863. https://doi.org/10.1038/13158

Gilbert, L., Gus, L., Rose, J. and Gottman, J. M. (2021) *Emotion coaching with children and young people in schools: Promoting positive behaviour, wellbeing and resilience*. London: Jessica Kingsley.

Gilbert, P. (2014) The origins and nature of compassion focused therapy. British Journal of Clinical Psychology, 53, 6–41. https://doi.org/10.1111/bjc.12043

Glicken, M. D. and Robinson, B. C. (2013) Chapter 2 – Understanding job stress, job dissatisfaction, and worker burnout. In *Practical resources for the mental health professional, treating worker dissatisfaction during economic change* (pp. 23–39). Academic Press. https://doi.org/10.1016/B978-0-12-397006-0.00002-6; https://www.sciencedirect.com/science/article/pii/B9780123970060000026; https://www.researchgate.net/publication/285180579_Understanding_Job_Stress_Job_Dissatisfaction_and_Worker_Burnout; or https://www.sciencedirect.com/science/article/abs/pii/B9780123970060000026?via%3Dihub

Gould, S. J. (2003) *The structure of evolutionary theory*. London and Cambridge, MA: Belknap Press of Harvard University Press. ISBN: 9780674006133

Gračanin, A., Bylsma, L. M. and Vingerhoets, A. J. J. M. (2014) Is crying a self-soothing behavior? *Frontiers in Psychology*. https://doi.org/10.3389/fpsyg.2014.00502

Greene, R. W. (2021) The explosive child: A new approach for understanding and parenting easily frustrated, chronically inflexible children (6th ed.). New York: HarperCollins Publishers.

Greenspan, S. I. and Shanker, S. G. (2004) *The first idea: How symbols, language, and intelligence evolved from our primate ancestors to modern humans.* Cambridge, Mass.: Da Capo Press

Gross, J. J. (1998) The emerging field of emotion regulation: An integrative review. *Review of General Psychology*, 271–299. https://doi.org/10.1037/1089-2680.2.3.271

Gus, L. and Wood, F. (2017) Emotion coaching. In D. Colley and P. Cooper (Eds.), *Attachment and emotional development in the classroom: Theory and practice* (pp. 83–99). London: Jessica Kingsley.

Hagman, G. (2016) *New models of bereavement theory and treatment: New mourning*. London and New York: Routledge.

Ham, J. and Tronick, E. (2009) Relational psychophysiology: Lessons from mother–infant physiology research on dyadically expanded states of consciousness. *Psychotherapy Research*, 19(6), 619–632. https://doi.org/10.1080/10503300802609672

Harris, K. M. and Udry, R. J. (2022) *National longitudinal study of adolescent to adult health (add health), 1994–2018 [public use]*. Carolina Population Center, University of North Carolina-Chapel Hill [distributor], Inter-university Consortium for Political and Social Research [distributor], 2022-08-09. https://doi.org/10.3886/ICPSR21600.v25

Häusser, J. A., Junker, N. M. and van Dick, R. (2020) The how and the when of the social cure: A conceptual model of group- and individual-level mechanisms linking social identity to health and well-being. *European Journal of Social Psychology*, 721–731. https://doi.org/10.1002/ejsp.2668

Häusser, J. A., Kattenstroth, M., van Dick, R. and Mojzisch, A. (2012) "We" are not stressed: social identity in groups buffers neuroendocrine stress reactions. Journal of Experimental Social Psychology, 48, 973–977. https://doi.org/10.1016/j.jesp.2012.02.020

Harvard Business Review. (2021) *The workplace health report*. https://championhealth.co.uk/wp-content/uploads/the-workplace-health-report-2022.pdf

Harvard Health. (2020) *Understanding the stress response: Chronic activation of this survival mechanism impairs health.* Harvard Medical School: Harvard Health Publishing. Understanding the stress response – Harvard Health.

Health and Safety Executive. (2022) Work related stress, depression or anxiety statistics in Great Britain', www.hse.gov.uk/statistics/

Hebb, D. O. (1949) *The Organization of Behavior: A neuropsychological theory*. New York: Wiley. https://pure.mpg.de/rest/items/item_2346268_3/component/file_2346267/content

Hefferon, K. and Boniwell, I. (2011) *Positive psychology: Theory, research and applications*. McGraw-Hill Education: ProQuest Ebook Central. https://doi.org/729517 [Accessed 27.04.2023].

Herbers, J. E., Cutuli, J. J., Supkoff, L. M., Narayan, A. J. and Masten, A. S. (2014) Parenting and coregulation: Adaptive systems for competence in children experiencing homelessness. *American Journal of Orthopsychiatry*, 420–430. Published online July 2014. https://doi.org/10.1037/h0099843

Herman, K. C., Hickmon-Rosa, J. and Reinke, W. M. (2018) Empirically derived profiles of teacher stress, burnout, self-efficacy, and coping and associated student outcomes. *Journal of Positive Behavior Interventions*, 20(2), 90–100. https://doi.org/10.1177/1098300717732066

Herman, K. C., Prewett, S. L., Eddy, C. L., Savala, A. and Reinke, W. M. (2020a) Profiles of middle school teacher stress and coping: Concurrent and prospective correlates. *Journal of School Psychology*, 78, 54–68. https://doi.org/10.1016/j.jsp.2019.11.003; https://pubmed.ncbi.nlm.nih.gov/32178811/

Herman, K. C., Reinke, W. M. and Eddy, C. L. (2020b) Advances in understanding and intervening in teacher stress and coping: The Coping-Competence-Context Theory. *Journal of School Psychology*, 78, 69–74.

Herman, K. C. and Reinke, W. M. (2015) *Stress management for teachers: A proactive guide*. (The Guilford Practical Intervention in the Schools Series).New York, NY: Guilford Press.

Hill, R. and Dahlitz, M. (2022) *The practitioner's guide to the science of psychotherapy*. New York: W. W. Norton and Company.

Hirschberger, G. (2018) Collective trauma and the social construction of meaning. *Frontiers in Psychology*, 9, 1441. https://doi.org/10.3389/fpsyg.2018.01441 and https://www.ncbi.nlm.nih.gov/pmc/articles/PMC6095989/

HM Government. (2022) *SEND REVIEW: Right support, right place, right time*. Online at https://www.gov.uk/government/consultations/send-review-right-support-right-place-right-time

Hohnen, B., Gilmour, J., Murphy, T., and Blakemore, S. J. (Foreword). (2019) *The incredible teenage brain: Everything you need to know to unlock your teen's potential*. London and Philadelphia: Jessica Kingsley Publishers.

Holden, C. (1979) Paul Maclean and the Triune Brain. *Science*, 204(4397), 1066–1068. https://www-science-org.oxfordbrookes.idm.oclc.org/doi/10.1126/science.377485

Holmes, E. (2022) *Therapeutic storywriting groups*. The Blog that Inspires Leaders in the UK Education Sector. The Optimus Blog. https://blog.optimus-education.com/therapeutic-storywriting-groups

Holmes, J. (1993) *John Bowlby and attachment theory*. London: Routledge (The Makers of modern psychotherapy).

Holmes, S. E., Girgenti, M. J., Davis, M. T., Pietrzak, R. H., DellaGioia, N., Nabulsi, N., Matuskey, D., Southwick, S., Duman, R. S., Carson, R. E., Krystal, J. H., Esterlis, I. and the Traumatic Stress Brain Study Group in *PNAS*. (2017) *Altered metabotropic glutamate receptor 5 markers in PTSD: In vivo and post-mortem evidence*. U.S. National Academy of Sciences, University of Yale: Yale News. https://neurosciencenews.com/ptsd-treatments-7108/ and https://doi.org/10.1073/pnas.1701749114

Horowitz, M. J. (2011) *Stress response syndromes: PTSD, grief, adjustment, and dissociative disorders*. Northvale, NJ: Rowman & Littlefield Publishers, Incorporated. Available from: ProQuest Ebook Central. [29 June 2023]. https://ebookcentral.proquest.com/lib/brookes/detail.action?docID=1117183#

Howard, S. and Johnson, B. (2004) Resilient teachers: Resisting stress and burnout. *Social Psychology of Education: An International Journal*, 7(4), 399–420. https://doi.org/10.1007/s11218-004-0975-0 [Accessed 12.04.2022].

Hoxby, C. (2022) *The fork in the road: Adolescence, education, economic fatalism, and populism with Caroline Hoxby*. Lecture. Image Adapted from Video Source: https://youtu.be/r3OH0hT-gBo University of California television (UCTV).

Hughes, D. (2006) *Building the bonds of attachment: Awakening love in deeply troubled children*. Lanham, MD: Jason Aronson.

Hughes, N. K. and Schlösser, A. (2014) The effectiveness of nurture groups: A systematic review. *Emotional and Behavioural Difficulties*, 19(4), 386–409. https://doi.org/10.1080/13632752.2014.883729; new.boxallprofile.org. (2023) *Boxall*. [online] Available at: https://new.boxallprofile.org/.

Human Genome Project. (2023) Cambridge. https://www.yourgenome.org/stories/evolution-of-the-human-brain/

Iacobucci, G. (2022) Covid-19: Pandemic has disproportionately harmed children's mental health. *BMJ*, 376, o430. https://doi.org/10.1136/bmj.o430

International Rescue Committee (2023) Supporting Refugees. https://www.rescue.org/uk/supporting-refugees-uk

Jané, S. E., Fernandez, V. and Hällgren, M. (2022) Shit happens. How do we make sense of that? *Qualitative Research in Organizations and Management*, 17(4), 425–441. https://doi.org/10.1108/QROM-12-2021-2261

Joshi, L. H. (2022) *Help your child cope with change*. Poland: Vie Books (Summersdale Publishers Ltd).

Kanjlia, S., Lane, C., Feigenson, L. and Bedny, M. (2016) Absence of visual experience modifies the neural basis of numerical thinking: Math study shows our brains are far more adaptable than we know. *Proceedings of the National Academy of Sciences*, 201524982. John Hopkins University, Baltimore, MD and Harvard University, Cambridge, MA. https://doi.org/10.1073/pnas.1524982113 and Absence of visual experience modifies the neural basis of numerical thinking | PNAS.

Kosner, A. W. (2019) *The mind at work: Karl Friston on the brain's surprising energy*. https://blog.dropbox.com/topics/work-culture/the-mind-at-work--karl-friston-on-the-brain-s-surprising-energy

Kosner, A. W. (2021) *The mind at work: Lisa Feldman Barrett on the metabolism of emotion*. https://blog.dropbox.com/topics/work-culture/the-mind-at-work--lisa-feldman-barrett-on-the-metabolism-of-emot

Krause, E. D., Mendelson, T. and Lynch, T. R. (2003) Childhood emotional invalidation and adult psychological distress: The mediating role of emotional inhibition. *Child Abuse & Neglect*, 199–213. https://doi.org/10.1016/s0145-2134(02)00536-7

Kübler-Ross, E. (1969) *On death and dying*. Abingdon: Routledge.

Kübler-Ross, E. (1997) *On death and dying* (1St Scribner Classics ed.). New York: Scribner Classics; London and New York: Routledge.

LeDoux, J. E. (1996) *The emotional brain*. New York: Simon and Schuster.

LeDoux, J. E. and Pine, D. S. (2016) Using neuroscience to help understand fear and anxiety: A two-system framework. *American Journal of Psychiatry*. Published Online. https://doi.org/10.1176/appi.ajp.2016.16030353

Levine, P. A. and Klein, M. (2006) *Trauma through a child's eyes: Awakening the ordinary miracle of healing*. Berkley, CA: North Atlantic Books.

Levy, T. (2016a) *The functions of attachment* [online]. Evergreen Psychotherapy Center: Attachment Treatment and Training Institute. Available here [Accessed 02.05.2018].

Levy, T. (2016b) *Disrupted attachment paves way for future problems* [online]. Evergreen Psychotherapy Center: Attachment Treatment and Training Institute. Available here [Accessed 02.05.2018].

Li, P. (2023) What is a Secure Base and How Can Parents Become One? https://www.parentingforbrain.com/secure-base/

Liddle, M., Boswell, G., Wright, S., Francis, V. and Perry, R. (2016) *Beyond youth custody*. http://www.beyondyouthcustody.net/wp-content/uploads/BYC-Trauma-Young-Offenders-FINAL.pdf

Lipina, S. J. and Colombo, J. A. (2009) *Poverty and brain development during childhood: An approach from cognitive psychology and neuroscience.* American Psychological Association. https://doi.org/10.1037/11879-000

Liver, P (2014) Childline Director: *Nothing is More Urgent than Addressing the Increased Unhappiness in Children*. TES Opinion. https://www.tes.com/magazine/archive/nothing-more-urgent-addressing-increased-unhappiness-children

Long, R. (2023) Positive psychology workshop. 'Global solutions to working with Vulnerable Children and Young People' at SEBDA International Conference 2023. Birmingham, UK.

Lyubomirsky, S. (2008) *The how of happiness: A scientific approach to getting the life you want*. New York: Penguin Press.

Lyubomirsky, S., King, L. A. and Diener, E. (2005) The benefits of frequent positive affect: Does happiness lead to success? *Psychological Bulletin,* 131, 803–855. http://sonjalyubomirsky.com/wp-content/themes/sonjalyubomirsky/papers/LKD2005.pdf

Ma, X., Edgecombe, G. D., Hou, X., Goral, T. and Strausfeld, N. J. (2015) Preservational pathways of corresponding brains of a Cambrian Euartropod. *Current Biology*, 25(22), 2969–2975. https://doi.org/10.1016/j.cub.2015.09.063

MacLean, P. D. (1970) The triune brain, emotion, and scientific bias. In F. O. Schmitt (Ed.), *The neurosciences: Second study program* (pp. 336–349). New York Rockefeller University Press.

MacLean, P. D. (1994) Human nature: Duality or triality? *Politics and the Life Sciences*, 13(1), 107–112. https://doi.org/10.1017/S0730938400022358. https://www-jstor-org.oxfordbrookes.idm.oclc.org/stable/4236012

Maguire, E. A., Gadian, D. G., Johnsrude, I. S., Good, C. D., Ashburner, J., Frackowiak, R. S. J. and Frith, C. D. (2000) Navigation-related structural change in the hippocampi of taxi drivers. *Biological Sciences*, 97(8), 4398–4403. https://doi.org/10.1073/pnas.070039597

Malinen, S., Hatton, T., Naswall, K. and Kuntz, J. (2018) Strategies to enhance employee well-being and organisational performance in a postcrisis environment: A case study. *Journal of Contingencies and Crisis Management*, 27. https://doi.org/10.1111/1468-5973.12227 [Accessed 24.07.2023].

McCallum, F. and Price, D. (2010) Well teachers, well students. *Journal of Student Wellbeing*, 4(1), 19–34. 19 School of Education University of South Australia Mawson Lakes, South Australia.

McGilchrist, I. (2009) *The master and his emissary: The divided brain and the making of the western world*. New Haven, CT: Yale University Press.

McKay, S (2020) Rethinking the reptilian brain https://drsarahmckay.com/rethinking-the-reptilian-brain/

McLaughlin, B., Gotlieb, M. R. and Mills, D. J. (2022) *Caught in a dangerous world: Problematic news consumption and its relationship to mental and physical ill-being. Health Communication*, 1. https://doi.org/10.1080/10410236.2022.2106086

Mehrabian, A. (1972) *Nonverbal communication*. Piscataway, NJ: Aldine Transaction.

Meins, E., Fernyhough, C., Wainwright, R., Clark-Carter, D., Das Gupta, M., Fradley, E. and Tuckey, M. (2003) Pathways to understanding mind: construct validity and predictive validity of maternal mind-mindedness. *Child Development*, *74*(4), 1194–1211. https://doi.org/10.1111/1467-8624.00601

Mental Health Foundation. (2023) Work-life Balance. https://www.mentalhealth.org.uk/explore-mental-health/a-z-topics/work-life-balance

Mentally Healthy Schools. (2023): Supporting Staff Wellbeing. Anna Freud: National Centre for Children and Families. https://www.mentallyhealthyschools.org.uk/whole-school-approach/supporting-staff-wellbeing/ [Accessed 19.02.2024].

Mercier, M. and Lubart, T. (2021) The effects of board games on creative potential. *Journal of Creative Behavior*, 55(3), 875–885.

Milburn, T. W. (1998) Psychology, negotiation, and peace. *Applied and Preventive Psychology*, 7(2), 109–119. https://doi.org/10.1016/S0962-1849(05)80008-3.

Mind. (2016) *How to deal with anger.* https://doi.org/53109 [Accessed: 05.06.2022].

Mind. (2023) https://www.mind.org.uk.

Momentous Institute. (2019) *Upstairs and downstairs brain upstairs and downstairs brain*. Momentous Institute. https://momentousinstitute.org/blog/upstairs-and-downstairs-brain

Morrison, I. (2016) Keep calm and cuddle on: Social touch as a stress buffer. Adaptive Human Behavior and Physiology, 2, 344–362. https://doi.org/10.1007/s40750-016-0052-x

Mosley, J. (1998) *Quality circle time in the primary classroom: Your essential guide to enhancing self-esteem, self-discipline and positive relationships.* Cambridge: LDA Publishers.

Music, G. (2016) *Nurturing natures: Attachment and children's emotional, sociocultural and brain development*. Taylor & Francis Group, London. Available from: ProQuest Ebook Central. [21 November 2022]. From online library https://ebookcentral-proquest-com.oxfordbrookes.idm.oclc.org/lib/brookes/detail.action?docID=4710029#

Myers, D. (1994) *Disaster responses and recovery: A handbook for mental health professionals.* National Center for Post-Traumatic Stress Disorder. US Department of Health and Human Services. https://www.google.co.uk/books/edition/Disaster_Response_and_Recovery/-sZPLe8CCIwC?hl=en&gbpv=1

National Childbirth Trust (UK) website. (2023) https://www.nct.org.uk/

National Child Traumatic Stress Network. (2023) https://learn.nctsn.org/

Neff, K. D. (2003) Self-compassion: An alternative conceptualization of a healthy attitude toward oneself. *Self Ident*, 2, 85–101. https://doi.org/10.1080/15298860309032

NHS. (2023) https://www.nhs.uk/

Nikoni, S. (2011) Brain areas and their functions. *(Health24, August 2011) in Health24:* Urban Child Institute (2023). Brain areas and their functions | Health24 (news24.com) Urban Child Institute: Health24. https://www.news24.com/health24/mental-health/brain/anatomy-of-the-brain/brain-areas-and-their-functions-20120721#:~:text=The%20brain%20can%20be%20divided,Hippocampas%20and%20the%20Mid%2D%20brain.

NurtureUK. (2023) *Nurture Groups*. [online]. Available at: https://www.nurtureuk.org/what-we-do/nurture-groups/

O'Brien, J., Forest, M. and Pearpoint, J. (1996) *SOLUTION CIRCLE getting unstuck a creative problem solving tool*. Toronto: Inclusion Press https://inclusion.com/site/wp-content/uploads/2020/03/Solution-Circle.pdf

Office for Health Improvement and Disparities. (2022) https://www.gov.uk/government/publications/covid-19-mental-health-and-wellbeing-surveillance-report

Office for National Statistics. (2021) https://www.gov.uk/government/publications/covid-19-mental-health-and-wellbeing-surveillance-report

Ofsted. (2019) Teacher Well-Being at Work In Schools and Further Education Providers. https://assets.publishing.service.gov.uk/government/uploads/system/uploads/attachment_data/file/936253/Teacher_well-being_report_110719F.pdf

Ofqual. (2021) *Learning during the pandemic: Quantifying lost time*. https://www.gov.uk/government/publications/learning-during-the-pandemic/learning-during-the-pandemic-quantifying-lost-time

Organisation for Economic Co-operation and Development (OECD). (2022) *Policy responses: Ukraine, tacking the policy challenges*. Supporting the social and emotional well-being of refugee students from Ukraine in host countries. https://www.oecd.org/ukraine-hub/policy-responses/supporting-the-social-and-emotional-well-being-of-refugee-students-from-ukraine-in-host-countries-af1ff0b0/

Ortega-Hernández, J. (2014) Making sense of 'lower' and 'upper' stem-group Euarthropoda, with comments on the strict use of the name Arthropoda von Siebold, 1848. *Biological Reviews of the Cambridge Philosophical Society*, 2014. (Published online December 21, 2014). https://doi.org/10.11111/brv.12168

Ortega-Hernández, J. (2015a) *Homology of head sclerites in burgess shale euarthropods*. University of Cambridge, UK. http://dx.doi.org/10.1016/j.cub.2015.04.034 published 7th May 2015

Ortega-Hernández, J. (2015b) *Clues contained in 500-million-year-old brain point to origin of heads in early animals*. https://www.cam.ac.uk/research/news/clues-contained-in-500-million-year-old-brain-point-to-the-origin-of-heads-in-early-animals published 7th May 2015

Parkes, C. M. (1972) *Bereavement: Studies in grief in adult life*. London: Tavistock.

Parkes, C. M. (2001) *A historical overview of the scientific study of bereavement*. In M. S. Stroebe, R. O. Hansson, W. Stroebe, and H. Schut (Eds.), *Handbook of bereavement research: Consequences, coping, and care* (pp. 25–45). American Psychological Association. https://doi.org/10.1037/10436-001

Pastoor, L. (2016), Rethinking refugee education: principles, policies and practice from a European perspective, *Annual Review of Comparative and International Education*, 30, 107–116.

Pastoor, L. (2019) *In-Service Teacher Training (INSETT) - Providing psyschosocial support to young refugees*, Norwegian Centre for Violence and Traumatic Stress Studies. https://one.oecd.org/document/EDU/WKP(2019)11/En/pdf

Pearson, N. (2014) *King of Cambrian predators had brain of a worm*. Natural History Museum. https://www.nhm.ac.uk/discover/news/2014/july/king-cambrian-predators-had-brain-worm.html

Perrow, S. (2023) Susan Perrow - Therapeutic Storyteller. https://susanperrow.com/

Perry, B. and Szalavitz, M. (2017) *The boy who was raised as a dog: And other stories from a child psychiatrist's notebook — What traumatized children can teach us about loss, love, and healing* (3rd ed.). United States: Basic Books.

Pierson, R (2013) Every Kid Needs a Champion. TED Talks Education. https://www.ted.com/talks/rita_pierson_every_kid_needs_a_champion?language=en

Pillay, S. (2016) The Thinking Benefits of Doodling. Blog at Harvard Medical School. Harvard Health Publishing. https://www.health.harvard.edu/blog/the-thinking-benefits-of-doodling-2016121510844

Porges. S. W. (2009) The polyvagal theory: New insights into adaptive reactions of the autonomic nervous system. *Cleveland Clinic Journal of Medicine*, 76 (Suppl 2), S86–S90. https://doi.org/10.3949/ccjm.76.s2.17; https://www.ncbi.nlm.nih.gov/pmc/articles/PMC3108032/#:~:text=The%20polyvagal%20theory%20proposes%20that,of%20behavior%20and%20psychological%20experience

Porges, S. W. (2022) Polyvagal theory: A science of safety. *Frontiers in Integrative Neuroscience*, 16, 871227. https://doi.org/10.3389/fnint.2022.871227 or https://www.ncbi.nlm.nih.gov/pmc/articles/PMC9131189/

QBI. (2023) *What is synaptic plasticity?* Australia: Queensland Brain Institute. What is synaptic plasticity? – Queensland Brain Institute – University of Queensland (uq.edu.au) or https://qbi.uq.edu.au/brain-basics/brain/brain-physiology/what-synaptic-plasticity

Ra, F. (2011) *Subjective Well-Being Definitions and Measures*. iswb.org. Available at: http://www.amazon.co.uk/kindle-ebooks. Downloaded on 28th March 2014.

Rae, T. (2012) *The anger alphabet: Understanding anger – An emotional development programme for young children aged 6–12* (2nd ed.). SAGE Publications. https://doi.org/4093389.

Ratcliffe, M., Ruddell, M. and Smith, B. (2014) What is a "sense of foreshortened future?" A phenomenological study of trauma, trust, and time. *Frontiers in Psychology*, 5, 1026. https://doi.org/10.3389/fpsyg.2014

Riley, K. (2022) *Compassionate leadership for school belonging*. London: UCL Press. https://doi.org/10.14324/111.9781787359567; https://discovery.ucl.ac.uk/id/eprint/10146072/; https://discovery.ucl.ac.uk/id/eprint/10146072/1/Compassionate-Leadership-for-School-Belonging.pdf [Accessed 19 February 2024].

Robertson, J. and Bowlby, J. (1952) Responses of young children to separation from their mothers II: Observations of the sequences of response of children aged 18 to 24 months during the course of separation. *Courrier du Centre International de l'Enfance*, 3, 131–142.

Rogers, B. (2011) Essential guide to managing teacher stress: Practical skills for teachers. Harlow: Pearson Education UK. Available from: ProQuest Ebook Central. [28 April 2023]. https://ebookcentral.proquest.com/lib/brookes/reader.action?docID=5138681

Rogers, C. R. (1959) A theory of therapy, personality, and interpersonal relationships: As developed in the client-centered framework. In S. Koch (Ed.), *Psychology: A study of a science. Formulations of the Person and the Social Context* (Vol. 3, pp. 184–256). New York: McGraw Hill.

Rose, J., Gilbert, L. and Richards, V. (2015) *Health and well-being in early childhood*. https://books.google.co.uk/books?id=HFTpCQAAQBAJ&lpg=PT136&ots=GsA0Na2m5p&dq=o'connor%20and%20russell%202004%20adverse%20childhood%20experiences&pg=PT136#v=onepage&q=o'connor%20and%20russell%202004%20adverse%20childhood%20experiences&f=false

Rosenshine, B (2012) Principles of Instruction: Research-Based Strategies That All Teachers Should Know. https://www.teachertoolkit.co.uk/wp-content/uploads/2018/10/Principles-of-Insruction-Rosenshine.pdf [Accessed 15.08.2023]

Sammons, A. (2019) *The compassionate teacher: Why compassion should be at the heart of our schools*. Melton, Woodbridge: John Catt Educational.

Segal, Z. V., Williams, J. M. G. and Teasdale, J. D. (2013) *Mindfulness-based cognitive therapy for depression: A new approach to preventing relapse (2nd Edition)*. New York, NY: The Guilford Press.

Seligman, M. E. P. (2002) *Authentic happiness: Using the new positive psychology to realize your potential for lasting fulfillment.* New York, NY: Free Press.

Seligman, M. E. P., Steen, T., Park, N. and Peterson, C. (2005) Positive psychology progress: Empirical validation of interventions. *American Psychologist*, 60(5), 410–421. https://doi.org/10.1037/0003-066X.60.5.410. American Psychological Association.

SEPSIS. (2023) Sharing stories of trauma can help healing: Faces of sepsis sharing stories of trauma can help healing: Faces of sepsis. Sepsis Alliance. https://www.sepsis.org/news/sharing-stories-of-trauma-can-help-healing-faces-of-sepsis/

ShapeofLife. (2023) *Amphioxus or, what we like to call Sir Lancelet.* Image on https://www.shapeoflife.org/news/featured-creature/2015/06/04/amphioxus; https://www.shapeoflife.org/sites/default/files/global/images/graphic-amphioxus.jpg

Shelley, L. M. and Beins, B. C. (2012) *Student handbook to psychology: Developmental psychology.* New York: Facts on File Inc.

Simon, N. S. and Johnson, S. M. (2015) Teacher turnover in high-poverty schools: What we know and can do. *Teachers College Record*, 117 (3), 1–36. https://psycnet.apa.org/record/2015-09773-007

Shonkoff, J. P. (2010) *Building a new biodevelopmental framework to guide the future of early childhood policy.* https://srcd.onlinelibrary.wiley.com/doi/abs/10.1111/j.1467-8624.2009.01399.x; https://doi.org/10.1111/j.1467-8624.2009.01399.x

Siegel, D. J. and Bryson, T. P. (2011) *The whole-brain child: 12 revolutionary strategies to nurture your child's developing mind.* London: Robinson.

Smith. (2016) *Using de-escalation techniques effectively. The Optimus Blog.* https://blog.optimus-education.com/using-de-escalation-techniques-effectively

Soboti, J. M. (2022) Building resilience: Helping emerging adults cope during the novel Coronavirus pandemic. *Clinical Social Work Journal*, 51, 24–33 (2023). https://doi.org/10.1007/s10615-022-00845-z or https://link.springer.com/content/pdf/10.1007/s10615-022-00845-z.pdf

Souers, K. and Hall, P. (2016) *Fostering resilient learners: Strategies for creating a trauma-sensitive classroom.* Alexandria, VA: Association for Supervision and Curriculum Development.

Sowell, E. R., Thompson, P. M., Holmes, C. J., Jernigan, T. L. and Toga, A. W. (1999) In vivo evidence for post-adolescent brain maturation in frontal and striatal regions. *Nature Neuroscience*, 2(10), 859–861. https://doi.org/10.1038/13154

Stallard, P. (2019) *Think Good, Feel Good: A Cognitive Behavioural Therapy Workbook for Children and Young People.* John Wiley & Sons, Incorporated, 2019. *ProQuest Ebook Central*, https://ebookcentral.proquest.com/lib/brookes/detail.action?docID=5561047.

Steffen, P. R., Hedges, D. and Matheson, R. (2022) The brain is adaptive not triune: How the brain responds to threat, challenge, and change. *Frontiers in Psychiatry*, 13, 802606. https://doi.org/10.3389/fpsyt.2022.802606 https://www.frontiersin.org/articles/10.3389/fpsyt.2022.802606/full

Stroebe, M. and Schut, H. (1999) The dual process model of coping with bereavement: Rationale and description. Death Studies, 23(3), 197–224. https://doi.org/10.1080/074811899201046. PMID: 10848151. https://pubmed.ncbi.nlm.nih.gov/10848151/

Suldo, S. M. (2016) *Promoting student happiness: Positive psychology interventions in schools.* Guilford Publications: ProQuest Ebook Central. https://doi.org/4439757. [Accessed 30.05.2023].

Sumners, C. (2018) *Synapses: Crucial connections: Synapses connect one neuron to another and are thus responsible for every thought, memory or movement—But how do they work?* Texas A&M University Health. How Do Synapses Work? – Texas A&M Today (tamu.edu) and Synapses: Crucial connections – Vital Record (tamhsc.edu).

Tajfel, H., Turner, J. C., Austin, W. G. and Worchel, S. (1979) An integrative theory of intergroup conflict. *Organizational identity: A reader*, 56–65.

Tang, Y., Benusiglio, D., Lefevre, A., Hilfiger, L., Althammer, F., Bludau, A. and Grinevich, V. (2020) Social touch promotes interfemale communication via activation of parvocellular oxytocin neurons. *Nature Neuroscience*, 23, 1125–1137. https://doi.org/10.1038/s41593-020-0674-y

Tang, E., Bleys, D. and Vliegen, N. (2018) Making sense of adopted children's internal reality using narrative story stem techniques: A mixed-methods synthesis. *Frontiers in Psychology*, 9, Article 1189. https://doi.org/10.3389/fpsyg.2018.01189

Taylor, J. (2023) Original images created by the author, Juliet Taylor, for use in this publication, 2023.

Taylor and Francis Group. (2022) *News addiction linked to not only poor mental wellbeing but physical health too, new study shows.* ScienceDaily. ScienceDaily, 24 August 2022. www.sciencedaily.com/releases/2022/08/220824102936.htm

The Circle of Security Network. (2023) https://www.circleofsecuritynetwork.org/

The Family Place. (2023) Specialist and flexible therapeutic interventions for families https://thefamilyplace.co.uk/

Thompson, P. M., Giedd, J. N., Woods, R. P., MacDonald, D., Evans, A. C. and Toga, A. W. (2000) Growth patterns in the developing brain detected by using continuum mechanical tensor maps. *Nature*, 404(6774), 190–193.

Togetherall. (2023) *Whatever's on your mind, we're here: We're a community of real people who understand.* https://togetherall.com/en-gb/

Tranter, M. (2021) *A million things to ask a neuroscientist: The brain made easy.* NeuroScientist.

Tronick, E. Z. (1989) Emotions and emotional communication in infants. *American Psychologist*, 44(2), 112–119. https://doi.org/10.1037/0003-066X.44.2.112

Tronick, E. Z. (2017) *Neurobehavioural development in infancy.* In D. Skuse, H. Bruce, L. Dowdney (Eds.), *Child psychology and psychiatry: Frameworks for clinical training and practice* (pp. 17–23). John Wiley & Sons, Ltd https://doi.org/10.1002/9781119170235.ch3

Unicef (2023) Rights Respecting Schools: Creating Safe and Inspiring Places to Learn. Unicef UK. https://www.unicef.org.uk/rights-respecting-schools/

Urban Child Institute. (2023) *Baby's brain begins now: Conception to age 3.* http://www.urbanchildinstitute.org/why-0-3/baby-and-brain

Van der Kolk, B. (2015) *The body keeps the score: Mind, brain and body in the transformation of trauma.* New York and London: Penguin Books.

Von der Embse, N., Ryan, S. V., Gibbs, T. and Mankin, A. (2019) Teacher stress interventions: A systematic review. *Psychology in the Schools*, 56(8), 1328–1343.

Wade, M., Parson, J., Humphreys, K. A., McLaughlin, K. A., Sheridan, M. A., Zeanah, C. H., Nelson, C. A. and Fox, N. A. (2022) The Bucharest Early Intervention Project: Adolescent mental health and adaptation following early deprivation. *Child Development Perspectives*, 16(3), 157–164. PMID: 36247832, PMCID: PMC9555391 doi: https://doi.org10.1111/cdep.12462

Walker, A. (2023) *Teacher retention commission: 8 proposals to stem exodus.* School week. https://schoolsweek.co.uk/teacher-retention-commission-8-proposals-to-stem-exodus/ [Accessed 06.06.2023].

Weir, K. (2020) *Grief and COVID-19: Mourning our bygone lives.* American Psychological Association. https://www.apa.org/news/apa/2020/04/grief-covid-19

WHO. (2020) *Mental health atlas 2020.* https://www.who.int/publications/i/item/9789240036703

Widgit Online (2023) https://widgitonline.com/en/home

Winnicott, D. W. (1973) *The child, the family, and the outside world.* UK: Penguin Random House UK.

Woodward, C. (2020) *Using WhatsApp as a support mechanism for community educators in Zimbabwe.* Retrieved July 17 2023 from https://www.learntechlib.org/p/218906/.

Workable. (2023) *Employee wellbeing: Caring for your people.* https://resources.workable.com/stories-and-insights/employee-wellbeing-caring-for-your-people#:~:text=More%20productivity%3A%20Employee%20wellbeing%20boosts,physical%2C%20mental%2C%20and%20financial [Accessed 30.07.2023].

Wray, J., Jaume, N. A., Oulton, K. and Sell, D. (2023) Talking with children and young people with 22q11ds about their mental health, behaviour, learning and communication. *Child: Care, Health and Development*, 49(1), 90–105. https://doi.org/10.1111/cch.13013

Young Minds. (2023) Young Minds: Fighting for young people's mental health. https://www.youngminds.org.uk/

Yurgelun-Todd, D. A., Killgore, W. D. and Young, A. D. (2002) Sex differences in cerebral tissue volume and cognitive performance during adolescence. *Psychological Reports*, 91(3 Pt 1), 743–757. https://doi.org/10.2466/pr0.2002.91.3.743

Zhao, Q., Yu, C. D., Wang, R., Xu, Q. J., Pra, R. D., Zhang, L. and Chang, R. B. (2022) A multidimensional coding architecture of the vagal interoceptive system. *Nature*, 603, 878–884. https://doi.org/10.1038/s41586-022-04515-5

Zunin, L. M. and Myers, D. (2000) as cited in DeWolfe, D. J. (2000) Training manual for human service workers in major disasters (2nd ed.). Washington, DC: Center for Mental Health Services. https://www.hsdl.org/?view&did=4017

Index

Note: **Bold** page numbers refer to tables, *italic* page numbers refer to figures.